Advance Praise

Experience the Trail afresh as a pair of mature newlyweds follow in the 200-year-old footsteps of Lewis, Clark and Company. In *Uncharted Moments*, Ton's lively prose style offers modern insights on history that shaped America's future. If you've ever longed to follow your dream, travel with Jeff and Carmen, who make an old journey new, learning their own lessons in teamwork, perseverance, and love undaunted.

—Laura Lee Yates,
author of *Bound for the Western Sea*

This is a very well-written and personal journey by a couple—newly married later in life— exploring America and their love along the Lewis and Clark Trail. They took full advantage of the Bicentennial's 15 Signature events, from Monticello to Astoria and back again to the lonely grave of Lewis on the Natchez Trace. They visited the places nobody should miss and then some. And they had the chance to hear some of the greatest scholars and elders along the trail.

—Clay Jenkinson, editor, *We Proceeded
On—The Lewis & Clark Quarterly*

For Lewis and Clark "buffs," at some magical moment, that usually occurs along "the Trail," the river of the intellect flows seamlessly into the emotions, and the Captains' epic journey becomes not just a story, but part of our being. Jeff Ton's masterful storytelling of his journey into this world of Lewis and Clark will entertain, amuse, and touch your soul!

—David J. Peck, D.O., physician and author of *Or Perish
in the Attempt* (University of Nebraska Press, 2011) and *So
Hard to Die: A Physician and a Psychologist Explore the Mystery
of Meriwether Lewis's Death* (Peck Family Trust, 2021)

Uncharted Moments is more than a travelogue. By retracing the Lewis and Clark Expedition by car, on foot, and by RV, Ton reflects on the people, places, and moments that shape us. Along the way, he shares earned insights on leadership, teamwork, and relationships—reminding us that a life well lived is built one meaningful moment at a time.

—Chris Burkhard, President of Placers Staffing
and host of the *Outside Insights* podcast

UNCHARTED MOMENTS

UNCHARTED MOMENTS

Love, Legacy, and the Lewis & Clark Trail

Jeffrey S. Ton

Published by Ton Enterprises, LLC
Copyright © 2026 Jeffrey S. Ton

For permission requests, contact:
Ton Enterprises, LLC
www.jeffreyston.com

Unless otherwise noted, all journal excerpts from the Lewis and Clark Expedition are quoted from *The Journals of the Lewis & Clark Expedition*, edited by Gary E. Moulton (University of Nebraska Press, 1983–2001). Spelling and punctuation have been preserved to maintain the original voice.

Photo Credits: Carmen Ton, unless otherwise noted

Maps: Jennifer Vogel, with assistance from the Lewis and Clark Trail Heritage Foundation. Lewis & Clark trail map used throughout: Google Earth | Data SIO, NOAA, U.S. Navy. NGA, GE | BCO | Image Landsat / Copernicus | Data LDEO-Columbia, NSF, NOAA

Cover: Jennifer Vogel

Tradepaper ISBN: 978-1-7353090-8-8
Hardcover ISBN: 979-8-9939158-0-7
Digital ISBN: 978-1-7353090-9-5
Audiobook ISBN: 979-8-9939158-1-4

Library of Congress Control Number: 2025923899

Contents

Notes to the Reader

This book is based on actual events and real people. In some instances, to protect individuals' privacy or maintain the integrity of personal moments, names have been changed or omitted. Some individuals are described rather than identified by name.

The experiences and emotions shared throughout remain authentic. The story is told with honesty, care, and deep respect for those who were part of it.

Throughout this book, I use a variety of terms to refer to Native peoples and Tribal Nations. When possible, I name specific tribes; when I use broader terms like "Indigenous peoples" or "Native peoples," I do so with respect and acknowledgment of the diversity, resilience, and sovereignty of these communities.

As you journey with us through these pages, you may notice subtle patterns—moments of reflection, guidance, and discovery. These are the quiet threads that weave our story together. Some passages hold up a mirror, revealing who we were and who we became. Others offer a mentor's wisdom, often from the river itself. And always, there is a map—not of roads, but of meaning—leading us toward the places, and people, that changed everything.

The Journey

Some journeys begin alone—and become something else entirely.

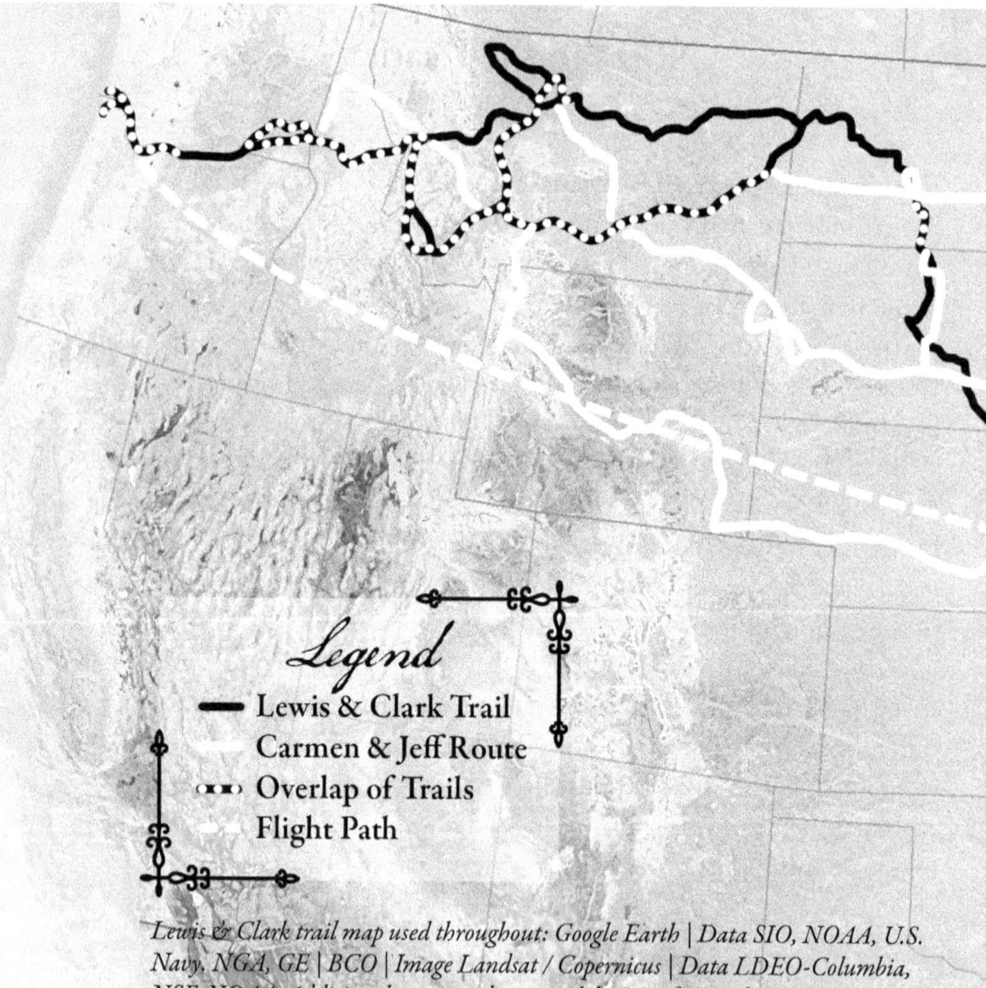

Lewis & Clark trail map used throughout: Google Earth | Data SIO, NOAA, U.S. Navy, NGA, GE | BCO | Image Landsat / Copernicus | Data LDEO-Columbia, NSF, NOAA. Additional routes and mapwork by Jennifer Vogel.

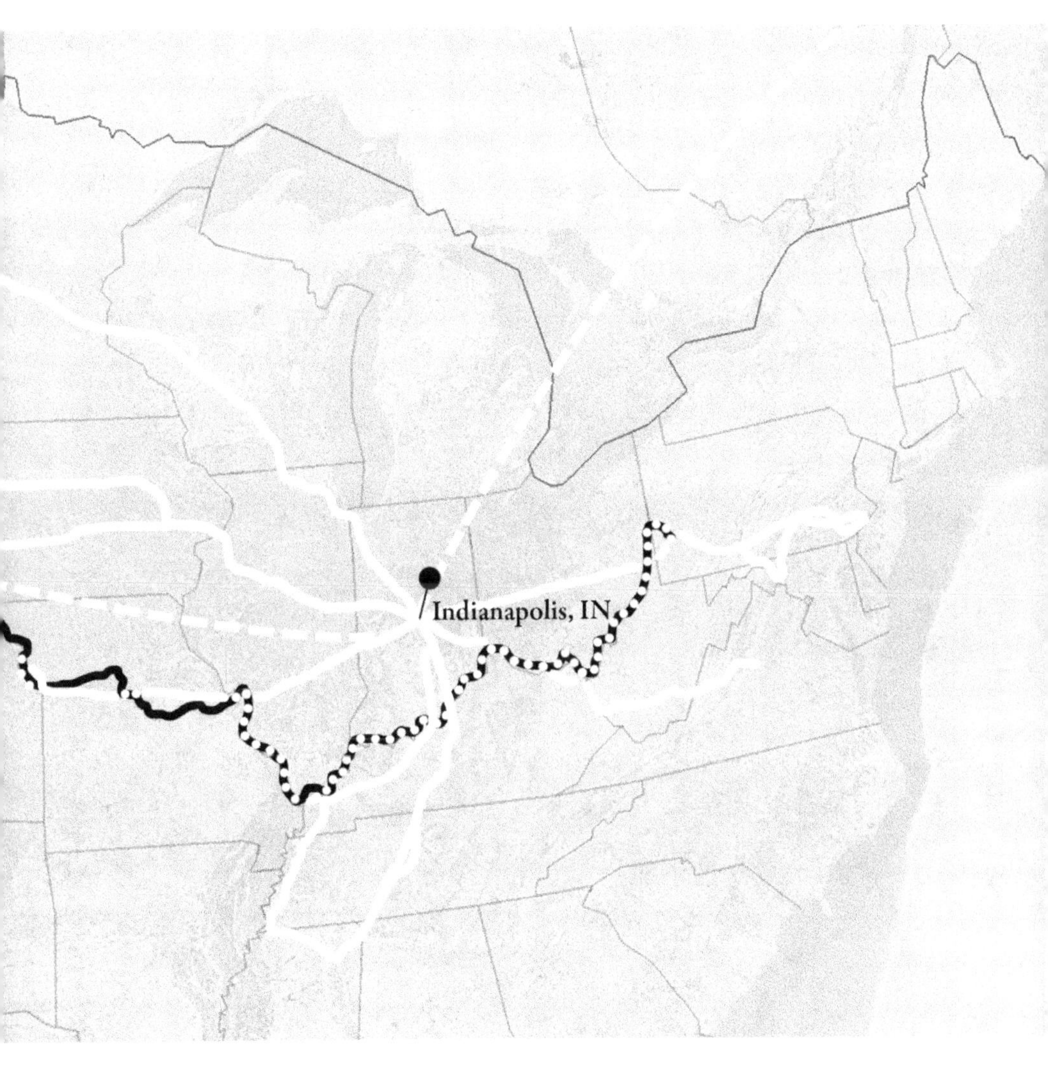

The journey unfolds in thirteen legs, covering each trip
we made, each marking a new bend in the river and a new
chapter in the story of love, history, and discovery.

Prologue

This is not the book I set out to write.

From 2003 to 2006, with two additional trips in 2007 and 2009, my wife, Carmen, and I followed the Lewis and Clark Trail. We traveled from Monticello in Virginia to Astoria, Oregon, and back to St. Louis, Missouri. Most long weekends found us on another stretch, trying to be where they had been, two centuries to the day. Along the way, we kept stumbling into what we called uncharted moments—those unscripted, sacred serendipities that happen because you're there and paying attention.

I wanted to write about those experiences for 20 years. I started more than once. Some of what you'll read comes straight from the journals I kept on the road. I thought I was writing a book about Lewis and Clark—about rivers and road trips, history and high-water marks. I thought it was a story about where we went.

Then life—and the terrain—changed. The calm river became a jumble of rapids. The miles got heavier.

Carmen is dying.

There. I said it, dammit.

She was diagnosed in 2023 with a rare, brutal progressive degenerative neurological disease—Multiple System Atrophy – Cerebellar (MSA-C). No treatment. No cure. A timeline none of us asked for. She walks with a rollator now. She speaks with effort. She writes only when she must. I retired to become her full-time caregiver. That's our life now. And still... this journey continues.

Because love doesn't end at the trailhead; it doesn't obey maps. It deepens. It roots itself like cottonwoods along the Missouri. The river kept teaching us—patience in the headwinds, humility at the confluence. And it taught us to listen: to the river, to each other, to the quiet between us.

In yet another neurologist's waiting room, searching for answers and not liking the ones we got, I realized...

This story is about Carmen.

About us.

The true epic wasn't in the maps or monuments. It was in the passenger seat beside me—the woman with the quiet strength, the knowing eyes, the unstoppable spirit.

My compass.

My co-captain.

We were newlyweds when we set out, barely a year into marriage. Those miles forged us. Lock two people in an aluminum-and-vinyl house hurtling down the highway for hours, and you either fray or you fuse. We fused. Somewhere between campgrounds and confluences, we fell in love with our country (despite its flaws), with this land—and with the Indigenous peoples whose presence and stories shaped it—and we fell deeper in love with each other.

So, this book isn't about what we saw.

It's about what we built.

Who we became.

And how sacred moments don't always come from crossing a continent—sometimes they come from holding a hand through the fog.

The Lewis and Clark Expedition
A Primer (or a Reminder)

In 1803–1806, after the Louisiana Purchase, President Thomas Jefferson sent his secretary, Meriwether Lewis, and frontiersman William Clark to lead the Corps of Discovery—about 30 men and one remarkable woman—up the Missouri River to the Pacific and back. Moving through the homelands of dozens of Indigenous nations, they traded, asked directions, and relied on Native knowledge to survive. Their journals are a window—brilliant and blinkered—into a world already old when they arrived, full of wonder, mistakes, and consequences we're still reckoning with.

This book follows our own journey along their route—not to retell their story, but to listen by the river, learn from those who were here first, and trace how love changes people who are willing to be changed.

WHO'S WHO ON THE JOURNEY

If you wish to know more about the people of the expedition and what became of them, Larry E. Morris's *The Fate of the Corps* offers a remarkable account of their lives after the trail. In these pages, I speak most often of four whose names echo beyond the expedition itself.

There is Meriwether Lewis—leader and observer, whose journals captured the wonder and the weight of discovery. William Clark—co-leader and steady hand, whose maps gave shape to the unknown. Sacagawea—Lemhi Shoshone woman, interpreter, and cultural bridge—who carried her infant son, Jean Baptiste ("Pomp"), through mountains and memory alike. And York—enslaved by Clark, yet a full participant in the journey—hunter, scout, and witness to a complicated American story that continues to unfold.

The expedition's survival owed as much to those they met as to those who served. Along the way, the Mandan, Hidatsa, Shoshone, Nez Perce, Chinook, Clatsop, and many others offered food, guidance, trade, and knowledge of the land. Without their generosity, the Corps might never have reached the ocean—or found their way home again.

THE EXPEDITION: ACROSS THE CONTINENT

In 1803, President Thomas Jefferson enlisted his private secretary, Meriwether Lewis, to explore the Missouri River to its source, follow the Columbia to the Pacific, and chart the lands of what would become the Louisiana Purchase. Lewis invited his friend William Clark to share command.

Lewis studied with leading scientists, gathered supplies, and commissioned a keelboat at Pittsburgh. He launched down the Ohio to meet Clark in Louisville, Kentucky. By October, they set off down the Ohio, turned north up the Mississippi, and built a winter camp across the river from St. Louis called Camp River Dubois. Along the way, they recruited a band of soldiers, boatsmen, and frontiersmen.

When spring came, the Corps of Discovery pushed up the Missouri—sailing, pulling, and poling against the current. They celebrated the first Independence Day west of the Mississippi at Independence Creek, met with the Oto, endured a tense encounter with the Teton Sioux, and reached the thriving Mandan and Hidatsa villages by winter. There in North Dakota, they built Fort Mandan and met a young Shoshone woman, Sacagawea, and her husband, Toussaint Charbonneau. Her knowledge of language and land would soon help to guide them west.

In April 1805, 33 souls and a Newfoundland dog named Seaman headed across the plains. They marveled at the White Cliffs of the Missouri River, struggled past the Great Falls, and crossed the Continental Divide at Lemhi Pass. Trading with the Shoshone for horses, they pressed on through the Bitterroot Valley and over the snow-covered Lolo Trail, where the Nez Perce (Niimiipuu) rescued and fed them after weeks of starvation.

After carving new canoes, they followed the Clearwater, Snake, and Columbia Rivers to the Pacific, building Fort Clatsop near present-day Astoria, Oregon. After a miserable winter of rain, they turned east in March 1806.

Dividing to explore new routes, they rejoined near the confluence of the Yellowstone and Missouri Rivers. When the Corps returned to St. Louis on September 23, 1806, they were weary, scarred, and forever changed. Their journey had carried them across a continent and into legend.

We Headed East to Explore The West

To: Monticello, Virginia
January 2003

*And in that quiet moment, I realized something simple and profound:
The rivers weren't just calling to me anymore. They were calling to her, too.*

"If therefore there is anything under those
circumstances, in this enterprise, which would
induce you to participate with me in it's fatiegues,
it's dangers and it's honors, believe me there is no
man on earth with whom I should feel equal pleasure
in sharing them as with yourself;"

—*Meriwether Lewis to
William Clark, June 19, 1803*

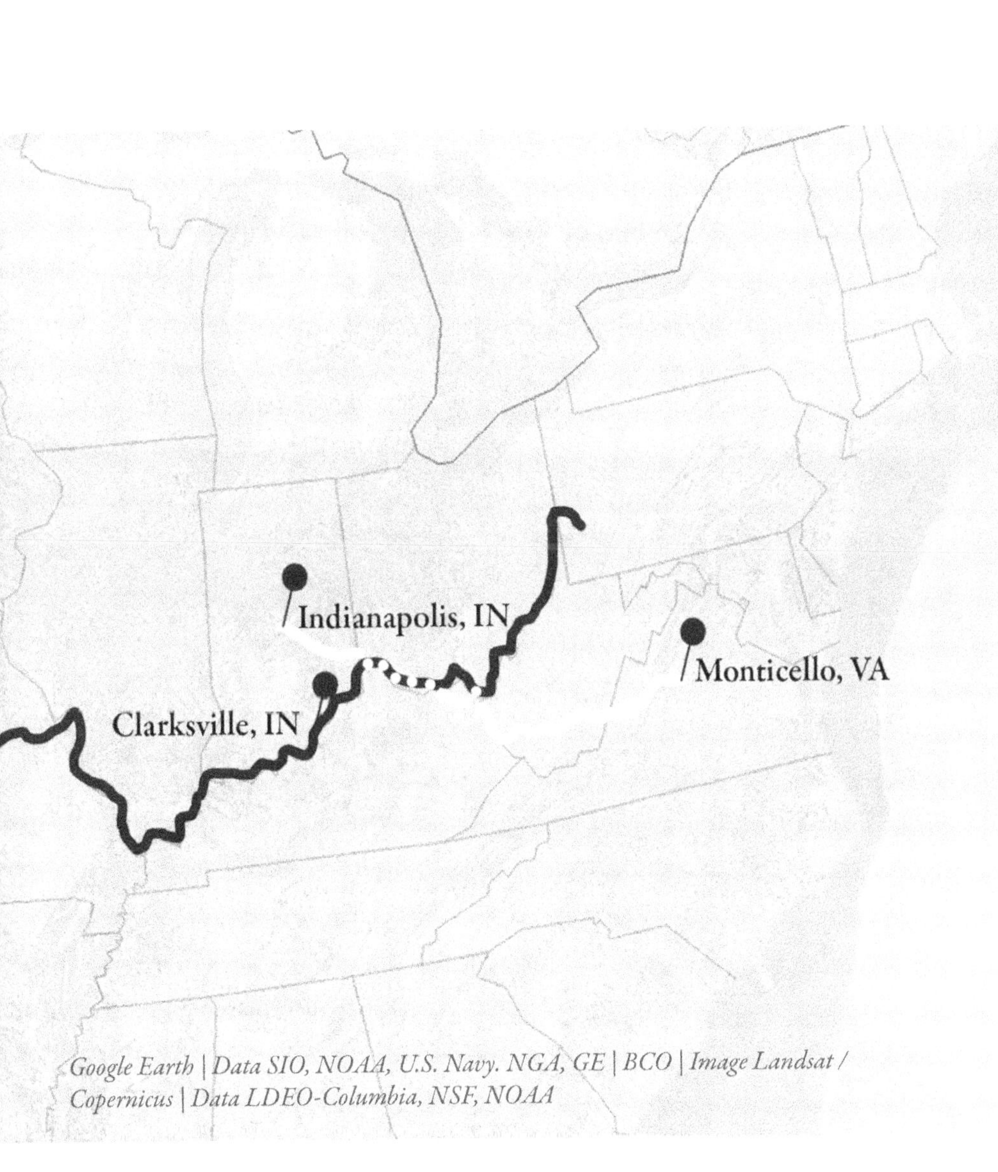

Google Earth | Data SIO, NOAA, U.S. Navy. NGA, GE | BCO | Image Landsat / Copernicus | Data LDEO-Columbia, NSF, NOAA

one

Farewell to a Friend

In November of 2002, Carmen and I were relaxing in our den, having just celebrated our first anniversary. I was surfing on our computer while Carmen watched the morning news. I took the opportunity to visit some of the Lewis and Clark Bicentennial websites. The Bicentennial Committee had revised its plan for 15 events to 12 signature events. The first would be at Monticello, Thomas Jefferson's home, in Charlottesville, Virginia, on January 18, just over two months away. The announcement went on to say that only 4,000 tickets would be available. The committee would use a lottery system to issue them. Anyone interested in attending had to submit a postcard to the committee postmarked before December 1.

Knowing we had not budgeted for a trip to Virginia in January, I turned to Carmen.

"Sooo," I said, trying to sound casual. "Remember that Lewis and Clark Bicentennial thing I kept rambling about this summer?"

And then later: "It's in January, at Monticello. They're doing a lottery for tickets. Postcards only. Postmarked by December 1st."

With each word, my enthusiasm deflated. "But it's probably a long shot... and even if we got in, we couldn't afford—"

"Let's enter," she said. "We'll figure it out later. We don't have much time. We don't have any postcards, but if we did, we would hand them to the post office clerk to ensure they get the correct postmark. It's the 27th, and tomorrow is Thanksgiving. We probably need to get to the post office on Friday."

I smiled. Carmen was already in problem-solving mode. "I can't go on Friday; I have to work. I could go on Saturday morning. Friday is Black Friday, anyway; it will be crazy..."

Carmen jumped in: "No, we don't want to wait until the last day; too much could go wrong. I'll go on Friday."

Wow, I really did marry an angel, I thought.

That is how Carmen found herself at the post office on Black Friday. When she arrived, the line was running out the door. Not to be dissuaded, Carmen cheerfully got in line. Twenty minutes later, when she was finally inside, she discovered the line snaked back and forth throughout the room.

Now, here is something you should know about Carmen. She can stand in line, any line—at the bar, at a restroom... any line—and come away with three or four new best friends. By the time she was halfway to the clerk, three people had shared their Thanksgiving plans, one had offered her a cookie, and another had confessed they had no idea what a Lewis and Clark was. When she finally got to the clerk, he stared at her in amazement. "A postcard? That's all you want?"

"Well, why don't you give me two, in case I mess one up?" she requested.

She carefully addressed the card and wrote our name and address on the back. After being assured it would receive that day's postmark, she slid the card into the mail slot in the post office vestibule. With her task completed, she headed home.

That evening, we sat down to relax with a couple of CC and 7s (Canadian Club and 7Up—Diet Sprite, in our case). We thought we had simply mailed a postcard.

We had no idea we'd just launched an expedition of our own.

A month later, my hands trembled as I tore open the envelope with a return address of Jefferson's West, Monticello, Charlottesville, Virginia. I braced myself for the letdown, fully expecting a polite rejection—a "thank you for your interest" form letter. For a moment, I stared at the folded paper inside, afraid to unfold it, afraid to let go of the possibility that maybe, just maybe, we'd been chosen. My heart pounded. My fingers hesitated. Then, I unfolded the letter and saw them—two tickets to the Lewis and Clark Bicentennial Inaugural Signature Event: Jefferson's West!

People who have won the lottery describe the moment as one of shock and disbelief. They sometimes double-check and triple-check the numbers before realization sets in. They scream. They cry. They laugh. They describe it as life-altering. I felt all of that and more. For someone just rebuilding his life, it felt like destiny had winked at us—a moment suspended between disbelief and wonder.

I turned to Carmen and said, "Oh my God! Oh my God! Oh my God! Our name was drawn. We got the tickets!" Then, reality began to set in. How were we going to get to Virginia? The event was only two weeks away, and we had to start planning!

That evening, I jumped online and did a quick MapQuest—yes, this was 2003, when planning a trip still meant printing out turn-by-turn directions from a website. The drive was 10 hours, a long and arduous journey. Since the event was on a Saturday, the best plan was to drive all day Friday, go to the event Saturday, and then drive home on Sunday. As we reviewed the event and exhibit materials, Carmen suggested we take Thursday afternoon off and drive as far as possible that night. This way, we would have most of Friday to sightsee and avoid the crowds on Saturday.

After making that decision, I spent the next week planning our weekend. We would leave on Thursday, January 16, and return on Sunday, January 19. I made a rough list of the exhibits, events, and historic places we wanted to visit.

Of course, the highlight would be the event itself. The inaugural event was to be held on the lawn of Monticello, the stately hilltop home of Thomas Jefferson. It was scheduled for January 18, 2003—exactly 200 years to the day after Jefferson penned his secret request to Congress, seeking funding for an expedition to explore a route to the Pacific. That letter had set in motion one of the most extraordinary adventures in American history.

The day would include speeches and performances by dozens of individuals, groups, and dignitaries. I was excited to see the names of many authors I had become familiar with over the last year or two: Moulton, Duncan, Baker, and Burns. If they were to build a Mount Rushmore honoring the scholars of Lewis and Clark—those whose passion brought the story to life for new generations—Stephen Ambrose would be there for his sweeping narrative, Gary Moulton for his definitive editing of the original journals, Dayton Duncan for weaving emotion into the documentary scripts, and Gerard Baker for elevating Indigenous perspectives into the national spotlight. Stephen Ambrose, Gary Moulton, Dayton Duncan, and Gerard Baker would all be immortalized there, with Ken Burns playing the role of sculptor Gutzon Borglum. Burns's documentary *Lewis & Clark: The Journey of the Corps of Discovery* featured all these men. They would all be speaking at the event, save Ambrose, who had passed away in October before his heroes could be celebrated.

WE HEADED EAST TO EXPLORE THE WEST

Finally, the day had arrived—the day those long-awaited tickets would become a journey. Armed with our road atlas, state maps of each state we would traverse courtesy of AAA, and our printout from MapQuest, Carmen volunteered for the first driving shift. It was midafternoon as she steered our Jeep Grand Cherokee onto the interstate. We were driving east to begin a westward story. We thought we knew the map. We didn't.

The first snowflakes began to fall. It was a beautiful, gentle snow.

The snow thickened into ropes, and the world narrowed to our headlights. Carmen leaned in, jaw set, hands steady at ten and two; the wipers kept time. Twice I offered to take the wheel. "I've got it," she said, not looking away. Semis ghosted past, a white roar in the dark. The heater clicked, my breath fogged the glass, and the road kept sliding under us like a river at night. I pulled my coat over me and listened to the thump of the blades, to her quiet breath—and let my eyes close.

Carmen and I first spoke on February 7, 1995, my 37th birthday. I was a software developer for a consulting company and one of the firm's top COBOL programmers. As such, when the company's recruiters were hiring a new consultant, I would get asked to do a technical interview and give my thumbs-up (or thumbs-down). That afternoon, my phone rang, and a new voice was on the other end. She introduced herself as Carmen Hillenburg, a recruiter for our company.

"Are you available for a technical interview this evening?" she asked.

"No, I really can't. It's my birthday, and I will be home with my wife and two sons," I laughed. "I could do it tomorrow evening if that works. If it has to be tonight, I can ask one of my team members to do it."

"Tomorrow should work. I will confirm with the candidate and let you know. Oh, and happy birthday!"

Over the next few months, I did several more interviews for her. During a call about an interview, she asked if I was attending the spring company meeting. I confirmed I was. She told me to find her and introduce myself. Two weeks later, I walked into the Marott ballroom, a well-known event space in Indianapolis. I was late. One of the drawbacks of being the senior person on the account was that when something broke, I had to fix it. I almost decided to skip the event, but—it was a free meal on the company, so why not?

As I walked in, one of my teammates approached me. "Hey, Jeff, someone here wants to meet you," he said. As he turned, Carmen stepped forward, introduced herself, and confidently shook my hand. She was stunningly beautiful. I probably mumbled something witty, like "It's nice to meet you," and averted my eyes nervously.

Over the following months, I conducted a few more technical interviews for her, and eventually, I heard she had left the company.

Time flowed forward, and a year or so passed, and my desk phone rang.

"Hello, this is Jeff Ton. Can I help you?"

"Hi, I don't know if you remember me, but this is Carmen Hillenburg."

Ah, gee, let me see—gorgeous blonde, long slender legs, piercing blue eyes, and a smile that could light up the city skyline... Nah, I don't think I remember her.

"Yes, of course, I remember you."

"Well, you always struck me as someone who doesn't always play by the rules..."

That was a curious opening line.

"...I have a favor to ask."

"After that line, what can I do for you?" I chuckled.

As it turned out, she was now working for a competing consulting company. She had transitioned from recruiting to business development. Could I introduce her to a couple of the managers and directors to help her get a foot in the door and possibly boost her sales numbers? Of course

I would and did. As the year progressed, I would see her in the office halls, heading to meet with this director or that manager.

My career was pivoting at the same time. I had worked for the same client since joining the consulting company in 1992, but I was seeking a more permanent opportunity. A new director had taken over our area. I'd known him for most of my time there. The department was struggling—our major project was years overdue and millions over budget. The previous director had brought in a new consulting firm, but the people they assigned weren't making progress.

The director asked if I wanted to join the client as an employee and take over the project. It sounded like a good deal to me.

Yes!

It took several months. The company I worked for wasn't exactly eager to give up the cash cow of my monthly billables. But eventually, it happened.

During my first few days in my new role, I made two life-changing phone calls. The first was to that new consulting firm, advising them that I was canceling the contract for cause and that their employees were no longer needed.

The second call was to Carmen.

"Hey, I need some resources for my team."

"Oh, that is great! I can meet you next Wednesday and discuss what you need."

"No, you don't understand. I just fired my entire team, and I need people tomorrow."

Over the next few months and years, we built one of the most incredible teams I've ever been associated with. Everyone on the team cared for each other... genuinely cared. That caring started with Carmen. In sales parlance, she was a farmer as opposed to a hunter. She nurtured her people, her clients, and her relationships. Her staff knew she would do anything for them, and therefore, they would do anything for her—and for me.

We didn't know it yet, but the roots of our shared adventure were already taking hold. Long before the first campsite, the first landmark, or the first historic speech, we had already built something extraordinary: a partnership.

As a team, we successfully turned the project around and implemented it. The river flows, and life goes on.

BUT WE'RE JUST FRIENDS

Our business relationship gave way to something quieter and more enduring: friendship. The easy kind that sneaks up on you. We started swapping stories—life slipping in alongside work.

That's when I learned her dad, Jim, had died not long after we met—and while he was still in the hospital, her husband filed for divorce. Cold. Calculated. She told it plainly, asking for understanding, not sympathy. Around the same time, my own marriage of 22 years was coming apart in public and unglamorous ways. I moved into a dim efficiency on the east side and tried to begin again.

She was dating. I was dating. We were both stumbling forward.

My friends kept saying, "You should ask Carmen out."

"No," I'd say. "She's a friend. And I'm her client. Complicated."

Her friends told her the same thing. She gave them the same answer. "It's complicated. He's a friend."

Then, over a routine lunch, she looked at me and said, "Would you like to go out—like, on a date?"

"I'm dating someone," I said. "It's getting serious." She tried to hide the discomfort. I missed the signal.

Life overlapped awkwardly after that—mutual parties, the relationship of mine that ended in a fireball, Carmen seeing someone new. When my former girlfriend moved to Florida, things were rough enough that I helped her pack and drove her there. Carmen and her boyfriend picked me up at the airport. Exactly as awkward as you'd imagine. Still, we were friends. When I bought a new canoe, she tossed me her Jeep keys without hesitation.

The chorus resumed. "You should date Carmen." "You should date Jeff."

No. We were friends. It was easy. Why risk it?

One night that became lore: A not-going-away party turned into too many Goldschläger toasts. Carmen drove me to her place, put me to bed at 5:30 like a battlefield nurse, and later found me wedged between the bed and the window after I tried to use the curtains as a rope. Morning came;

she told it kindly. From then on, whenever anyone said "Goldschläger," we did the hand chop: "Goldschläger? No." And still—somehow—we were just friends.

Early that summer, she called, "Where are you? I stopped by your office."

"I'm home. Little procedure."

"What happened?"

"Vasectomy."

"You did what?!" A flash of something moved in her voice. We were still "just friends."

That fall, I took her to Rick's Boatyard for her birthday. The waiter called it a "very romantic table." In unison: "Oh no—we're just friends." Weeks later, after a movie at her house, I asked, "So… when did we start dating?"

She giggled. "About two months ago, silly."

Others noticed the shift. In Carmen's kitchen, her mom, Judy, looked me in the eye: "You better take good care of her." I took it to heart.

We took a short Vegas getaway later that November—laughter, shows, hand in hand through the canals—and still didn't rush the line. On the flight home, I asked, "Am I being patient, or just pathetic?"

"You're being patient. And kind. And a gentleman," she said, taking my hand. "Maybe that's what I've needed."

December settled the question. After a wine-tasting with friends, she leaned across the console. "I'd like you to take me home." The kiss wasn't rushed. It felt like something that had been waiting for the right moment. We pulled into the garage, stepped inside, and faced each other. For a second, the world paused. Our eyes met.

BAM!

The Jeep dropped hard into a pothole hidden beneath the snow. My teeth clicked. Carmen caught the skid in two minor corrections, and we were back in the groove before I found a word.

We'd been crawling for seven hours on a drive that should've taken four. Carmen had to be spent. We stopped for gas and switched. We'd planned to stop in West Virginia; instead, we decided to push into Virginia to make up time, hoping to leave just an hour's drive for the morning. I pulled back onto the highway.

A few miles later, the snow just… stopped. Pavement appeared. For the first time since Indianapolis, the needle reached 65. The storm had stalled on the far side of the mountains, and the descent east put us back on schedule. Around 1 a.m., at the Virginia line, we stole a line from the captains and decided to proceed on to Charlottesville. The night clerk allowed us to check in without charging for the extra night. We stumbled upstairs and slept.

While we sleep, allow me to offer a little context—the kind that kept pulling me back, year after year. I promise, this matters.

JANUARY 1803: THE LETTER

When Jefferson became president in 1801, America was young and stretched thin—16 states, about 5 million people, 1 in 5 enslaved—and beyond the Appalachians lay the homelands of many nations. What gripped me was how precarious it all felt: no inevitability, no finished map. Rivers were the arteries; New Orleans was the heart. When Spain ceded Louisiana back to France in 1800, Jefferson read the danger: If Napoleon held the Mississippi's mouth, the republic might remain a coastal idea.

On January 18, 1803, he sent Congress a confidential request: Fund a small expedition up the Missouri. The maps they'd carry labeled that river with one electric word—conjectural—a dotted line into blank space; courage and questions where certainty should be.

Jefferson turned to Meriwether Lewis—his trusted aide—to piece together a plan from journals, rumors, and winter conversations. That's the moment that keeps pulling me: Someone chose to proceed without guarantees.

In a Charlottesville hotel, on the eve of Monticello, Carmen asleep beside me, I felt it too—the pull of the unknown. We were already stepping in.

two

Step Right Up, History's About to Begin!

We awoke to find Charlottesville covered in a blanket of snow. The storm had followed us across the mountains, as if determined to stay part of our journey—but by now, it had lost most of its fury. We learned the hills of West Virginia had been pummeled—ten inches in six hours. Here in Virginia, we were greeted by just two inches... and an arctic blast. Temperatures were holding in the mid-teens, with predictions of even colder air arriving the next day—the day of the ceremony. Did I mention the ceremony was outside? Brrrr.

But before all that, we had a full day of sightseeing planned—a day I'd been looking forward to for weeks.

Our first stop was the Charlottesville Visitor Center. It was our jumping-off point for history, but also something more. This trip was about stepping into the story together. For me, since discovering the Lewis and Clark story, history has never been just facts and dates. It's breath. It's movement. It's presence. Being in the places where something happened allows me to feel the echo of it, like the lingering hum of a bell that was struck long ago.

We bought our President's Pass tickets, which provided access to Charlottesville's historical locations, and headed to the main attraction: "The Tent of Many Voices," set up in the visitor center parking lot. It was the first official stop for Corps of Discovery II: 200 Years to the Future, the National Park Service's traveling tribute to Lewis and Clark's journey. As we walked toward the tents, I felt a flutter of excitement. I had waited years for this moment, and now here we were, stepping into it together.

The exhibit consisted of three tents. The first two walked us through the story of the expedition using narrated headsets and immersive murals. The images showed encounters with Indigenous nations, sweeping landscapes, and moments of sheer discovery. What struck me most was how much care was taken to show the story from multiple perspectives—especially the voices of the Indigenous nations whose lives were forever changed by that journey. The third tent was for the speakers—storytellers providing context.

For Carmen, this was her first real dive into the story. Aside from the Ken Burns documentary she'd gifted me for Christmas—and, of course, listening to me ramble on for hours—she hadn't explored much of it before. But she was wide-eyed with curiosity, peppering me with questions as we made our way through the exhibits. Watching her want to connect with this part of me was deeply moving. It was like she was falling in love with the story—she was falling deeper into the journey we were on together.

And that's what this was, after all: a journey. One that mirrored, in some small way, the very story we were here to honor. Theirs was by river; ours was by road. Theirs was into the unknown; ours was into a growing understanding of each other. But both were rooted in wonder.

WHEN IN DOUBT, BUY THE WINE

After leaving the visitor center, our next stop was Michie Tavern—a place that felt like it had one foot planted in the colonial past and the other in a storybook. It was initially built in 1784 by Corporal William Michie, a Revolutionary War veteran who transformed his home into a gathering place for food, drink, and spirited conversation. I imagined Jefferson, Monroe, Madison—maybe even a young Meriwether Lewis—stopping in for a pint, their muddy boots thudding across the wooden floors as they paced the room and debated politics and philosophy by firelight.

That's what I love about places like this. They speak to you if you're willing to listen. Sometimes I swear I can feel the conversations lingering in the air.

We stepped into the main tavern building.

The rooms were dark wood and thick walls. Time seemed slower here. Each room had a small button you could press to activate a narration. As we made our way through the sitting room, the sleeping quarters, and the ballroom, I found myself picturing those long-ago travelers—stiff from the road, thawing by the fire, sharing rumors of frontier skirmishes or political shifts back east.

Then we reached *our* room—the one that made my heart skip a beat.

Inside were artifacts and reproductions related to the Lewis and Clark Expedition. Some were period items: a musket from Harpers Ferry, a map from 1845, and an envelope signed by Jefferson. But others were directly tied to the journey: a copy of the *Gazette of the United States* from 1806, the first public announcement of the expedition's *departure*. The date leapt off the page—*February 29, 1806*. I looked at Carmen, and we both smiled. We were there to commemorate Jefferson's request to Congress in 1803. By the time this newspaper was printed, they were already hunkered down for a miserable winter on the Pacific coast.

One detail I couldn't step past: a Jefferson peace medal. Jefferson's silhouette was on one side; on the other, a handshake with the words PEACE AND FRIENDSHIP intertwined—one sleeve a military cuff, the other a bare wrist. Since the founding of our country, peace medals had been presented to chiefs during treaty negotiations or visits. The medals came in sizes, distributed according to the giver's perceived stature of the recipient, a built-in hierarchy in a "gift." To Americans, the medal signaled allegiance; for Native leaders, it could carry obligations—and risks—among neighbors and rivals. The hands promised parity; the cuff didn't. That quiet asymmetry is what lodged in me.

We finished the tour in the tavern's wine cellar, where we happily discovered we could purchase a bottle of Jefferson wine from vines that traced their lineage back to Jefferson's own vineyard. Of course, we bought a bottle. History tastes better when you can take it home with you.

THE COMPASS AND THE FLOWERS

From the tavern, we wound our way up the little mountain, Monticello. The road curled through bare trees dusted with snow. At the visitor center, we learned what the name really means: "Monticello" encompasses more than just the house; it is the entire hill. We also learned that each Signature Event would be issuing its own commemorative lapel pin. We started our collection on the spot, buying one for the Signature Event and one for Monticello itself.

No cars go to the top, so we waited for the shuttle. One last bend and the house appeared—quiet, snow soft on the lawn, red-brick walks cleared to a ribbon. It felt less like arriving at a place than at a moment. You could almost hear hooves in the hush.

The house is intentional to its bones—Roman forms filtered through Jefferson's taste, the famous dome that ended up on the U.S. nickel. Inside, the entrance hall opened like a museum: maps, taxidermy, and objects gathered from Indigenous nations the Corps encountered. Jefferson admired Native cultures, even as policies he supported pushed Native peoples off their lands. That tension breathes in these rooms.

Two hides stopped us. One, a Missouri River map painted on buffalo skin—likely from the winter at Fort Mandan, when Mandan and Hidatsa knowledge carried the captains forward. The other, a battle scene in pictographs—vivid, immediate. Not artifacts; stories.

We passed Jefferson's great clock—marking the days and not just the hours, the counterweights dropping through a hole cut in the floor to finish the week—and followed the tour through the greenhouse and sitting room to the library. Thousands of volumes, many chosen by Jefferson himself. It felt like a chapel.

Then the loaned exhibit from the Smithsonian caught my eye: their journals. Real pages. Faded ink. Rain-smudged margins. The humanity in the mess—the scraps, corrections, and attempts to make sense—gave me chills.

And then the unexpected: William Clark's compass. Not a replica. His. I pictured him under a hard sky, wind on his face, taking a reading and sketching a line with cold fingers. Beside me, Carmen had gone perfectly still—but not for the compass. She was reading a case of pressed flowers from the journey, the captains' notes in a careful hand. She traced the names like a poem. Native plants have always been her doorway; I felt something shift. She wasn't just along for the ride anymore. She was in it, too.

Our guide gathered us. We moved through the parlor and dining room, but our minds stayed behind glass: mine with the compass; Carmen's with the flowers. Out of the west-facing windows, thousands of folding chairs dotted the snow. Crews hurried over the stage and podium. The thrill hit me again: After years of reading and dreaming, we were about to join a national moment born from a single letter to Congress.

We walked down past the family cemetery. Through the gate, you can read Jefferson's chosen epitaph—Declaration, Virginia Statutes for Religious Freedom, University of Virginia—no mention of the presidency. The selection says plenty.

As much as we admired his intellect and vision, the contradictions were impossible to ignore. He wrote "all men are created equal" while enslaving people. He praised Native cultures while backing policies that dispossessed them. And we now know—through scholarship and DNA— that he fathered children with Sally Hemings, whom he enslaved. Brilliant, conflicted, flawed. Maybe that's why he still holds me—not because he was perfect, but because he wasn't.

THE BUST, THE DEAL, AND THE DESTINY

After lunch, we made our way to Highland—James Monroe's home (formerly Ash Lawn–Highland). Monroe, the fifth president of the United States and a longtime friend of Jefferson, lived here with his wife, Elizabeth. The house sits quietly in a grove just down the road from Monticello, and at first glance, it doesn't shout its significance. But the closer we looked, the more we realized how much of Monroe's life—and the fate of the country—was tied to this place.

James and Elizabeth Monroe lived here from 1799 to 1826. They purchased the home largely because of Monroe's close friendship with Jefferson. In fact, it was Jefferson who picked the site and even sent his gardeners to help establish the orchard before the Monroes moved in. The original walkway and gardens were designed to provide a direct view from Monroe's front door to Jefferson's dome atop Monticello.

There was something touching about that—a friendship etched into the landscape.

Inside, the house is modest compared to Monticello, but still elegant in its own way. One of the first things we saw made us look twice: a bust of Napoleon—a Roman-style rendering, complete with a laurel wreath, as if the emperor had just walked out of a marble temple.

Carmen and I exchanged a look.

"Napoleon?"

"Napoleon."

It turns out, Napoleon gave these busts as gifts to friends and allies. Seeing one here felt... strange. I was already thinking about Monroe's critical role in the Louisiana Purchase, and now, here was the man himself—bronzed and brooding—watching us from the mantel.

The irony wasn't lost on us.

Monroe had been sent to France by Jefferson, along with Robert Livingston, to negotiate for the port of New Orleans. Monroe was confirmed by Congress just days before Jefferson penned the letter we were here to celebrate. Monroe and Livingston were authorized to spend up to $10 million. That was the plan: Buy the mouth of the Mississippi, secure access for American commerce, and get out clean.

But Napoleon—battling war and bankruptcy—had other ideas.

Instead of selling just the port, he offered the entire Louisiana Territory: 530 million acres for $15 million. That's less than three cents an acre. Monroe didn't wait for permission; he just said, "Yes!" Just like that, everything changed.

Carmen and I stood in that house, retracing Monroe's steps, marveling at how a single negotiation—held across an ocean, under candlelight—reshaped a continent. The land deal was bold and risky. Many thought it was wildly unconstitutional because the Constitution did not explicitly grant authority to acquire foreign territory. But Jefferson moved forward. So did Monroe. And because of that decision, Lewis and Clark were sent west. Everything we were here to experience—this entire journey—flowed from that moment.

And standing in Monroe's house, I felt a surge of connection—to the politics, the policy, and the people. To the weight they carried. To the impossible choices they made. To the fact that, like all of us, they were doing the best they could in the middle of uncertainty.

That thread—of conjecture and courage—was becoming the heartbeat of this trip.

THE RIVER IS MY CHURCH

From there, we headed to our final stop of the day: American Rivers' powerful exhibit, "Discovering the Rivers of Lewis and Clark."

The display was simple in design but profound in its impact. A winding mural traced the journey of the Corps of Discovery—not by land but by water—river by river, current by current. It was a reminder that this wasn't an overland trek—it was a river voyage.

And for me, that mattered.

Years earlier, on a cold Canadian river, I had learned that water will teach you if you're quiet enough to listen; that day's mural pressed that lesson back into me. The rhythm of the water. The stillness. The way nature presses in close and quietly. I grew up in pews, son of a minister; after life bent in ways I didn't expect, the sanctuary that still held me was current and quiet. The river became my place to listen.

That's why this exhibit hit me so hard.

The exhibit went beyond naming the Missouri, the Columbia, the Yellowstone, and the Snake. It showed what two centuries have done to them—dams and diversions that drowned villages and sacred places, salmon runs collapsed, treaty waters narrowed. Homelands were on those walls. It was sobering. Heartbreaking. Infuriating. But not without hope. Panel after panel lifted up the people working the other direction—tribes, towns, scientists, nonprofits—unbuilding, replanting, reopening.

Carmen and I walked it slowly, in the kind of silence that isn't empty. At the end, we didn't need to say much. We both knew: Do something.

In the years that followed, we would spend weekends on the White River, back in Indiana, hauling tires and refrigerators from a two-mile reach until the tally topped ten tons. We even launched a small effort of our own to keep the work going. It's still one of the most meaningful things we've done together.

And it started here—on a snowy Virginia afternoon, in front of a mural of rivers that still speak.

THE DINNER TABLE AND THE TRAILHEAD

By the time we left the river exhibit, we were running on fumes—but still buzzing with everything we'd seen, everything we'd felt. It had been a long day of walking, learning, remembering, and imagining. Our feet were tired, our hands were cold, and our brains were full—but our hearts were full, too.

We needed a meal to match the moment.

We found a warm, quiet restaurant nearby—one of those cozy places with low lighting, local wine, and soft music humming under the conversation. We ordered dinner and a bottle of something red from a local vineyard and sank into our seats like we had just returned from an expedition of our own.

I remember thinking, *How did we get here? Not just to this restaurant. But to this life.*

We'd started as coworkers. Then friends. Now here we were, sharing wine after a day of wandering through history and wonder. Carmen had started this journey humoring my fascination, but somewhere along the way, it became hers, too.

I looked across the table at her, cheeks pink from the cold, eyes still bright from the museum. She reached for her glass. I reached for mine.

Whatever tomorrow held—the ceremony, the speeches, the bitter cold—we were already part of the story.

three

On Jefferson's Lawn

The next day dawned exactly as predicted—eight degrees. Carmen and I bundled up like Arctic explorers. By the time we left the hotel, we looked like Randy from *A Christmas Story*—layer upon layer of sweaters, scarves, coats, and puffy arms we could barely lower. The only thing missing was someone to tip us over and see if we could get back up.

The sun, ironically, was blindingly bright. So we added sunglasses to our outfits, which made us look absurdly cool for people about to freeze to death.

Because parking at Monticello was limited, we were assigned to park at Piedmont Virginia Community College, then take a shuttle to the top of the mountain. The buses ran in staggered waves to accommodate the crowd. Ours dropped us off nearly two hours before the ceremony. Did I mention it was eight degrees? And that the event was outside?

We spotted a warming tent off to one side of the lawn and made a beeline for it—but first, we staked our claim. We draped our blankets across two cold, hard plastic chairs, surprised to find so many seats still empty.

Inside the warming tent, we discovered where everyone had gone. The place was packed. People huddled in clusters, clutching hot chocolate, trying to will the heat into existence. The term *warming tent* turned out to be optimistic at best—our breath still crystallized on our scarves.

Eventually, we returned to our seats, joining thousands of others gathered to commemorate the 200th anniversary of the Lewis and Clark Expedition. We'd come east to learn how to go west—with our ears open. We were surrounded by people from all across the country—white, Black, Indigenous—students, teachers, retirees, historians, and curious citizens bundled against the cold.

As we waited for the program to begin, my mind drifted. *Proceed on.* A phrase that echoes from the Journals of Lewis & Clark. A phrase they often used. Putting one foot in front of the other. I realized that, in addition to commemorating an event from the past, we were celebrating something timeless: The human spirit. Courage. Perseverance. The daring to go into the unknown. In the wake of 9/11, still raw in all of us, these were qualities we were aching to reclaim. The idea that we could "proceed on"—even when the path was uncertain, even when the world had shifted beneath our feet—felt especially meaningful that morning. This ceremony wasn't about nostalgia. It was about drawing strength from history and using it to face the future.

Things kicked off with a burst of sound and color—the Lewis and Clark Fife and Drum Corps, a group of kids from St. Charles, Missouri, took the stage in full period attire: bright red coats, white trousers, black boots, and tall cylindrical stovepipe shakos, some adorned with feathers and fur. It was rousing and joyful—and somehow made the cold seem a little more bearable.

Dayton Duncan served as the master of ceremonies, guiding us through performances, stories, and reflections. We heard from authors whose books I had devoured in summers past. They shared not only stories of the Corps of Discovery, but also their own stories—how they had traveled the trail, what they had found. Indigenous dancers moved across the stage. Two fife and drum corps filled the air with music. Flags and banners from Indigenous nations rippled in the wind.

It was more than a ceremony.

It was a reminder.

That the spirit of exploration, of curiosity, of community—it still lived.

Even at eight degrees.

THE LETTER HEARD "ROUND THE WEST"

Then came the moment I'd been waiting for.

Dr. Gary Moulton stepped up to the podium to read Jefferson's letter to Congress—the one that launched it all.

It's not a long letter. It doesn't shout. It doesn't pound the table or wave a flag. It's measured, careful, precise. A budget request, really. But tucked inside those sentences is a vision that would change the course of the nation.

Jefferson asked for $2,500.

That's it.

Twenty-five hundred dollars to send a small group of men into a vast, uncharted wilderness stretching from the Mississippi River to the Pacific Ocean. I've spent more than that on home repairs. And here he was, casually suggesting we fund a journey across half a continent.

He wrote: "An intelligent officer, with ten or twelve chosen men … might explore the whole line, even to the Western Ocean."

As if it were just a weekend hike. As if the Rocky Mountains weren't a thing. As if woolly mammoths and Indians descended from Vikings weren't rumored to be out there.

But that was Jefferson's genius—and his gamble. He saw more than a river or a trade route. He saw a future.

And here we were, 200 years later, wrapped in blankets and snow, listening to those words as if they'd just been written. Carmen didn't say anything, but I could feel her beside me, fully present.

AN UNCHARTED MOMENT

The sky that morning was crystalline—bright, vivid, and endlessly blue. The bare branches of the winter trees reached upward like ink strokes on a canvas, their skeletal forms etched against the cold sky. Here and there, a dusting of frost clung to them, catching the sunlight like glass. It felt like the world had been polished.

Then Ken Burns stepped forward.

He approached the microphone slowly, hands folded in front of him, his voice much softer than we expected. Perhaps it was the weight of the moment. His task was not easy. He was here to honor his friend, Stephen

Ambrose—the historian who had written *Undaunted Courage*, the definitive book on the Lewis and Clark Expedition, and the driving force behind the idea of a national commemoration.

Ambrose had died just three months earlier. The weight of his absence was heavy on everyone's hearts. His wife and children were in the audience. And though it wasn't labeled as such, this moment had the feeling of a memorial service.

Ken spoke with quiet affection and deep reverence. He talked about friendship. About vision. About the courage of chasing a story all the way to its edge.

And then—something happened.

As Ken spoke, a lone hawk appeared in the sky behind the crowd. It soared silently, high overhead, its wings held still against the thin mountain air. It glided across the entire gathering—from the back of the lawn, over thousands of heads in the crowd, and beyond the dome of Monticello, disappearing into the blueness beyond.

Carmen and I were frozen in place—and not because of the cold. At first, we thought it might be part of the ceremony. A planned gesture. But as we whispered to each other, we realized: It was the first bird we'd seen all day.

We looked around. No one else had seemed to notice. No heads turned. No cameras followed.

But we saw it.

Later along the trail, we'd hear from Native speakers that some Nations read hawks as strength or warning—sometimes change. That morning, we only felt the lift.

We didn't need confirmation. The hawk wasn't in the program—but it was part of something.

To us, it was Stephen Ambrose—responding to his friend's tribute, acknowledging the journey he helped inspire, and offering a silent blessing to the years of commemoration ahead. A reminder that stories don't end. They echo.

And more than that—it was the first of many moments we would come to recognize on our journey. Small, strange, serendipitous encounters that carried a kind of weight. Things we didn't plan. Things we couldn't explain. But things we wouldn't forget.

We came to call them uncharted moments.

Some were directly tied to Lewis and Clark. Others happened simply because we were there—off the beaten path, open to whatever the trail would give us.

That was the first.

But it would not be the last.

THE RIVER BEGINS TO BEND

During intermission, I waited by the garden wall, sunlight bouncing off the snow. A man—John, newly retired, new to town—started chatting. I surprised myself by staying in the conversation: where we'd been, what drew us here, how good it felt to stand in this moment. When Carmen came back, I was mid-story. She slipped her arm through mine and smiled, the kind that says *I see this*. It would take years to name it, but the river had already started to bend—her steadiness at my side, the Lewis and Clark story in my mouth—and my voice not hiding.

The second half of the program braided ceremony and symbol. The U.S. Army 1802 Color Guard set the tone; Monacan elders offered blessings and songs. Banners along the stage carried the names of nations the Corps met—some we knew, most we didn't yet. Drums moved through the cold air, followed by a high school senior's earnest anthem. Standing on Monacan homelands, we felt the map tilt from routes to relationships.

The keynotes—Tex G. Hall and historian James P. Ronda—looked forward as much as back: reconciliation, shared memory, responsibility. I made a mental note of two words that jumped out at me: Listen first. It was the beginning of a vow we'd try to keep.

At the very end, the organizing committee for the next Signature Event was introduced, comprising representatives from Clarksville, Indiana, and Louisville, Kentucky. The rivalry between the two cities over who gets to claim the official "departure point" of the expedition was already on full display.

As the flag recessional played, led by the Charlottesville Municipal

Band and the Fife and Drum Corps, we stood in silence, watching each flag retire, one by one. It was a stirring, dignified close to the ceremony.

And then—back to reality. We stood in long, shivering lines to be packed onto buses for the ride down the mountain. Even in the cold, people were buzzing with energy—chattering about what they'd seen and heard. Or maybe it was just our teeth.

By the time we got to the car, it felt like we were thawing out in stages. We cranked the heater to full blast and sat in silence for a few moments, letting the warmth settle back into our fingers and toes.

What a day.

It was incredible to be there. But what made it unforgettable was that my beautiful wife was with me every step of the way. She was as curious, engaged, and inspired as I was.

That night, with the heater roaring and the snow glowing blue in the moonlight, we drove back to the hotel—frozen, exhausted, and full.

Tucked into our room, HBO aired the Rolling Stones from Madison Square Garden. We cranked it and danced barefoot across the hotel carpet, laughing like we were there. I used to rock alone; Carmen was now in the mix—riff for riff. To the neighbors: sorry, not sorry.

I married a person who says "turn it up"—and reaches for the dial.

TWO HEARTS, ONE RIVER

The next morning, we packed up and headed home—back to Indiana, back to reality. But not before beginning to dream up the next chapter.

Indiana in October.

As we drove, Carmen and I started making plans. Real plans. We made a pact right there in the car: we would attend as many of the Bicentennial Signature Events as we could over the next three years. We would chase the story together.

Somewhere between the hills of Kentucky and the banks of the Ohio, I looked over at her... and fell in love all over again.

When we crossed into Indiana, we took the scenic route—the Ohio River Scenic Byway—instead of the interstate. It took a bit longer, but we didn't care. The road wound alongside the water, giving us glimpses of the same river Lewis and Clark once followed. We stopped at one of the locks, hoping to watch a barge pass through. We waited, but the river was quiet.

Still, we lingered.

We walked to the far end of the lot and stood there in the cold, watching the water move.

Of Grief and Gravestones

To: the Natchez Trace and Hohenwald, Tennessee
July 2003

We don't always know what's sacred until we're standing in it.

Indianapolis, IN
Hohenwald, TN

four
Race to the Hills: The Natchez Trace

The next Bicentennial event was scheduled for October—over 10 months away. After the excitement of the inaugural event, waiting felt nearly impossible. There would be little to do except dive deeper into Lewis and Clark's exploration—or so we thought.

At the time, I worked for Thomson Multimedia (Technicolor), leading a significant project to outsource our application development and support. Through this project, I'd formed a friendship with the vice president of business development at Capgemini, the company we'd partnered with. He happened to share Carmen's passion for IndyCar racing. He and his wife, who lived near Nashville, Tennessee, invited us to the July IndyCar race. Carmen had been a huge IndyCar fan since childhood—she'd attended every Indy 500 since she was a kid. Frankly, my fandom was new and entirely thanks to her. Carmen got Lewis and Clark from me; I got IndyCar and much more from her.

We came for racing and rivers; the Trace would teach us about endings, vigilance, and the quiet ways strangers can wound—and heal—on the same day. We would be entering the homelands of the Natchez, Chickasaw, and Choctaw Nations—following a road first made by their feet and purposes long before ours.

I knew Meriwether Lewis had died along the Natchez Trace in Tennessee in 1809. After digging, I discovered he'd passed away near Hohenwald,

Tennessee, about 60 miles southwest of Nashville. I didn't realize how close the ancient trail network was to Nashville, with the modern Natchez Trace Parkway's northern terminus only 17 miles from downtown Nashville.

"Hmmm, what if we went down a couple of days before the race?" I mused. We could drive the scenic 60-mile stretch of the Natchez Trace Parkway and camp minutes from the Meriwether Lewis Death and Burial Site (a unit of the Parkway). Since the rivers still called strongly to us, I was excited to discover a canoe livery offering trips down the Buffalo River, just a short drive from our campground.

This was our first actual proof of the now-long-standing joke in our family: "You can turn *any* trip into a Lewis and Clark trip!" With a brand-new tool in my toolkit—Microsoft Streets & Trips—I mapped out our next adventure. Streets & Trips allowed us to plot routes with multiple stops—a significant leap forward. After mapping out the journey, it produced printable maps and turn-by-turn directions. Those instructions ranged wildly: sometimes excruciatingly detailed, sometimes frustratingly vague, and occasionally flat-out wrong. Carmen still preferred her paper maps and trusty road atlas. But I loved this high-tech approach to planning our next adventure.

CHASING SHADOWS ON THE TRACE

Our fascination with Meriwether Lewis deepened as we prepared to visit the Natchez Trace. I'd been drawn to him—part explorer, part mystery, forever tethered to the romantic tragedy of his final days, as I read *Undaunted Courage*. Now, as I shared the stories with Carmen, she was fascinated with his life as well.

Meriwether Lewis has never been just a name in a textbook for me. He was a young Virginian, raised in the turbulence of a new nation, mentored by Thomas Jefferson, and marked by both brilliance and restlessness. What struck me wasn't his résumé—it was the contradictions. Soldier and dreamer. Trusted secretary and troubled soul.

When I first learned that Lewis died under mysterious circumstances along the Natchez Trace in 1809, it didn't feel like a line in a history book. It felt like an unfinished story. Suicide or murder, no one can say for sure. What I can say is this: The mystery followed me. It tugged at me each time we packed the car or traced another mile of the trail. In Lewis, I saw the leader of an expedition, but also a man burdened by doubts and shadows. Maybe that's why his story has always felt less like history and more like a mirror.

I imagined Lewis on that final ride, exhausted, perhaps ill, burdened by debts and disappointments. I wondered about his thoughts, his fears, his dreams. Did he sense he was writing the final lines of his adventure? Or did fate intervene in ways we'll never fully understand?

I knew we'd revisit Lewis's final days when our travels brought us back there in 2009, the 200th anniversary of his death. But first, Carmen and I had our adventure waiting along the Natchez Trace—a journey through history, and through our hearts.

FOOTPRINTS AND FELINES

The Natchez Trace has been traversed for over 10,000 years, initially by the Natchez, Chickasaw, and Choctaw Nations for hunting and trade. It stretched from present-day Natchez, Mississippi, through a corner of Alabama, to near Nashville, Tennessee. Centuries later, American boatmen returning home from trips downriver used these same trails. They sold their boats in New Orleans and journeyed back north on foot or horseback, staying at rustic inns called "stands." It was at one such place, Grinder's Stand, that Lewis met his mysterious fate.

Carmen and I started our journey at the northern end of the Natchez Trace Parkway, just outside Nashville, on a sweltering July day. Our first stop was the Double Arch Bridge at Birdsong Hollow, an impressive concrete structure soaring 155 feet above the valley floor.

As we traveled further down the Parkway, we stopped at a roadside pull-off to explore one of the original sections of the trail. Wagon ruts—or at least what we imagined as ruts—were still faintly visible. We walked a short distance under a dense canopy of branches, feeling an unexpected chill. I realized Meriwether had never passed this spot; he had approached from the south, while we started from the north.

A bit farther down, we reached Jackson Falls. A soft mewing drew Carmen's attention at the trailhead—a tiny kitten hiding nearby. She gently coaxed it out, but the kitten kept a cautious distance. As we descended the trail to the waterfall, the kitten quietly followed. The cascade was gentle, softly trickling over rocks about 60 feet above.

Climbing back up the steep trail in 90-degree heat left us exhausted and soaked with sweat. Our little feline companion stayed close behind. Carmen tried offering milk (we know better now) from our camping supplies, but the kitten vanished when other hikers passed. Concerned and silent, we continued our drive down the Parkway, wondering about the kitten—and perhaps about the fleeting, fragile moments that punctuated history and our journey.

Animals find Carmen. They always have—from childhood terriers and cats to the Scotties we loved as adults. Each and every animal she let into her heart remains there. No wonder that kitten stayed with her all afternoon.

EVENING AT GRINDER'S STAND

We reached the Meriwether Lewis Death and Burial Site—part of the Natchez Trace Parkway—in the stillness of midafternoon. As we drove into the neighboring campground, a gentle quiet hung in the air, the sort that makes you lower your voice instinctively. The moment we passed the sign marking Grinder's Stand, I felt something inside me shift, an odd mingling of reverence and unease. This was more than a campsite—it was a place of unresolved whispers, where history had paused and left behind unanswered questions.

We chose a site near the back, overlooking a small gorge. Tall trees surrounded us, their leaves whispering, a quiet backdrop to our preparations. Carmen and I moved gently, almost deliberately, as we pitched the tent and gathered firewood. It felt as if we were guests, visitors who should tread lightly, careful not to disturb whatever fragile peace hovered here.

The campground managers, a friendly retired couple from Michigan, paused at our site during their rounds. We exchanged pleasantries, but it quickly became apparent they recognized our pilgrimage for what it was. Almost immediately, they asked the question lingering in everyone's mind when they come here: "Do you think Lewis was murdered—or was it suicide?"

The words hung between us, and I felt their weight: murder, suicide. I realized then that those words had haunted this place for two centuries, weaving themselves into every conversation, every quiet moment spent around a campfire. Their question wasn't idle curiosity; it felt more profound, more personal, as if the answers might ease a burden they had carried during their time here.

We talked, our voices soft, almost reverent, considering possibilities, doubts, and mysteries. They were convinced Lewis had been murdered; something in their tone suggested it troubled them, as if an injustice lingered unresolved.

They left us with a friendly wave and promised to return with extra firewood. Alone again, I noticed Carmen quietly staring into the trees, lost in thought. I gently touched her shoulder.

"You okay?"

She looked back at me, nodding slowly. "It's strange," she whispered. "It feels like we're camping in someone else's memory."

I knew exactly what she meant. The campground felt suspended between history and imagination, a space that belonged as much to Lewis's unresolved spirit as it did to travelers like us, who came seeking something intangible.

A DOOR OPENS

Later, we decided to head into nearby Hohenwald to pick up ice and explore the local museum. On the edge of town, we pulled into a tired quick-mart. Inside, the lights were dim and the air stale; three men clustered near the counter, loud and loose with their jokes. My gut tightened. I kept my eyes down, paid for ice, and asked for directions to the museum.

When I pushed back through the door, Carmen was already wheeling the Jeep around, jaw set. I tossed the ice in and climbed in, and she pulled away. Only when we'd slipped into an empty lot did she speak—hands still white-knuckled on the wheel. One of the men had exited the shop and saw Carmen bent over the cooler, rearranging the contents. He started toward her, calling out, "Hey, Blondie, got anything in that cooler for me?" She didn't wait for him to get any closer. She had thrown the cooler in the Jeep and peeled around to pick me up. We sat there, breathing, as anger and adrenaline ebbed, then turned the car toward town.

We continued into town, quieter now, still absorbing the tension of that moment. When we finally found the Lewis County Museum and Nature Center, our spirits lifted, only to sink again when we realized it had closed 15 minutes earlier. Carmen sighed, the frustration heavy on her face—but as we turned away, a door unexpectedly opened.

"Hey, you folks want to see the museum?" asked a friendly voice—a man in a suit, emerging with a warm smile. He explained he was the board chairman, and despite the after-hours board meeting in progress, he welcomed us inside anyway.

We followed him gratefully into the cool, welcoming interior, hesitantly passing through the boardroom, where everyone paused their meeting to greet us warmly. Their genuine kindness was a balm to our shaken nerves, restoring some of the day's earlier warmth.

In the quiet space of the exhibit rooms, we studied the historical relics connected to Lewis, each artifact reminding us of the deeper story behind our journey. Our exploration eventually led us into the final room—a startling display of mounted exotic animals. We exchanged a glance, quietly uncomfortable, and quickly moved through the unsettling exhibit.

We both understand the process of hunting and where food comes from. This, though, was spectacle—trophies taken for taking's sake—and it turned our stomachs.

Leaving the museum meant retracing our steps back through the boardroom, where, once again, everyone paused to bid us farewell. They seemed sincerely glad we'd visited, sharing smiles, directions, and that ever-present question about Lewis's death. They told us we needed to stop by the display of the original monument stones that had marked Lewis's grave. They explained that a few years before our visit, the monument's base had been replaced with new limestone bricks in preparation for the Bicentennial. The Lewis County Museum obtained the original stones and placed them in a park in Hohenwald.

Walking back outside, Carmen slipped her hand gently into mine, her touch grounding and reassuring. We'd come here seeking history but found ourselves experiencing something more profound—a reminder of how vulnerable we can be, yet how unexpectedly kindness can appear just when it's most needed. We'd come for history and left steadier—shaken by one encounter, steadied by another.

We quickly found the stones a short drive from the museum.

Reading from a brochure we had picked up at the museum, we learned that Hohenwald is the county seat of Lewis County, Tennessee. The county was created to honor Meriwether Lewis in 1848. The state set aside funds for a monument to be built above Lewis's grave. His body was exhumed so that he could be identified. Even though several experts proclaim murder, there are differing accounts of what was found when his remains were examined.

The monument was built. The base was constructed from limestone bricks stacked in a somewhat pyramidal fashion. A column, broken in half to symbolize a life cut short, was erected on top of that platform. To provide further protection, an iron fence was built around the monument. The barrier remained until the Civil War, when parts were appropriated to make horseshoes.

By the early 1900s, the grave and its surroundings were in disrepair. Vandalism and neglect had taken their toll. In 1925, President Calvin Coolidge declared the site a national monument. It was then transferred to the National Park Service in 1933. By that summer, the Civilian Conservation Corps was established nearby, and they began cleaning up the area and establishing trails.

Beginning in 1996, as the 200th anniversary of his death approached, descendants of the Lewis family asked the federal government to exhume his remains and perform an examination to answer the "murder or suicide" question once and for all. Because the grave is on National Park land, the Department of the Interior had to approve it. In 2008, that approval was granted. However, two years later, without notice, the department reversed its decision and denied the request.

We stood a while before the rough limestone that had guarded his grave for more than a century and a half, then drove back to the Parkway in silence.

THE FINAL RESTING PLACE

Upon entering the park, we drove to the site of Lewis's grave. His monument stands in the middle of a large clearing immediately adjacent to the remnants of a portion of the Trace. We silently walked across the clearing and paid our respects to this great explorer. After several minutes, we made our way over to the replica of the stand itself. It is a small, two-room cabin located at the southern end of the clearing. Inside was a small display telling Lewis's story. Outside the cabin, the foundation stones of the original stand were visible a few paces away.

Carmen and I then walked across the clearing to the trail itself. She must have sensed my desire to walk a few steps down the trail alone because she made some excuse about it being too hot—she'd wait in the shade. So, with a shiver running up my spine, I made my way a few hundred yards down the path, stopped for a moment, and returned, retracing what were to be his final steps. It was deathly quiet, if you'll excuse the expression... not even a whisper of a breeze.

We returned to our campsite in silence and began to prepare dinner. It was many minutes before we spoke. We drank a toast to Meriwether and enjoyed our dinner.

That night by the fire, with the night sounds wrapping the dark, we talked about our day. I could tell by the way she brought up the room of exotic animals that the image was still troubling her. Carmen drew a clear line. "It's not hunting I have a problem with," she said. "It's killing for the sake of it."

Then she told me where that line came from. Her grandparents ran a small slaughterhouse and grocery—work done to feed people: family, neighbors, strangers. They worked hard and helped quietly; you had to be paying attention to see it. After her parents divorced, she and her mom lived with them for a while. Grandma Delmo—her mother's mother—ran the house and the store. Papaw George would shake his head, roll his eyes, and sip his "milk," telling them, *You'll understand when I'm gone.* Later, they did—dozens of empty vodka bottles hidden around the house.

There was polish in that world, too. Grandma Margaret—technically her great-grandmother—had been a nanny for Freddie Ayres, of the L. S. Ayres family, which founded the Indiana-based department store chain of the same name. With her, Carmen learned the unshowy kind of manners: how to carry yourself, how to show respect for yourself and for others. From both Delmo and Margaret came the everyday arts—cooking, baking, tending a garden, loving flowers—skills stitched to purpose.

What I heard, under the crackle, was Carmen's compass, set long before we met.

THE RIVERS ARE CALLING OUR NAMES

We packed our gear after an excellent breakfast of eggs, bacon, and toast over an open campfire the following day. The camp managers drove up in their golf cart as we did so. They were very excited as they presented us with a roll of Lewis and Clark Trail stickers. After thanking them, we headed a few more miles south to the Buffalo River Canoe Outfitters. The owner loaded our canoe and gear and drove us to the put-in site for a seven-mile trip. During the ride, he asked what had brought us to the area. And, of course, when he heard we were there to visit Lewis's grave, he asked us if we thought it was murder. It seemed everyone in this area could be divided into two groups: those who believed he was murdered... and those who were wrong.

The Buffalo River crosses the Natchez Trace several times as it winds toward the Duck River and ultimately the Tennessee River. It was easy to imagine Lewis on horseback crossing the river, hooves clacking on rock as the water splashed around his mount's legs. The scenery is spectacular.

Over time, the river cut through limestone, sandstone, and shale, carving bluffs and tucking caves and sinkholes into the hills. Along the banks, rich, weathered soils feed dense green forests pressed to the water, with farm fields and pastures stepping down from the ridges.

The banks were thick with lush vegetation, giving the area an almost rainforest feel. The abundant plant life is mainly due to the weathering of the shale into rich, fertile soil. Dense forests abound in the riparian corridor. Farm fields and pastures dot the valley, some coming to the river's edge, with hills in the distance.

The river ran about three feet deep in most places, with a few darker pools—enough current to carry us without much work. The river set its liturgy: bow hush, eddies murmuring amen.

We stopped for lunch on a gravel bank inside one of the river's meandering turns. There is something about a pita bread sandwich, chips, and an ice-cold beer alongside a river that makes it taste like a steak dinner at the finest restaurant in town.

After lunch, we pushed off from the bank and headed downstream. As we rounded a turn, we encountered an entire herd of cattle standing in the water. The farmer had extended the field's fence into the river to ensure the cows could cool themselves in the water, but not wander downstream. You have to think that the fence gets ripped out multiple times yearly during high water.

Carmen was now an old pro at the bow. I smiled—remembering two early paddles before we were a couple. I was living in an apartment on a small lagoon of the White River in Indianapolis. Many evenings and weekends during the warmer months, I would paddle upstream a couple of miles or more and then return to the lagoon.

In the spring of 2000, I invited my good friend Carmen to go canoeing. She arrived at my apartment dressed to the nines—her hair perfect, nails done, makeup elegant, and a sweater tied just so. Me? Shorts and a sleeveless T-shirt; I had to show off my new dreamcatcher tattoo.

She looked at me. I looked at her. She apologized for the way she was dressed. "No, no! You look great!" I stammered, "You won't even have to paddle. I will do all the work."

With that, we climbed into the canoe and pushed off. Rather than paddling upstream first, I decided we would head downstream. The river was flatter and slower in that direction, so there was less chance of getting my passenger wet. We had a lovely afternoon, but I wasn't sure she would ever say yes to another trip. Her friends were amazed that I got her out on the river at all.

The next summer, we visited my parents at their place in Green Lake, Wisconsin. I asked Carmen if she would like to go canoeing while we were there. "I know the perfect river," I told her. "The Mecan River is just a short drive from Green Lake. It is a small river with a very gentle flow." She enthusiastically agreed.

We opted for a several-hour trip. Paul and Leanne Harvey own and operate Mecan River Outfitters on a beautiful property with a log lodge that the Harvey family built. We arrived on a slow day, and Leanne was our shuttle driver. After explaining where the take-out point was, she dropped us off and drove the van back to the lodge. We threw our gear into the canoe and pushed off from shore. I quickly realized that I had oversold the ease of paddling this river.

Yes. It was a narrow river. And yes, the current was steady but not overly fast. But I had forgotten how much the river meandered, turning left and right, then back left again, often doubling back on itself as it cut through the forest. Many of the bends were choked with deadfall trees, known as "strainers," and the trees that lined the banks hung low over the water's surface, creating "sweepers." This was going to be a very technical paddle, and the bowsman—that is, Carmen—was going to have to work hard to keep us out of trouble. I began to instruct her on the maneuvers she would need to perform. I was devastated. I knew she would never trust me to take her canoeing again.

Ten minutes became twenty, then half an hour, and we navigated a dozen river turns. I was pissed at myself for getting us into this situation. But then I heard it. We had just maneuvered through a particularly challenging turn when I heard it. The sound of giggling came from the front of the canoe. Carmen was having a blast! I knew then that I was going to marry this woman!

Meanwhile, back on the Buffalo in July 2003, the paddle was nowhere near as challenging. It was very relaxing and almost uneventful—almost. We were in sight of the take-out point, with one final turn of the river to navigate. However, we (meaning me) underestimated the river's strength. It had picked up speed over the last half mile. I overcorrected the turn and the current caught the stern of our canoe, pushing us right into a strainer—one of the most dangerous situations you can find yourself in on a river. We were pinned against the trunk of a fallen tree. The river pushed us with all its might into the branches, where our canoe would likely tip over and we could become entangled in the potentially deadly limbs.

Pinned to the trunk, every reflex said lean away. We leaned in—exposing hull, not gunwales—held the paddles to the bark, and waited for the current to blink. It did. The bow inched free, the river grabbed us, and we slid back into the main flow.

Sheepishly, we looked around to be sure no one had witnessed our little excitement. Within minutes, we were standing on shore at the take-out. Panting, with our hearts still racing, we unloaded the canoe.

I got a little nervous as we hauled our gear up the bank. About 10 guys in their 20s and 30s were on a multi-day river trip. They had stopped at the outfitters to buy ice to restock their beer coolers. They stood around, talking loudly, laughing, and looking in our direction. My mind immediately jumped back to the previous encounter with the locals at the gas station. They were looking at us, but in my mind, they were staring at Carmen.

To give them a wider berth, we took a different path from the river to the livery shack, carrying our next load of gear. As we passed by a large tree, we both stopped short. On the side of the tree, working its way up the trunk, was the largest snake we had ever seen. It was a rat snake, about four feet long. They are commonly called chicken snakes due to their fondness for eating chicken eggs. Giving him a wide berth, we were relieved we had not encountered him on the water or when we had stopped for lunch earlier in the day.

We loaded our gear in the Jeep and headed toward Nashville. As we passed the burial site, we decided to take a final loop through the park. At the end of the park road, a narrow stream slipped out of the trees—the place where Lewis was first laid to rest before his remains were moved. We stepped in and waded upstream and back, the water cooling our shins. Sunlight sifted through the leaves and broke into bright coins on the surface. Butterflies lifted at our passing; others held fast on the bank, paired and still. The woods went quiet around us. We stood longer than we meant to, letting the moment steady us.

As we headed back to the Parkway, we made a final pass around the clearing where Meriwether lay and proceeded to Nashville.

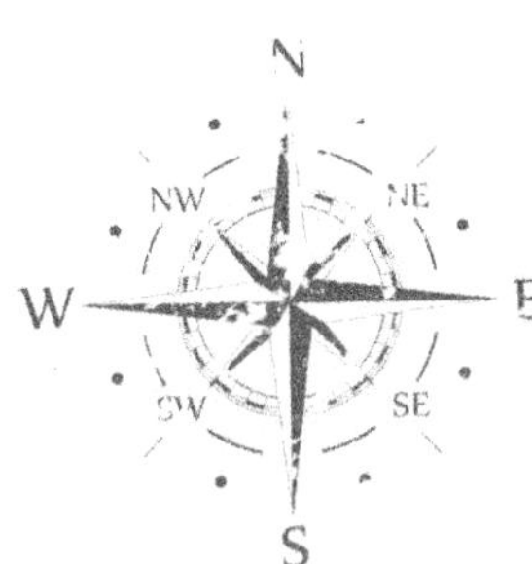

City of Light

To: Paris, France
September 2003

*Serendipity doesn't ask permission—it just shows
up with goat cheese and a bottle of wine.*

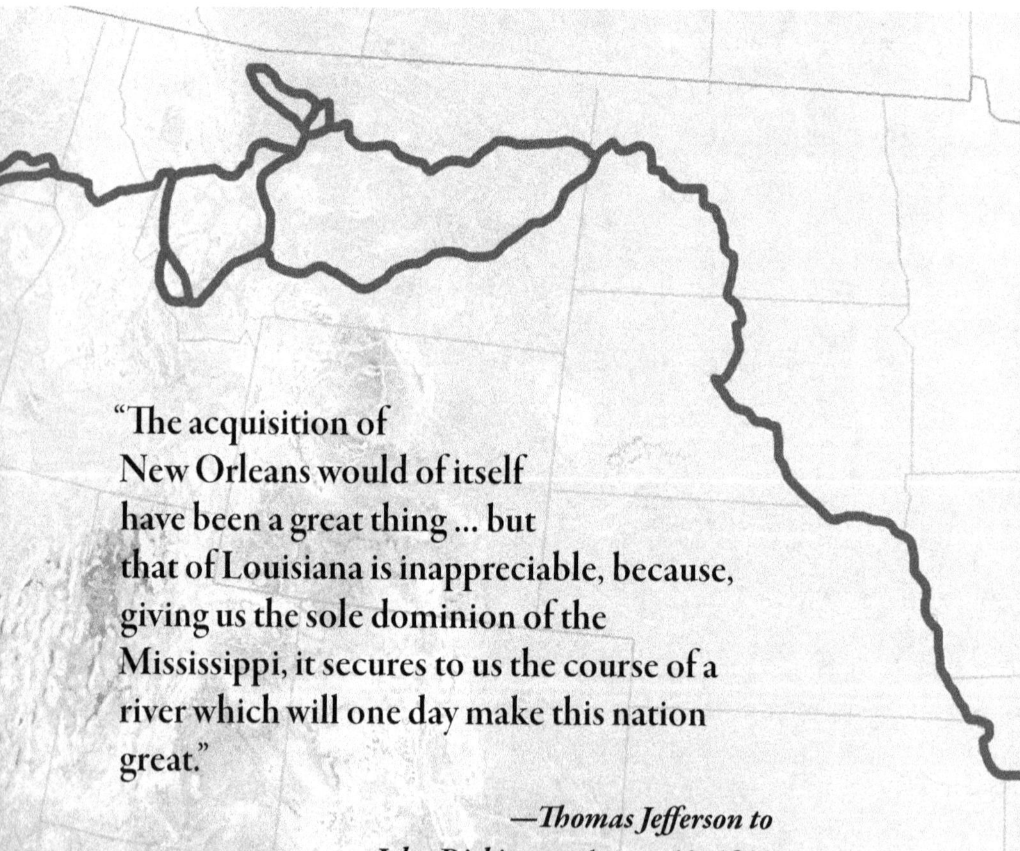

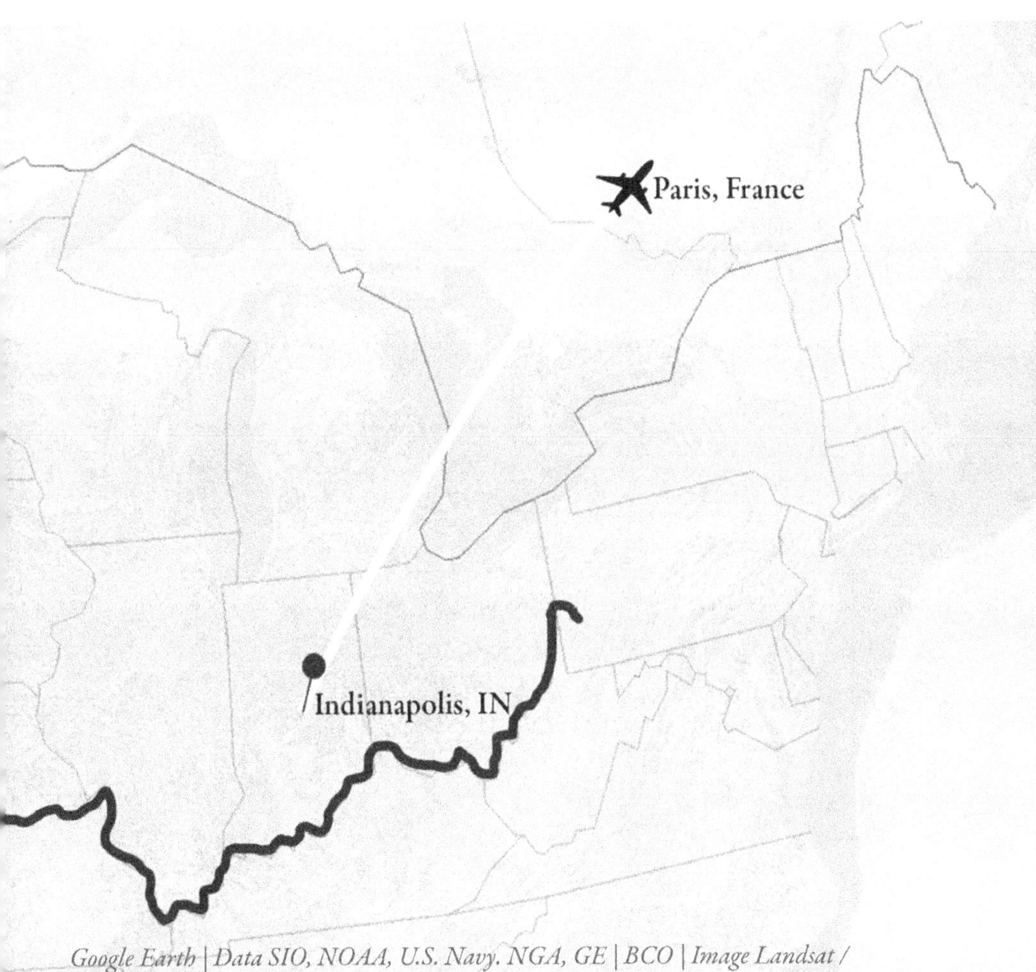

Paris, France
Indianapolis, IN
Google Earth | Data SIO, NOAA, U.S. Navy. NGA, GE | BCO | Image Landsat /
Copernicus | Data LDEO-Columbia, NSF, NOAA

five

Thanks for the Country, Dude!

In September 2003, our journey took another unlikely turn. I'd been promoted to director at Thomson Multimedia (formerly RCA), now French-owned, which meant regular trips to Paris. By my third visit, we arranged for Carmen to fly over to see the city for the first time, and I took a couple of days off to show her around. There I was in Paris—La Ville-Lumière—about to be joined by the light of my life, the most beautiful woman I had ever met, and my mind was on... Lewis and Clark!

Why? The Louisiana Purchase, that's why. Napoleon! He sold our country the land through which Lewis and Clark would travel. Carmen was joining me in the city where the Lewis and Clark story truly begins. Can I admit to feeling giddy with excitement?

Paris wasn't on our Lewis and Clark Bicentennial route, but it nudged my compass. Even here, the river story pressed in—Napoleon's city, the doorway to a purchase I still treated like a tidy chapter heading. I didn't yet know how incomplete that frame was. What I did know was that joy was about to land at Charles de Gaulle Airport.

On the morning of her arrival, I caught a taxi across the street from my hotel in Boulogne and headed to the airport. My heart was racing as we wound through early-morning traffic. I couldn't wipe the smile off my face. It felt like the day after Carmen and I officially started dating—walking the halls at work, grinning ear to ear, thinking, *I'm dating Carmen Hillenburg!*

At the arrivals door, I wore that same grin. I waited. Finally—there she was—my beautiful wife in this beautiful city. A scene from our wedding flashed: the curtain parting, her smile finding me as she walked toward me. Only this time, the terminal doors opened, and she walked toward me with that same smile and those sparkling eyes.

A TABLE IN THE SKY

We grabbed a taxi back to Boulogne to drop her luggage before our day of adventure. As we crossed town, her eyes lit at first glimpses of Paris. With each new sight, she squeezed my hand and pointed like a kid seeing fireworks: the Stade de France, the skyline of La Défense, Roland-Garros, the lush green of the Bois de Boulogne.

Bags stowed at the Hôtel Acanthe, we headed to the Métro for our whirlwind day. First stop: the Eiffel Tower and lunch at Le Jules Verne, the restaurant on the tower's second floor.

We emerged from the Métro to the Seine shimmering before us, pulling us toward the tower like a slow current. With every step into the Champ de Mars, Carmen's excitement built. I felt it in the squeeze of her hand, saw it in the look that says, *Is this real life?*

At the base, street vendors peddled souvenirs, and a dozen languages braided the air. We made our way to the south pillar, where the private elevator to Le Jules Verne awaited. It's one thing to say a restaurant is on the second floor; it's another when that second floor is more than 400 feet in the air.

Sunlight poured through floor-to-ceiling windows. From our table, the city unfurled: Sacré-Cœur, Les Invalides, Montmartre. The Seine stitched it all together like a silver ribbon. I watched Carmen's eyes dance from landmark to landmark and thought, *Even here, even now, the river has found us—two river rats in Paris, lifted high above it all.*

The restaurant was elegant in that quiet, understated way the French excel at. A low hum of conversation, soft classical music, the clink of silver on china—the small choreography of grace.

The maître d' nodded, and a young waiter led us to our table. As we sat, Carmen reached for her menu, but her eyes kept drifting to the view. I leaned in and whispered, "Can you believe we're here?" She just smiled and shook her head—wide-eyed, wordless wonder.

After an indulgent lunch of pastries, bisque, duck, and filet, we ended the French way—with espresso. I lifted my cup and toasted: "To rivers, and chocolates, and wild ideas like love in midlife."

She touched her tiny cup to mine, smiling. "And to lunches in the sky with people you adore."

In that moment, I didn't care if we saw another thing all day. I was exactly where I wanted to be.

CATHEDRALS AND CANDLELIGHT

After our leisurely lunch, we descended by elevator—reluctant to leave the dream, eager for what came next. What better way to follow a visit to the clouds than to step into the sacred? Our next stop: Notre-Dame.

We strolled to the Trocadéro Métro, stealing one last glance at the Eiffel Tower, its iron limbs stretched confidently into the sky. When we emerged at the Hôtel de Ville stop, the Seine shimmered before us—as if it had been waiting. We crossed the Pont d'Arcole with the towers of Notre-Dame rising like sentinels ahead.

The west façade loomed—three portals carved like living scripture. The Portal of the Last Judgment gazed back, solemn and sure. Above them, the Gallery of Kings stood in stony witness. We traced each figure with our eyes, breathing in the grandeur—and the contradiction.

Notre-Dame is both fortress and sanctuary, art and armor. A monument to faith—and a symbol of power. It reminded me of Jefferson's Monticello, of imperial tombs, and of my own upbringing in the church: a structure built to honor God, heavy with human imperfection.

Inside, the air was cool and hushed. Sunlight spilled through stained glass in slow, deliberate beams. Candles flickered in side chapels—small flames against centuries of stone and silence. We found a quiet enclave with a hundred votives. Light danced across the walls. Carmen stepped forward, taper in hand.

She lit a candle for her Granny.

Pearletta Gruhl Hitchell—born 1909—raised Carmen's father, Tom, on her own in the 1930s. Strong. Independent. I've always imagined she helped shape those same qualities in Carmen. Pearletta passed in 1999.

Carmen lit a second candle—this one for her dad, Jim.

Something in me cracked—not from sadness, exactly, but from awe.

Tom, her biological father, had been more tangle than tether—four marriages, hurt that ran deeper than words, a childhood that saw too much. Jim Crain adopted her when she was 11: the man who chose her, raised her, protected her. I never met him, yet I feel like I know him; I see him in her steadiness, in how she carries people forward long after they're gone. In 1995—the year Carmen and I met—Jim was diagnosed with glioblastoma. His treatments followed. So did her divorce. Life re-threaded itself.

That's how Carmen Gruhl became Carmen Crain, then Carmen Hillenburg... and now Carmen Ton.

Watching her in that moment, praying quietly in the shadow of this ancient church, I realized something: Her faith had never been loud. It never needed stained glass or steeples. It lived in her steadiness—in how she remembers, heals, and loves.

And the church became a metaphor. For all its contradiction and grandeur, the holy had always lived in the quiet places: soft light; a steady hand; a woman lighting candles for people who shaped her.

We stepped back into the Paris sunlight, blinking against the brightness, carrying something new. Not heavy—but holy. A small flame we didn't have before.

Something uncharted.

CHEESE, WINE, AND THE LIZARD KING

What better way to follow a visit to a cathedral than a visit to a cemetery? From sacred stone to sacred silence. From a monument to faith... to a monument to flame. We were still riding the high of Notre-Dame's quiet holiness when we turned our attention to something more rebellious.

As middle-aged rock 'n' rollers with a shared affection for the myth-makers of our youth, we had to visit Père Lachaise—the final resting place of Jim Morrison, rock god, poet, wanderer, the Lizard King himself.

As we rode the Métro, Carmen's wheels started turning.

"You know what we should have done?" she asked, eyes sparkling. "We should've brought a bottle of wine to toast Morrison."

And there it was. That flash. That uncharted moment.

We popped out of the station and scanned the corner. There, like a stage set, stood the tiniest wine shop I'd ever seen. Inside, it was a scene from a different century—walls lined with bottles, an elderly woman behind the counter with a twinkle in her eye and stooped shoulders that told stories of decades.

"Bonjour," she greeted us.

"Parlez-vous anglais?" we asked.

"Non, parlez-vous français?" she teased, with a soft chuckle.

What followed was a symphony of gestures, mangled French, broken Spanish, and belly-laughing humanity. We selected a bottle of red. Carmen pointed at a soft cheese in the case.

"Chèvre," the woman said.

Blank stares.

"Chèvre," she repeated.

We shrugged.

"Chèvre!"

Finally, with a sparkle in her eye and an impish grin, she looked right at us and said,

"Baaaaa."

Ahhh... goat cheese. Of course. Chèvre.

We laughed. We bought the wine and the cheese.

Then Carmen paused. "Uh... how are we going to open our wine?"

One more round of pantomime, one more shared smile, and with the grace of a Parisian sommelier, our hostess opened the bottle, slid the cork partway back in, and handed it to us like she was sending us off to a wedding.

She kind of was.

A communion. A celebration. A tribute.

Across the street, the cemetery sprawled before us like a city for the dead—cobblestone paths winding between crypts that whispered names like Wilde, Chopin, and Bizet.

We paused at Bizet's crypt. Carmen stood quietly, her fingers brushing the cool stone. She was named after his famous opera, and in that moment, it felt like more than a coincidence. It felt ancestral, almost—as if she were standing in a place that had been waiting for her.

She's always felt the spirits of places more keenly than I have. Where I see names and dates, she senses presence. History speaks to her in scent, in sound, in something deeper than memory.

We moved on, past Wilde's bold Art Deco tomb and Chopin's weathered marker. But I kept glancing back, watching her. She was listening—to the stories etched in stone.

And then, tucked between gravestones and fading graffiti, we found Morrison.

His grave was worn, almost forgotten. Vandals had chipped away at anything that wasn't nailed down. Messages were scrawled on nearby stones—lyrics, tributes, nonsense. It was chaotic. Beautiful. Honest.

We found a bench nearby, poured our wine into two plastic water cups, unwrapped the chèvre.

"To Jim," Carmen toasted.

"To Jim," I echoed.

We clinked. Or rather... tocked.

The sound was faint, but it carried something that lingered longer than taste: reverence. Not the cathedral kind. The kind born of grit, grief, rebellion, and poetry.

The cheese was creamy. The wine was smooth. A gendarme kept a watchful eye from the path nearby. But we weren't here to cause trouble. We were here to remember. To feel. To be human in a place where humanity often gets polished out of marble.

It felt like Jim was there, smirking at our plastic cups and our goat cheese picnic. It felt like we were exactly where we were meant to be.

A scrap of a Doors lyric flickered—highway ghosts at first light—and then the city exhaled.

We sat a while, letting Paris move around us—plastic cups, a wedge of chèvre, Morrison's stone, the low shuffle of feet on gravel. When we finally stood, we didn't speak. We didn't need to. The little *tock* of our cups seemed to hang in the air, enough benediction for the day.

HÔTEL DES INVALIDES AND THE CONTRADICTIONS OF GREAT MEN

Hôtel des Invalides and our Lewis and Clark connection were just a short Métro ride away, but something had shifted in us. We had just come from a quiet communion in Père Lachaise—a plastic-cup toast to poetry, rebellion, and mortality. The city was beginning to feel less like a postcard and more like a pilgrimage.

The sun was starting to dip, casting long shadows across the 7th arrondissement. From the Métro platform, we glimpsed the golden dome gleaming above the rooftops. It pulled us toward it like a beacon. Hôtel des Invalides—part military hospital, part church, part crypt. And beneath its gilded crown: the tomb of Napoleon Bonaparte, the man who, with a stroke of a pen, sold the Jefferson administration half our country. It wasn't his land to sell. It was—and is—home to nations whose names we were only beginning to learn.

It was nearly closing time, so we didn't linger in the courtyards. We walked with purpose, past columns and cannons, heading straight toward the dome. Inside, the light dimmed. We stepped into a grand rotunda—a circular hush of stone and reverence. We could look up to the intricate ceiling. Or we could look down.

At Napoleon. Well, at his tomb.

It sat like a sunken monument to ambition—massive, imperial, undeniable. We descended into the crypt and stood in silence. The sarcophagus was polished to a hard shine, throwing back the room's light.

It couldn't have been more different from Morrison's grave, and the contrast pressed on our chests.

Here, power was preserved. Institutionalized. Celebrated. There, it had been vandalized, stripped down, reclaimed.

Here, the marble whispered "Victory. Empire. Legend." There, the crumbling stone had murmured "Mortality. Music. Memory."

"Wow," I whispered to Carmen, my voice almost swallowed by the vault. "This ties back to the bust we saw at Monroe's house." The same stylized laurel crown. The same Caesar-like pose. Even across an ocean and two centuries, the image endured. Napoleon wanted to be immortal. It seemed he had succeeded.

Standing there—inside grandeur that felt more like theater than truth—the irony wouldn't let go. The man who rose from a revolution against opulence had entombed himself in the very symbols that sparked it. The contradictions echoed off the walls.

It landed then: The day ran on contradictions.

Napoleon, Jefferson, Lewis, Clark—heroes with flawed hearts and complicated legacies. Carmen and I—carrying our own. Wounds and wonders. Faith and doubt. Independence and longing. We were only beginning to see them—in the men we followed and in ourselves. We had a lot to learn—about them, about each other, about what we were becoming.

When we stepped back outside, the dome had cooled from gold to an ember glow, and the evening felt heavier and somehow clearer.

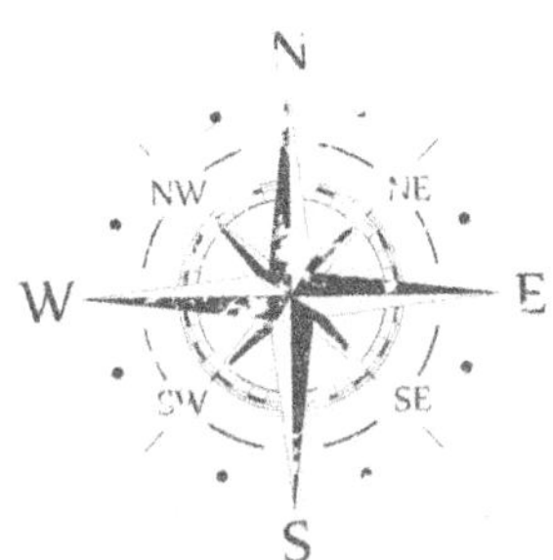

The Last Jeep to Clarksville

To: Clarksville, Indiana, and Louisville, Kentucky
October 2003

Some roads lead us home before we even know where we're going.

"This is an undertaking fraited with
many difeculties, but My friend I do
assure you that no man lives whith whome
I would perfur to undertake Such a Trip &c.
as your self..."

—*William Clark to
Meriwether Lewis, July 18, 1803*

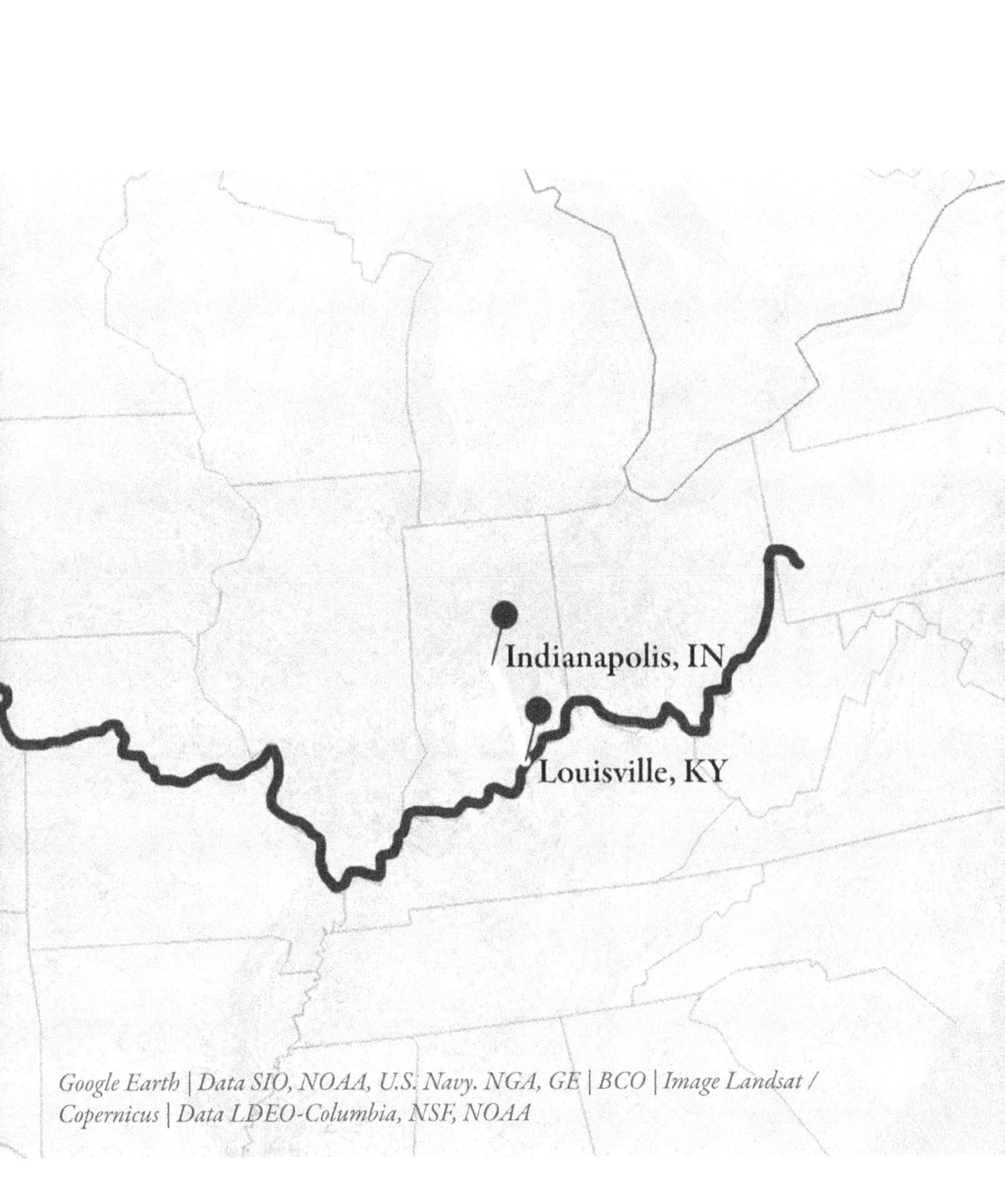

Indianapolis, IN
Louisville, KY
Google Earth | Data SIO, NOAA, U.S. Navy. NGA, GE | BCO | Image Landsat /
Copernicus | Data LDEO-Columbia, NSF, NOAA

six

Remembering Granny

Ten months after Monticello, the next Signature Event was finally close to home—On the Threshold of Discovery, Louisville and Clarksville. We planned the final weekend: the reenactment, the river, the boats.

In 1803, Lewis left Monticello, threaded east for supplies and instruction, then turned west and floated the Ohio River, reaching the Falls of the Ohio on October 14. In 2003, the commemoration ran from October 14–26; we circled the last days on our calendar and packed the car.

The Falls sit across from Louisville, Kentucky, on the Indiana side, in the shadow of the Clark name. Everywhere you turn down here, a Clark story waits—John and Anne Rogers Clark, George Rogers Clark of Revolutionary War fame, and William, our famed explorer, whose son and grandson were Meriwether Lewis Clark (Sr. and Jr.). James Alexander Thom's *From Sea to Shining Sea* was one of the sparks that lit this whole fire for me; for a minute, I'd even dreamed of quitting my job and canoeing the entire trail from Clarksville. Saner heads prevailed.

Between Paris and this weekend, my Granny died. Sara (Hickey) Ton was 96—sharp, wry, and tougher than the Nebraska wind she was born into. Carmen loved her immediately and thoroughly. That mattered because joining my family hadn't been easy for Carmen. As a second wife and new stepmother, she walked in carrying hope for siblings and found everyone in the midst of their own storms. Holidays were the worst—traditions already spent elsewhere, inside jokes that moved too fast, a sense of being almost there.

Granny saw her. Maybe she recognized the outsiderness. Perhaps it was the way Carmen listened—really listened. They became buddies, the kind who sit close at noisy gatherings and trade stories. We visited often. Carmen would guide the conversation, ask about the pictures on the wall, laugh with her, and walk the hall when walking was still possible. I'd known Granny for 44 years and learned more by watching them talk than in all my years of being her grandson.

When it came time for the funeral, I reread Granny's journals and asked Carmen to help shape the words. We built a eulogy out of transitions—how she moved through seasons, and what she learned from each. I spoke; Carmen read pieces of Granny's voice. It felt right: memory speaking for itself.

A few days later, my mom handed Carmen one of Granny's favorites—a silver ring that looks woven, like strands worked into a small nest. Mom held it a second longer than you might expect and said, eyes shining, "She wanted you to have this, Carmen. She was a special lady, and you are a special woman."

Maybe some of the ice was melting.

Carmen didn't say anything. She just brushed her thumb across the band, like learning its story by touch. The ring settled in—on her hand, in our life, in our family.

THE UNVEILING OF TIME ITSELF

We spent the two-hour drive down I-65 talking about Granny—her journals, the service, the silver ring on Carmen's finger. Time slid by, and at 1:30 p.m. Friday we eased off the interstate toward downtown Jeffersonville for the 2:00 unveiling of a Thomas Jefferson statue. We'd never watched a statue meet its public.

On the square, the fife and drum corps from St. Charles, Missouri, marched in—snare hits ricocheting off brick—and the crowd tightened. The Discovery Expedition of Saint Charles reenactors followed, a quick flash of the Trail to come. A student troupe offered a few earnest lines from their Lewis and Clark musical, then the sculptor spoke briefly about form and intent.

And then Thomas Jefferson arrived.

Yes, an actor—but the carriage made belief easy. He welcomed us as citizens of his young republic and mentioned laying out Jeffersonville's grid directly east of Clarksville—greens woven with homes and civic space.

Carmen leaned in. "I kind of like him," she whispered, and her eyes did that glimmer I know.

William Clark was called next. The reenactor stepping forward was Charles "Bud" Clark, a direct descendant. In a simple, right-feeling gesture, "Jefferson" granted Clark the captaincy Lewis had promised but the War Department hadn't (later formally corrected under President William Jefferson Clinton). The crowd exhaled—an old knot untying in public.

We paused to shake the president's hand. Carmen apologized for missing him at Monticello in January. Without missing a beat, he smiled. "Ah—Washington called. I was delivering a rather important funding request." Carmen shot me that twinkling look.

The statue's drape fell. Jefferson stood bronze and composed, hand resting on a drafting compass, gaze set over the town he had imagined. For a second, everything went quiet. I felt Carmen's thumb graze the ring—once—like reading a line of text by touch.

We proceeded on.

MAP IN HAND, WONDER AHEAD

We crossed the river into Louisville and checked into the Galt House—our home base for the weekend, a place with history in its bones. We dropped our bags, layered against the chill, and walked a few blocks to Filson on Main, an extension of the Filson Historical Society, for "A Toast to the Lewis and Clark Exhibit," including a reception and a talk by Gary Moulton. James Holmberg and Dayton Duncan would be signing books at the event, as well.

I've always been drawn to maps—the way lines and rivers tell a story before a single word is read. Clark's maps, especially, felt like a hand on the shoulder. I couldn't wait for Dr. Moulton's "William Clark: Expedition Mapmaker."

But just inside, wine glasses in hand, we learned Moulton's brother had died unexpectedly. Gerard Baker—a National Park Service leader and Mandan–Hidatsa historian—would speak instead. We'd heard him in Monticello and trusted his grounded voice, even as the room absorbed the change.

Before the lecture, we wandered the exhibit: letters and tools, fragments of lives under glass. The letters between William Clark and his brother Jonathan stopped us—ink loops and slants that Holmberg had painstakingly decoded for his book aptly titled *Dear Brother: Letters of William Clark to Jonathan Clark*. Tucked nearby was a surprise we instantly pocketed as trivia gold: Churchill Downs was founded by Meriwether Lewis Clark Jr., William's grandson. We added the track to our weekend map.

When the cocktail hour ended, we found seats. Despite the late notice, Baker spoke from the heart—funny, steady, unflinching. As a citizen of the Mandan–Hidatsa Nation, he reminded us that stories look different depending on whose eyes you use. He invited us to start with listening.

We came for maps; we left with a new way to listen. What began that night was a spring that would widen, mile by mile, into a river.

Afterward, we stopped at the signing tables. Holmberg's enthusiasm for the letters was contagious; Carmen told him about our January trip east, and he listened with kind eyes. Dayton Duncan looked tired—distant, we thought—but his inscription told another story:

> To Jeff and Carmen,
> Drive on in your adventure!

He had been listening after all.

Before we left, we introduced ourselves to Bud Clark, William Clark's descendant. He signed our copy of *Dear Brother*—a small, steady link in a long chain.

Of Tombstones and Horse Tracks

Saturday morning, we started early at Cave Hill Cemetery, east of downtown Louisville. After winding through the hills, we found George Rogers Clark and a cluster of Clarks, the air as still as a held breath. Just steps from that weight, a wild peacock pecked at the grass with regal indifference—iridescent blues and greens, oblivious and alive. History humbles; nature keeps going.

We couldn't spot Meriwether Lewis Clark Jr. at first. One quick stop at the office for a map, and there he was, tucked among the Churchill stones. Of course! He had married a Churchill! We stood a minute longer than we needed to, reading names, doing that old thing Carmen and I do—imagining the lives inside the dates.

From there, we drove to the farm site called Locust Grove, once home to William's sister Lucy Clark Croghan and, in the end, to their brother George Rogers Clark himself. We skipped the film and caught up with a docent who loved "GRC" the way only a Kentuckiana kid can. I'd devoured a biography as a boy—wrote a book report, even—and the surprise attack he led against British troops with his Vincennes march lived in my bones: winter water to the chest, frozen ground, audacity. Carmen remembered it, too, from fifth-grade Indiana history; the frigid crossing sticks.

The highlight was George Rogers's bedroom, furnished much as it was when he died. Our guide walked us through those last days—a fall into the fire across the river, the leg amputation, the slow narrowing of a life to a single room—until February 13, 1818. Hand on the doorframe, I could feel a chapter of history close.

By midday, we were at the Louisville riverfront: vendor tents, the brown Ohio sliding by, the Tent of Many Voices pitched against the wind. We scanned the schedule, chose Hasan Davis for his portrayal of York, enslaved by Clark, and then found seats.

He didn't lecture; he embodied. Humor, edge, dignity. York's labor, York's skill, York's gaze across the same rivers we'd been chasing. He let silence do part of the work and then asked us to hear the story with different ears. The spring that started at Filson widened here.

He didn't redraw the map; he changed how we read it: Start with who was already there.

Out on the water, the Corps of Engineers barge offered trail exhibits, even a replica of Lewis's iron boat. We walked it briefly, grateful, but our heads were still with York.

After a quick lunch, we drove to Mulberry Hill, the John and Ann Rogers Clark home site. We expected reverence and found a city park—pickup basketball, kids on swings, the ordinary holiness of a Saturday. Only a modest marker hinted at what had been.

We walked toward a small grove and, behind a chain-link fence, found the Clark family cemetery—John and Anne resting inside a clutch of weatherworn stones. Horseshoe pits and playground chatter drifted over the fence. It felt more like a secret than a memorial.

We took a few photos, read the names out loud, and tried to picture the house that once stood here. How many people had picnicked 10 feet away, never knowing? Public memory in one ring of fence, private upkeep in another. If we wanted to honor the past, we'd have to keep looking for the places where the signs grow faint.

TWIN SPIRES, TWINNED FATES

The next stop was Churchill Downs—twin spires like trumpets of tradition. Until that weekend, we hadn't known that William Clark's grandson, Meriwether Lewis Clark Jr., founded the track. This weekend continued to teach us about roots—and their shadows.

It was packed. The Breeders' Cup was unfolding two thousand miles away in California, but Churchill Downs felt like the epicenter—crowds pouring in to watch the telecast and place their bets, the grandstand buzzing as if the horses were circling this track. We parked in a satellite lot and rode the shuttle in. Through the gates, the museum traced the track's arc from Clark Jr.'s vision to the modern Derby. Reverence, celebration—and then a plaque that stopped us:

Like his namesake, Meriwether Lewis Clark Jr. died by suicide.

We looked at each other, silent. Carmen's thumb found Granny's ring and rested there. All weekend, we'd been brushing shoulders with ghosts—some bronzed, some barely signed. Here was another: expectation, legacy, and the quiet unraveling you don't see from the grandstand.

We joined a short tour—stables, the sheen of thoroughbreds, the dirt oval stretching under a hazy afternoon sky. The place thrummed with bettors watching California; the air buzzed, but the plaque kept echoing.

We didn't know it then, but we'd be back for the Derby itself one day—an unexpected gift from a business acquaintance.

So many names on this journey carried two stories: one told in marble and bronze, the other whispered in journals and the spaces between dates. We were learning to read both.

eight

Their Journey Begins... and So Does Ours

Sunday morning greeted us with a steady downpour. Across the river in Clarksville, a statue unveiling was scheduled—a sculpture of Lewis and Clark's symbolic handshake, two centuries to the day since their historic rendezvous. We stared out our hotel window at the unrelenting rain, the streets slick with reflection. We decided to forgo the statue. There would be other days to see it. But we wouldn't miss the closing ceremonies at Clark's Cabin.

We came to witness a reenactment; the river insisted we were part of it.

Crossing the Ohio, we wove through back streets toward the cabin, only to find barricades and closures. We left the car at the Falls of the Ohio Interpretive Center and took the shuttle.

As we stepped off the bus, the morning air was alive with something old. Canvas tents dotted the clearing; a veil of woodsmoke curled through the damp. Wet leaves and earth, a hint of coffee and stew. You could *hear* the 19th century—boots in mud, iron on iron, the creak of wheels, a cadence half-remembered. Reenactors moved with quiet purpose, warming hands at tin mugs, tending leather and bone and pelt. A child squealed; a camera clicked. The past and present held space without rushing to separate.

Across the clearing stood the cabin, modest and stoic on the bluff above the Ohio. The structure wasn't original, but its presence loomed. Inside, a fireless hearth anchored one wall. The loft's small windows watched.

Our guide spoke softly, as if the timbers were listening. Here, William Clark once cared for his aging brother, George Rogers. Here, Meriwether Lewis stepped ashore to begin the journey west. Before Lewis and Clark, there had almost been another expedition—led by George Rogers Clark himself. Politics and hesitation stalled it. Decades later, he wasn't the bold young general but a man fading from memory, cared for by his younger brother, watching others set out on the road he didn't take.

A warrior turned witness—the pioneer who stayed. Body failing, name eclipsed—and still part of it, in the smoke and footfalls and hush.

We left the cabin in silence. Outside, a cannon roared. A flintlock cracked. We wandered the camps, laughed with traders, listened in—but our hearts stayed up at the cabin, with the man who almost was.

AT THE EDGE OF THE RIVER

We walked down the ramp just before the ceremony. Along the shoreline waited replicas of the keelboat—the expedition's heavy workhorse, built to haul men and supplies upriver—and a pirogue, long and maneuverable, their low silhouettes cutting the fog like memories made manifest—wooden ghosts of a journey that once shaped a nation.

The Discovery Expedition of St. Charles would retrace the route—storytellers in motion. We paused at the gunwales: weathered boards, coiled rope, the smell of river water in the grain. These boats carried dreams and doubt, ambition and fear. They carried conjecture.

Familiar faces from Monticello and the Jefferson statue unveiling gathered: Scott Mandrell as a thoughtful Meriwether Lewis; Peyton "Bud" Clark, William Clark's descendant. Nearby, descendants of George Shannon, the youngest member of the expedition, compared notes. The past breathed through the bloodlines in front of us.

We couldn't board, so I drifted to the water's edge. The Ohio spread, brown and alive. I knelt, touched it with both hands, and let it slip through my fingers—cool, steady, endless.

In that moment, I didn't see reenactors. I saw companions. I didn't see replicas. I saw readiness. I pictured Carmen and me in a canoe, pushing off, paddles catching the river's pulse. It wasn't a tourist's thought. It was something deeper. A calling.

Far off, fifes trilled; snares found the beat. The fife and drum corps announced the start.

Reluctantly, I stood and walked back up the ramp. Carmen had found two seats near the front. We wiped the wet chairs and sat as the canopy rippled in the breeze.

Part of me stayed with the river, waiting.

THE CEREMONY: ECHOES AND CONTRASTS

The Discovery Expedition presented the colors with crisp, solemn movements. A student cast rose for the anthem—young voices, steady. But what stayed with us was the Flag Song.

The combined tribal drums began—not showy, not theatrical, but rooted. As hands struck taut hide in unison, flags of nations the Corps encountered were carried forward one by one. The air thickened and stilled; you felt it in your chest before you understood.

A small paradox caught my eye: Those keepers of an old rhythm sat on plastic-and-metal folding chairs—the kind from church basements and PTA meetings. Old and new, sacred and ordinary, woven into a single breath. The drums told a story of survival and adaptation, of holding on and pressing forward. Carmen's thumb brushed the ring.

Speakers followed—Stephenie Ambrose Tubbs, honoring her father; Gerard Baker, blending historian's care with a Native son's voice; and Amy Mossett, offering welcome with fire and grace. Dignitaries spoke: former Indiana First Lady Judy O'Bannon, Congressman Baron Hill. For a moment, my mind drifted to a letter I'd once sent Mr. Hill about paddling the Trail. Now we sat in the mist by the Ohio, listening—heartbeats in time with the drum.

Not paddling yet. Maybe... almost.

UNCHARTED: THE MOMENT BETWEEN

It was nearly time. The Corps would push off—down the Ohio, up the Mississippi, into the pages. But before the first paddle met water, something happened—an uncharted moment.

The program listed: *Reenactment—General George Rogers Clark (Hal Stearns).*

A lone drum broke the stillness—*boom-tap-boom*—and drew every eye. The fife and drum fell in.

"Forward, march," called Meriwether Lewis.

Boots found the dirt in unison, straps creaked, cartridge boxes jingled. The line approached the stage—history in motion.

"Halt... Attention!"

Then George Rogers Clark.

He didn't stride. He shuffled. His blue coat still carried the weight of glory; the gold epaulettes caught a thin gray light.

He moved down the line, returning salutes with something quieter than ceremony. A nod. A knowing.

And then—William.

The youngest brother. Caretaker now. The man about to go where George Rogers did not. William saluted. George Rogers answered. Their eyes held.

It wasn't rank passing. It was weight. And hope. And heartbreak.

For a breath, we were all witnesses to what was and what might have been. To what was given and what was lost. The frail brother who once lit the flame, and the younger one who would carry it west.

"To the left—wheel... Forward, march."

History moved on.

WHERE IT REALLY BEGAN

When the Corps left the stage, the crowd surged toward the ramp. We hurried, too, but trees walled the view; the shore funneled into a narrow tunnel. By the time we reached the water's edge, the boats were already pulling away to a chorus of "Hip, hip, hooray!"

We had missed the launch.

I stood catching my breath. Then I heard it—the low hum of outboards.

Motors. The illusion cracked. For all the buckskins and careful ritual, the boats didn't rely on oars today. I felt a little cheated—and stayed anyway.

We watched in silence as the boats moved across the Ohio and disappeared around the bend toward Illinois. As the last ripple vanished, it hit me.

This is where it really began.

Not across the river from St. Louis. Here. In Clarksville's muddy water under gray skies. Here, plan became reality. Maybe this was the most fitting way for it to begin after all—not with a flawless view, but with a scramble, an improvisation, a not-quite-as-planned moment that still carried the weight of something sacred.

An uncharted moment, just the way it should be.

The World Is Different Now

To: St. Louis, Missouri
March 2004

In the shadow of the Arch, we watched history fold in on itself—Spain, France, America. And somewhere between the handshakes and the pageantry, we felt the world shift.

"[I] took possession of Upper Louisiana
in the name of the French Republic on the
9th day of March; and on the next day,
I assumed the country and Government
in the name of the United States."

—Amos Stoddard, March 10, 1804

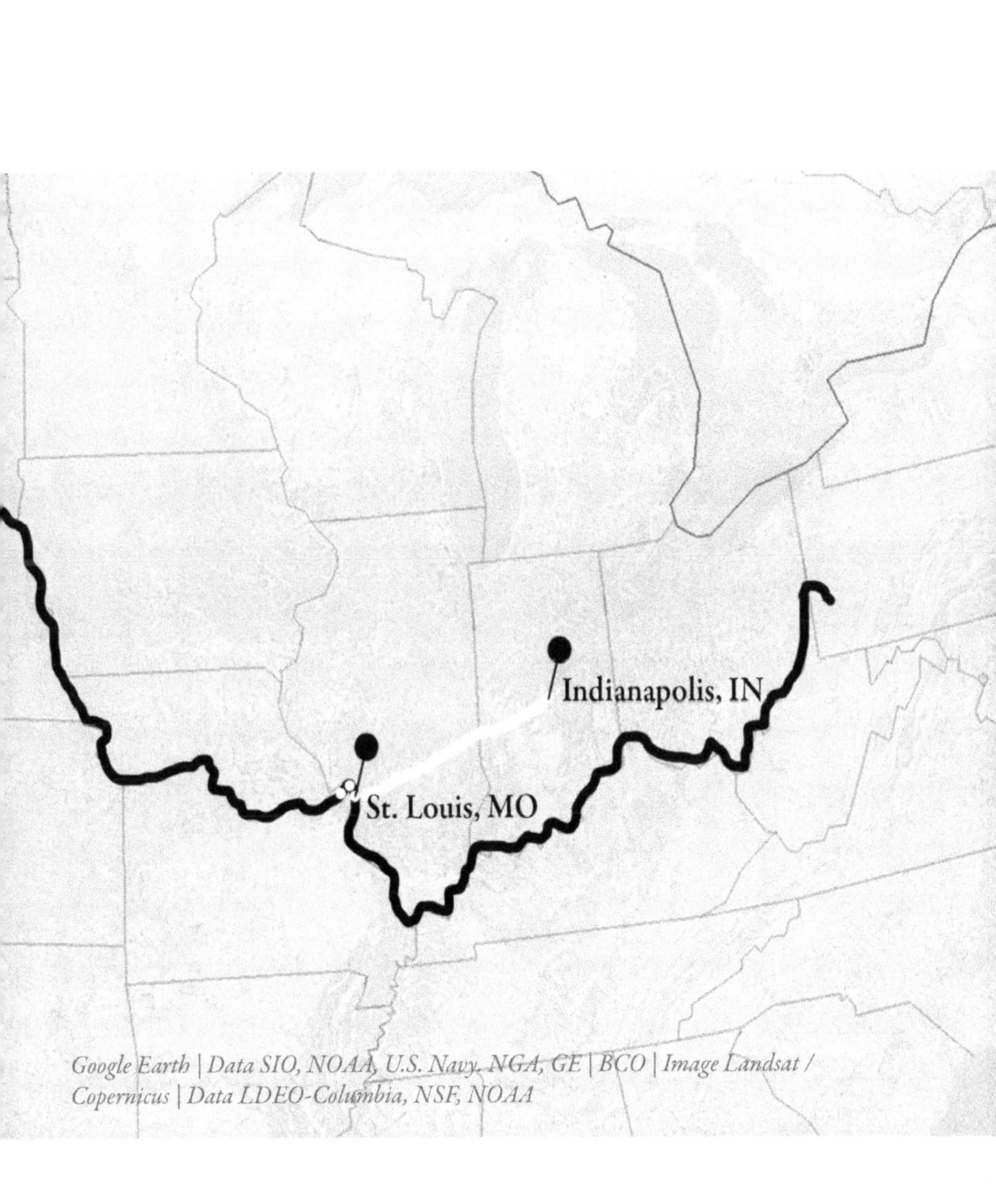

Indianapolis, IN
St. Louis, MO
Google Earth | Data SIO, NOAA, U.S. Navy, NGA, GE | BCO | Image Landsat /
Copernicus | Data LDEO-Columbia, NSF, NOAA

nine

March Feels Like September

Signature Events along the Lewis and Clark Trail crowded the 2004 calendar—seven major commemorations from March through October. There was no way we had the vacation—or the stamina—to chase them all.

With the first three clustered near the trail's eastern gateway, we started plotting: St. Louis, for sure. Kansas City over the Fourth of July felt right. The rest? We'd see what the year allowed.

In the pre-smartphone era, we printed our Microsoft Streets & Trips maps, highlighted timelines with color-coded ink, and dog-eared brochures. We were already anticipating goosebumps and gravel roads.

Then came February.

Over pasta and wine with Tom and his wife, Kathleen, a long-promised wedding gift finally took shape: Barcelona to Italy and the south of France, through the Straits of Gibraltar, ending in Portugal—a dream trip.

And the dates? May—exactly when two Signature Events were scheduled in the St. Louis area.

Carmen and I locked eyes. That glance held heartbreak and gratitude in equal measure. We nodded and smiled—of course, we said yes—but inside, we were torn. We'd never planned to attend every event, but to miss two so close to home felt like watching a canoe slip around a bend without us.

On the drive home, I tried to be lighthearted. "We're not passing on the gift of a lifetime," I said. "There'll be a tricentennial in a hundred years." She gave me the smile that says *We'll find our way, even if it isn't the one we planned.*

MARCH 11, 2004

The first Signature Event of 2004—the Three Flags Ceremony (March 9–14)—marked the handover we call the Louisiana Purchase: Spain to France to the United States: three flags, one land, infinite consequences.

We'd planned to leave for the Illinois–Missouri border on the 12th, a Friday, but with the cruise looming, we bumped everything up: Hartford, Alton, St. Charles—compress the learning, widen the lens.

That Thursday morning, the world shifted. Ten bombs tore through Madrid commuter trains during rush hour—nearly 200 dead, more than 1,000 wounded. In the early hours, blame pointed one way; by afternoon, it pointed another. Grief didn't care which flag it wore.

We read in silence, packed the car, and headed west on I-70.

Only three years removed, the weight of 9/11 still lived in the bone— raw, unsettled, just below the surface. Now Madrid. And we were driving toward a ceremony meant to celebrate diplomacy among Spain, France, and the United States. All three tied to the Purchase. All three now tied again by fear and uncertainty.

History isn't tidy. Maps draw neat borders; grief ignores them.

THE DAY THE SKY FELL

Like so many Americans, we remember exactly where we were on September 11. As we drove, we shared our memories of that day.

We'd lingered over coffee; my first meeting wasn't until 9 o'clock. I kissed Carmen goodbye at 8:30 and drove to our office—The Atrium, a glass-walled headquarters that loved to tell a story about itself. Inside, a knot of people stared up at a TV: flames from a hole in the North Tower. A plane, the crawl said. I called Carmen. She answered in tears.

We were still on the phone when the second plane hit, live. Silence. Breath caught. Then the Pentagon. Then the fall of one tower, then the other. The fourth plane in a Pennsylvania field. We closed the office. I drove home fast.

We clung to each other on the couch like the world might give way. In some ways, it already had. Names we'd never said before—bin Laden, al-Qaeda—moved into our daily language—nearly 3,000 lives. The sky went quiet. The world did not return to what it had been.

In the months that followed, words like *coalition* and *WMD* crowded the headlines. Allies aligned and argued. We were guests in a complicated world, still learning what that meant.

And now to St. Louis, to a ceremony about flags changing hands over lands already lived in. We hadn't yet learned how little those flags meant to the people already there—the many nations whose consent was never sought. We were guests; we didn't know how to say it yet.

Buffeted by the wind, the car steadied. Carmen found my hand across the console and squeezed—*bridges, not bombs.* Outside, clouds churned. Inside, the air wasn't empty; it was attentive.

As we crossed into Illinois, we chose wonder over worry and turned to the day ahead. First stop: the Sacagawea statue at Lewis and Clark Community College north of Alton, Illinois. Then south to the Wood River site. From there, Cahokia's old post office. Finally, the Arch and the Museum of Westward Expansion, on the Missouri side. Saturday, a few more museums and St. Charles. Sunday, Bellefontaine Cemetery and the Three Flags Ceremony before heading home on I-70.

A packed trip—just the way we liked it.

At the hotel in Alton, I spread a stack of maps and visitor guides across the desk like treasure charts. Tracing routes, circling landmarks, I found two more stops worth adding. Tomorrow just got tighter—and richer.

ten

Standing at the Confluence

We were up early and overcaffeinated—the kind of morning that makes you think you can outrun the itinerary. First stop: Lewis and Clark Community College. We'd pictured a modest campus of boxy buildings; instead, we found stone and stillness—ponds, small bridges, and a century-old main hall with quiet confidence.

A student guessed the statue was behind the main building. Before we could wander far, a campus security guard in a white truck waved us over and offered to guide us. As we walked the old corridors, he shared scraps of the school's past. It had started as a Catholic boarding school. Carmen's eyes lit—she'd gone to a Catholic girls' boarding school, too. Familiar hallways carry their own ghosts.

Out back, there she was: a bronze figure of a young Native woman walking west, her infant bundled tight. The guard said the model had also posed for the Native American $1 coin and was rumored to be a descendant of Sacagawea. The sculpture felt grounded and forward at once. We didn't speak. We didn't need to.

We took a few photos and proceeded on.

CAMP DUBOIS: WINTER'S EDGE OF WONDER

In Alton, the Clark Bridge fanned over the Mississippi like harp strings. High-water marks on a nearby grain elevator told another story—mud lines stacked like memoranda from floods past. We crossed, looped beneath the span, and returned to Illinois, chasing down a "Lewis and Clark Trail Site No. 1" that refused to reveal itself until Carmen spotted a gravel track behind a utility shed.

Camp Dubois waited there—winter quarters, 1803–1804—a square of rough-hewn logs, simple cabins, smoke in the wood. A reenactor waved us in and walked us through the captain's quarters and the blacksmith's station. The talk was of gear, routines, fidelity to the most minor details; the feel was sharpened blades, long nights, and the thrum of *almost*. Even the power lines overhead couldn't break the spell.

We stayed nearly an hour and left—behind schedule, but ahead in spirit.

THE RIVER WAS CALLING

Our next stop was the Lewis and Clark State Historic Site, which overlooks the confluence of the Missouri and Mississippi Rivers. The museum is surrounded by miles of land once owned by Standard Oil, the horizon still dotted with old refinery towers—a strange juxtaposition of industrial legacy and natural history.

At the reception desk, I struck up a conversation with two older volunteers who had that easy Midwestern kindness. The museum had only recently opened. The observation tower—meant to offer sweeping views—wasn't finished yet, and the trail to the riverbank had been washed away by flooding and was closed.

I was crushed.

I had wanted to see the confluence, even if the modern riverscape bore little resemblance to what Lewis and Clark saw two centuries earlier. One volunteer clocked my face and slid over a scrap of paper. He drew a backroad route across the bridge to a park on the Missouri side—we could see it from there.

We toured the museum, watched the earnest film, and followed his hand-drawn map across the bridge. What we'd taken for the river was only the navigation canal; the true channel lay beyond. The park opened into wetlands and reforested prairie, gravel under our tires and then under our feet. A fire truck rolled in behind us; a few firefighters, on break, had come to see the rivers, too.

At a confluence, the map surrenders to the water; names are stories, but the current decides.

And there it was.

To our left, the Missouri—broad, muscular, brown with spring run-off—poured into the Mississippi. The meeting churned and braided, small whirlpools etching circles into the surface. Hypnotic. The power of it—the movement, the merging—pulled at something inside me.

We stood at the overlook, gazing at the place where the Missouri meets the Mississippi, river haze lifting like memory. Carmen leaned in and said softly, "It's funny, isn't it? Technically, this river we're looking at should be called the Missouri." I turned, eyebrows raised. She smiled, that *I-read-something-you-didn't* smile. "The Missouri's longer, and it brings more water into the Mississippi than the other way around. Geologically speaking, some say the Mississippi is actually a tributary of the Missouri."

"So... we've been following the main river all along?" I asked, half-teasing. She nodded. "Makes you wonder how different things might be if names were based on science instead of stories."

We went quiet, watching the muddy swirl where two great rivers embraced—thinking of all the decisions shaped not by facts, but by who got there first.

We later learned we were standing within homelands we couldn't have named then—Illiniwek communities like Kaskaskia and Peoria along the Illinois side, and the wider Osage watershed across much of the Missouri. We were guests; the water already knew.

I imagined Lewis and Clark on the opposite bank, watching this same meeting of rivers. What were they thinking? Were they bracing for thousands of miles *against* this current, anxious about the Nations they would meet, the terrain, the hunger?

Or perhaps, like me, the river was calling them.

Maybe it wasn't worry that filled them—but wonder.

Maybe, like us, they heard the voice of the water beckoning them forward. Not with answers, but with mystery. Not a destination, but an invitation. *Come. Discover. Dare.*

On the walk back, we finally looked up—really looked up—and saw thick tangles of grass, branches, and debris caught high in the trees, 20 or

30 feet overhead. Ghosts of floodwaters past. The quiet language of rivers at their angriest.

Before leaving, we stopped at the boat launch. I walked down alone, crouched at the edge, and dipped my fingers in. The Missouri was cold and dark, always moving. Something inside me moved with it.

This was the river that would become a character in our story—a ribbon twisting through time, wild and unknowable. We had maps, sure. But like the Corps of Discovery, we had no way of knowing what lay ahead around the next bend.

And yet... we proceeded on.

HANGRY UNDER THE ARCH

By midafternoon, we aimed for the Arch—and straight into traffic. Hunger frayed our edges. The riverfront restaurants I remembered were gone, so we hunted for blocks until a Subway appeared like a truce. Sandwiches first; mood repaired.

Security lines, coats off, tray for keys—some changes in two centuries are easy to see. In the tiny tram car, we squeezed in with a wide-eyed college student and a quiet Indigenous couple.

"Here for the Three Flags Ceremony?" I asked.

"We're Osage," the woman said. "We came for the stories."

"So did we," I said.

At the top, the narrow windows framed a long view: the Mississippi like polished steel to the east; to the west, St. Louis stretching from courthouse to ballpark. The metal shell creaked once—just enough to remind us even monuments breathe.

Below, the Museum of Westward Expansion drew us to the Lewis and Clark panels and the wall of Presidential Peace Medals—decades of tokens lined in a row. Whether those gifts held meaning is a longer conversation; the sight of them, together, still landed. Near the center, Jefferson stood beside the Louisiana Purchase papers—a hinge and its door.

We stepped back into the late light feeling both smaller and steadier. The weekend would bring more adventures. For now, the day's current had done its work.

eleven

When Three Flags Flew as One

We opened the day with a quick pass through the Missouri History Museum—a headset tour, a few artifacts, the low hum of reverence you feel in rooms that outlived their makers. Lunch at the Meriwether Café, then a glance at the forecast. Rain later. We flipped the plan: save indoor exhibits for the storm; head for the river while the sky still held.

Museums can catalog a story, but the river remembers it.

FACING WEST WITH THE CORPS

St. Charles wears its history proudly—a river town that still feels small. In 1804, the Corps paused here after leaving Camp Dubois, waiting for Lewis, who was in St. Louis tending to some last-minute business, to catch up. During the Bicentennial, the reenactors called it home.

At the Lewis & Clark Boathouse and Museum, the replica keelboat sat on the ground floor—stem to stern within reach but just out of bounds. Upstairs, the museum's highlight stopped us: a handmade diorama that ribboned from Camp Dubois to the Pacific and back. Miniature lodges exhaled tiny curls of cotton at Mandan—winter smoke you could almost smell. Labels traced triumphs and hazards. We lingered, chin-tilted, moving west with the figures as if we didn't already know the next bend was conjectural.

Outside on the observation deck, the Missouri rolled past—wide, muddy, relentless. Just looking at that current made my shoulders ache. Once upon a time, I'd imagined a full retrace by canoe. Staring at that river, I knew I'd last 20 minutes before searching for a riverside bar—with Carmen laughing beside me.

We walked to the statues of Lewis, Clark, and Seaman, then drifted to the water's edge, blocking out the 21st-century signs. Bare trees across the bank, a long brown muscle of current. It felt possible that what we saw was close to what they saw.

LISTENING TO THE WATER

From St. Charles, we drove to Bellefontaine Cemetery—William Clark's resting place. A caretaker traced the route on a map; we threaded the lanes beneath budding trees until the bluff opened to the river.

The grave rises on a marble platform, an obelisk set above the valley. At the entry, a bronze bust of Clark—the gaze steady, the expression caught between resolve and something gentler. His descendants ring the site like a living family tree.

Carmen read the markers, then gave me the gift she's learned to give—space—and walked back to the car.

I stood with Clark. Stared into his eyes—bronze, yes, but somehow deeper in that stillness. I've always identified more with him, though I couldn't have told you why. Looking out to the Mississippi, I imagined him standing on this bluff, too, counting miles upstream as the same water slid past on its way to the Gulf. Power, will, and a quiet compassion that only shows itself when you stop talking long enough to feel it.

We were guests in a landscape that taught before we had the words.

THE RIVER REMEMBERS BOTH SHORES

Back in Forest Park, we stepped through Art of the Osage. One detail rooted me: the tradition of an Osage bride wearing a U.S. military uniform—honor braided with history's contradictions. Meaning bends like water—cutting one bank while carving another. The truth is layered; we were still learning to acknowledge our role as guests on Osage land and in Osage stories.

THE FLAGS WOVEN TOGETHER BY HISTORY: PAST AND PRESENT

Sunday began wet and gray, but by the time we reached the Arch, the pavement had dried as if the city had wrung itself out. Security lines again, then steps facing east toward the river.

A long queue curled beside a booth selling the brand-new Lewis and Clark nickel. We let it be for the moment, bought a French bicentennial coin and a canceled postcard, and found seats in the sun.

The program opened with African American drummers and a poet whose words came raw and exacting—slavery, dispossession, wounds named out loud. It startled us, then steadied us. Truth-telling isn't the enemy of healing; it's the first step toward it. Osage singers followed with a Flag Song; the St. Charles fife and drum kept time; a local duo sang French and frontier airs.

While the music played, Carmen made a friend on the steps (as she does). The woman turned out to be the diorama artist from the previous day. When she learned we'd missed the Wood River and St. Charles pins, she offered to mail them to us. The trail has a way of repaying kindness with kindness.

Carmen noticed the nickel line had vanished and jogged down, returning five minutes later empty-handed: sold out. Half a million coins gone in hours. A mother nearby had waited 90 minutes for her son and offered us one. Carmen asked if we could buy two; the woman smiled and handed us an entire roll. Grace passed hand to hand.

Then the ceremony.

From downriver, the white pirogue of the Discovery Expedition eased toward the stage. Both captains stepped ashore—pageantry, yes, but fitting for the moment. Spain's flag rose first; the Army band played the anthem. The Spanish ambassador spoke of brotherhood and shared history, just three days after Madrid's trains were bombed. By the time he finished, tears had traced both our faces. The ovation lasted and lasted.

France's flag followed, and His Excellency Jean-David Levitte spoke with grace about a long, complicated friendship—condolences for Madrid, a hand extended despite Iraq-era strain.

Another ovation, shorter but sincere.

Then "The Star-Spangled Banner," the American flag high on the third pole, and remarks about standing together—past complicates, future shared. Three flags in one wind—Spain, France, United States—over a river that remembers longer than any anthem.

The river below rolled on. Like history. Like hope.

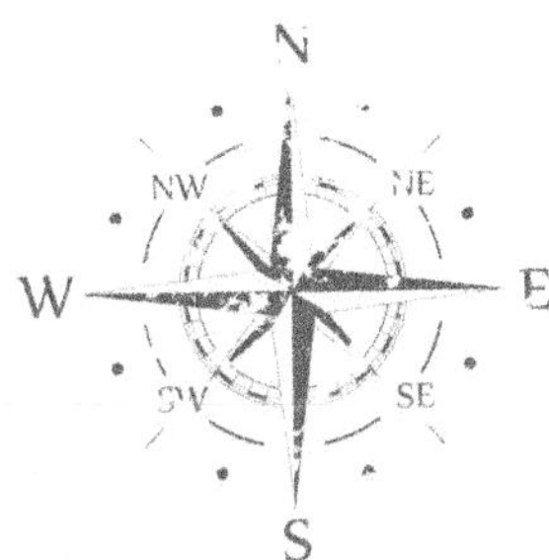

Two Questions and a Plan

To: Kansas City, Missouri; Leavenworth, Kansas; and Atchison, Kansas

July 2004

We didn't just come to witness history—we came to make decisions about our own.

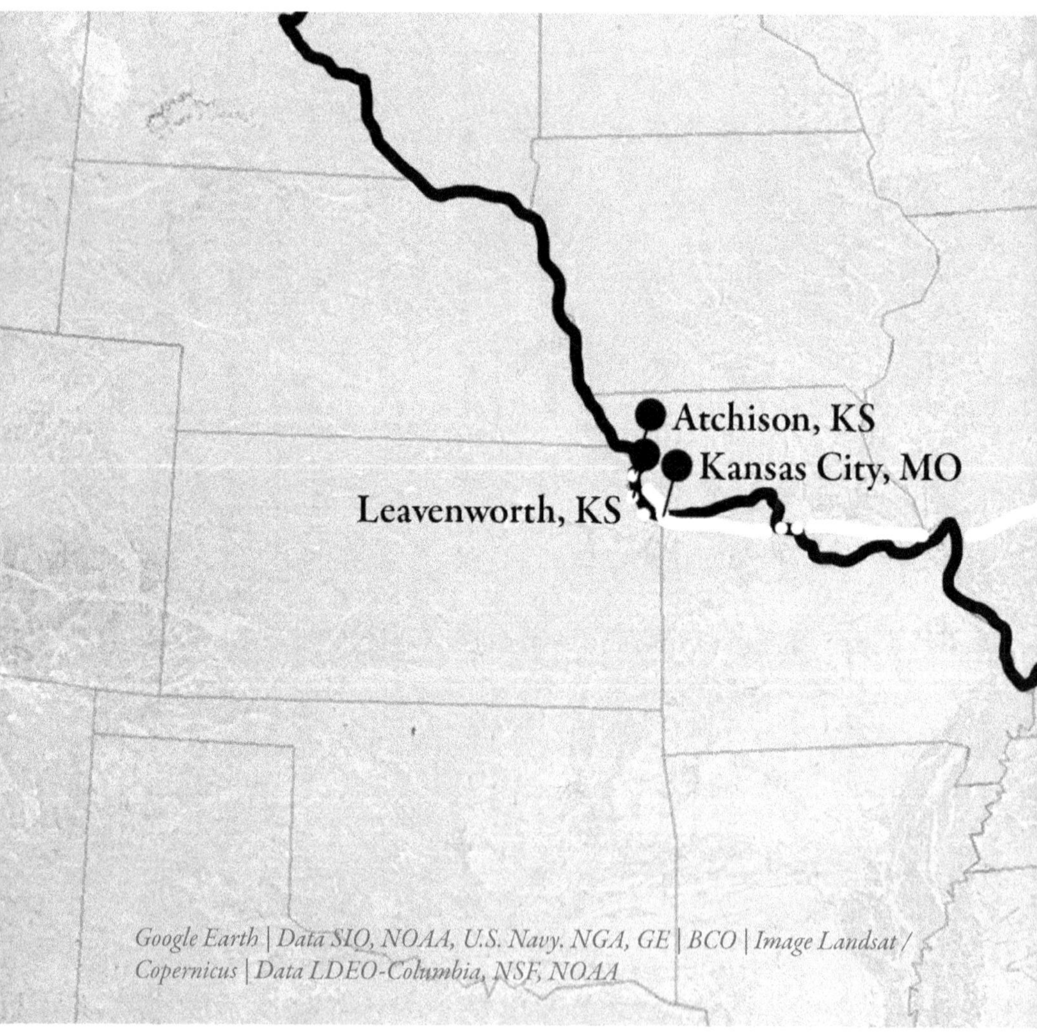

Google Earth | Data SIO, NOAA, U.S. Navy. NGA, GE | BCO | Image Landsat / Copernicus | Data LDEO-Columbia, NSF, NOAA

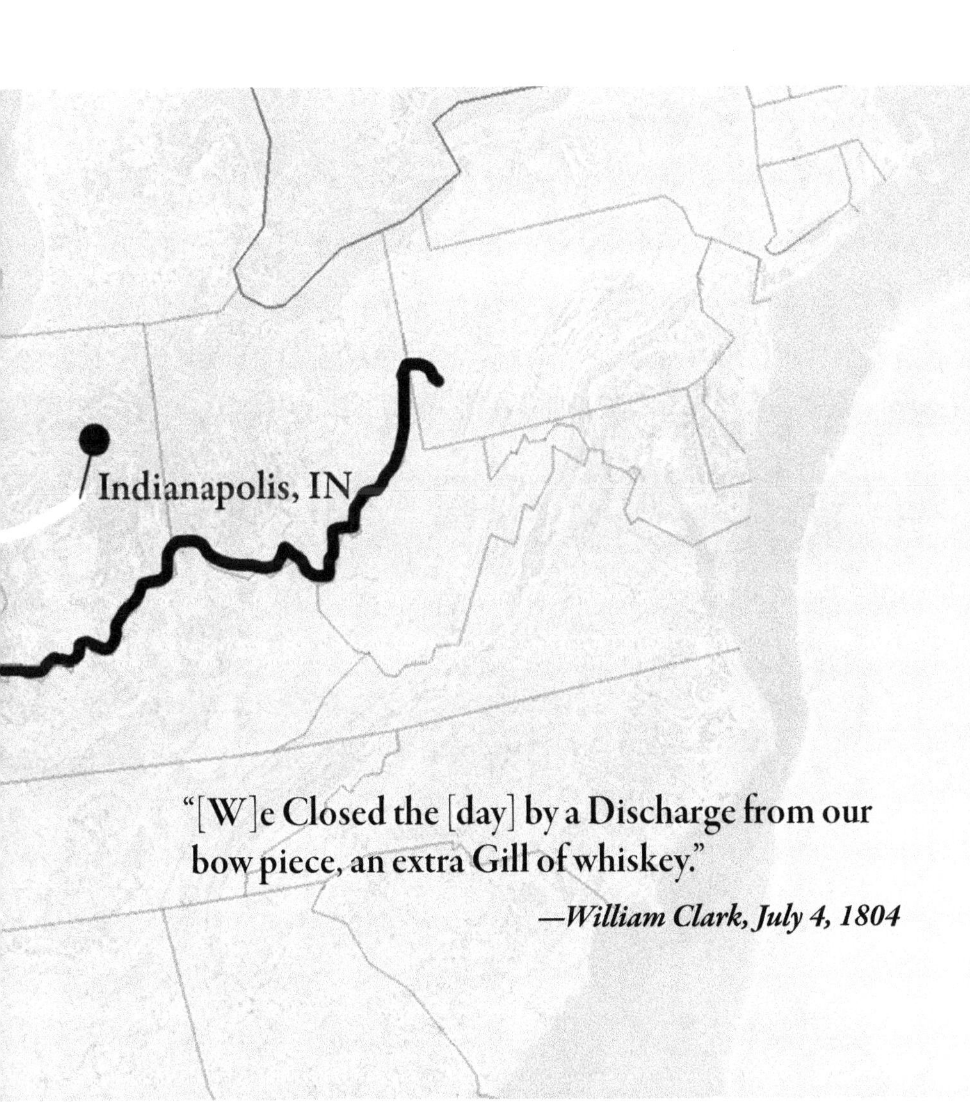

"[W]e Closed the [day] by a Discharge from our
bow piece, an extra Gill of whiskey."

—*William Clark, July 4, 1804*

twelve

Kansas City Here We Come

After missing the two previous Signature Events because of our cruise that spring, Carmen and I were more than ready to get back on the road. The longing to reconnect with the trail—and with that quiet sense of purpose it always stirred in us—had been building for weeks. So, just after six in the morning on July 2, we pulled onto I-70 and headed west with the rising sun to our backs. This leg would ask us two questions—what comes after the trail, and how we'll keep traveling it.

This bicentennial event, A Journey Fourth, ran from June 19 to July 11, stretching across Kansas City, Missouri, and Leavenworth and Atchison, Kansas. But the weekend of the Fourth was the centerpiece—commemorating the first Independence Day ever celebrated west of the Mississippi. For us, the Fourth had always been more than fireworks and flags. We couldn't imagine a better way to honor both stories—ours and theirs.

As we drove, we made a couple of quick side trips—missed pages from our earlier chapters. First, the Lewis and Clark Historic Site in Wood River, Illinois, where Carmen cheerfully dashed inside to track down the commemorative pin we had missed back in May. She came out smiling, mission accomplished. "One more gap filled," she said, dropping it into our growing collection. It was just a pin, maybe, but also a tether—a way to say *We were here. We still care. We're still on the journey.*

Carmen also remembered that the river overlook had been closed

91

due to flooding when we visited back in March. This time, it was open. We drove down the short road and parked. Before us lay the very point where the Wood River, the Mississippi, and the Missouri converged— three waters, each with its own source, each with its own story, merging into something greater. We stood quietly, gazing across to the other bank, where just months ago we'd stood with the firefighters, watching this same water from the opposite shore.

It felt like a reunion—with the river, yes, but also with something deeper. We had gone abroad, wandered distant shores, and returned changed. This was our recommitment. The trail was still waiting.

From there, we headed into St. Charles and made another quick stop at the Boathouse. Carmen found the second missing pin while I poked around the gift shop. That's when we discovered it—a CD set narrating the course of the Missouri River as it winds through the state. It promised stories, mile by mile, bend by bend, following the river westward. We looked at each other and laughed. "We just have to get this," I said, already picturing us driving with the windows down, a voice on the speakers guiding us like a modern-day Clark with a good microphone.

We were officially back on the trail—slightly older, a little wiser, and just as wide-eyed.

MORE THAN A BOONDOGGLE: WHERE THE RIVER RESISTS

We set off again, leaving I-70 behind and dropping south onto Missouri Route 94, hoping to hug the river's edge and let the trail unfold more slowly. At first, traffic clogged the road—stoplight after stoplight—winding through small-town congestion with no river in sight.

Half an hour later, the suburbs gave way to farmland and gentle hills. A public access site finally brought us to the Missouri's bank. The gravel crunched underfoot as the water came into view.

The river here was quiet, restrained. You could see what the Corps of Engineers had spent decades trying to do: wing dams—angled fingers of rock and concrete reaching into the flow. They looked like someone had tried to comb the river into submission.

Carmen stood beside me, hands in her pockets, watching the current slip past the wing dams. Something was unsettling about a river boxed in like that. Tamed, but not peaceful. Controlled, but not understood.

I leaned on the railing, thinking about the river's old wildness—the bends and braids that once shifted with every season. The Army Corps had tried to make it a commercial superhighway. The numbers told a different story. Barges rarely passed here anymore. For all our attempts to shape it, the Missouri kept reminding us it would never be fully known or owned.

In that moment, the river became a metaphor for so much else—grief, healing, even love. All of it wild and winding. And Carmen, ever steady, didn't try to fix the silence or explain the moment. She just stood with me in it.

Eventually, we turned back toward the car. Our little detour cost us two hours and gained only 30 miles, but it still felt worth it. The map might call it a boondoggle; the river called it something else. A pause. A lesson. A reminder that the straight path isn't always the truest.

We rejoined the interstate, quieter, more thoughtful.

We proceeded on.

FORT OSAGE: STORMS AND STILLNESS

A sudden storm overtook us near Columbia—rain lashing the windshield, traffic slowing to a crawl. Around 3:30 p.m., we pulled into Fort Osage, perched on a bluff above the Missouri. The fort was built under William Clark's direction several years after the expedition. On June 23, 1804, Clark had noted this site in his journal and later returned to establish a foothold in the territory—strategy, presence, control. Perhaps the bluff had stayed with him.

We stopped at the visitor center to buy tickets. The woman at the counter looked like she'd been through a storm of her own. When I asked whether they sold commemorative pins, she snapped, "No, we don't." I smiled and mentioned our collection, trying to lighten the moment. "Yeah," she muttered, "I don't know why people do that."

Ohhhhhh Kaaaaay...

We walked the short path to the fort in silence, the wind still heavy in the trees. The reconstructed structure stood proud—simple, solid, sure of itself. Our first stop was the trading post. In the early 1800s, these were known as factories, and the men who ran them were factors—government agents building alliances through trade. Inside, a warm, animated interpreter greeted us and began sharing stories—buckskin tanning, pieces of eight, the rhythms of barter. His enthusiasm was a welcome contrast to our earlier exchange, proof again that a place is only as cold or as kind as the people you meet.

Past the trading post, a replica whipping post stood in the yard, iron shackles still fastened—justice or cruelty, depending on who stood in those restraints. We climbed into the blockhouses at each corner for the view. From up there, you could see why Clark was drawn to this spot. The river stretched wide below, a winding artery of possibility.

We hiked down to the river's edge and looked back at the fort rising above us. Flags flew at half-staff in honor of former President Reagan, who had died just days earlier. The moment was quiet, the air heavy with history, past and present.

Rain returned as we climbed back up. We ducked inside, dripping and laughing, and watched a short film about the fort's origins. The small museum offered more artifacts, more glimpses into a time when bluffs like these were outposts at the edge of the known world.

We wandered through the gift shop. About 10 minutes before closing time, our "favorite" clerk announced she was closing. I politely said we were still shopping. "It doesn't go in my pocket, so I don't care." We paid, and she locked the door behind us. On the walk to the car, Carmen laughed. "Well," she said, "if we ever wondered what a career in public service feels like, we just got a snapshot."

We drove on—amused, a little annoyed, but mostly thoughtful. Fort Osage offered more than facts about early expansion. It reminded us, again, that people shape places—and that every story has its share of storms and stillness, generosity and indifference. The important thing is to keep moving forward.

IN THE FOOTSTEPS, BETWEEN THE RAINDROPS

It took the Corps of Discovery three days to reach what is now Kansas City; we made the drive from Fort Osage in just under an hour. Our hotel was in Platte City, Missouri, just across the river from Leavenworth,

Kansas—a strategic location, given that this Signature Event was spread across Kansas City, Leavenworth, and Atchison. We had a full weekend ahead, but first on the agenda was a book signing downtown.

Another downpour pinned us in a parking lot, then softened. We found a garage and headed out. Moments later, it sprinkled again. We passed one restaurant but kept going, deciding on George Brett's a few blocks down. The skies opened once more before we reached the door. Our umbrella was no match for the wind-driven rain. We arrived soaked and laughing, like two kids who'd just run through the sprinkler.

The meal was excellent—clothes dried, warm food, the steady thrum of conversation settled us. Stepping back into the evening, the city glistened from the storm.

As we walked toward the bookstore hosting the book signing, our shoes squeaking on wet sidewalks, I felt the day catch up to me. Just hours earlier, we had been standing inside a recreated frontier fort, learning how buckskin was tanned and how the rhythms of trade shaped a continent. Now, we were brushing raindrops from our jackets, weaving through traffic, surrounded by the modern hum of downtown. It was one of those quiet collisions that happened often on this journey—where centuries brushed shoulders, where the sacred and the ordinary shared the same street.

We arrived at the bookstore just in time. The panel featured four authors. I bought two books—a broader Chouteau prehistory and William E. Foley's *Wilderness Journey: The Life of William Clark*. Foley signed my copy; for a moment, history felt like a living hand you could shake.

We stepped out into the damp Kansas City evening, rain lingering in the air like a memory. Carmen slipped her arm in mine as we walked to the car, quiet and content. We left the city behind and made our way to the hotel—ready for the next chapter of this journey that was, more and more, becoming our own.

thirteen

Guests in Another Story

The opening ceremonies were held at Kansas City's Berkley Park on July 3. We left our hotel under gray, brooding skies that threatened to soak the day before it even began. The riverfront, just a few blocks from the heart of the city, was quiet when we arrived—too quiet, as it turned out. We were early.

The on-duty police officer at the entrance wasn't letting anyone in yet. Carmen, with that gentle, grounded confidence of hers, rolled down the window and leaned forward. "We just drove a long way," she said with a warm smile. "Would it be okay if we waited along the park road?"

He paused, then waved us through.

She turned to me with the little grin that always gets me: "The worst they can do is say no."

We parked, pulled out our umbrellas and blankets, and waited in the morning stillness. After about half an hour, the lot officially opened, and we made our way to the field. Dozens of vendor tents lined the banks of the Missouri, and at the center, a wide stage faced a sea of empty chairs. We claimed two and settled in, letting anticipation hang in the humid July air.

And then—without warning—the sky cracked open.

Paratroopers from the U.S. Air Force burst through the cloud cover, their chutes blooming like wildflowers against the storm-gray sky. They descended in near silence and landed in a clearing just behind the crowd.

The timing felt too perfect, as if the sky itself had been waiting to release them. It was the most awe-inspiring presentation of colors we had ever witnessed.

Then came the flags—state after state, nation after nation. The procession of tribal flags was particularly moving, each one carried with solemn dignity. To the best of our later understanding, this riverfront lies within Kanza (Kaw) homelands. We didn't note others at the time, and we wish we had.

At the front, our now-familiar St. Charles fife and drum corps struck up their tune. The fifes cut through the heavy air like a voice calling across time. By now, we recognized many of their faces. We were no longer just attendees; we were companions in a story still unfolding.

There were speeches by local dignitaries and musical interludes by the U.S. Marine Corps Choir, harmonies rising like prayers. General William Wallace, recently returned from Iraq, delivered a keynote that carried us back to the Three Flags Ceremony—service, sacrifice, carrying history forward.

Then the unmistakable thrum of military helicopters—a low, vibrating chorus that shook the ground as a formation flew overhead. Thunderous, impossible not to feel.

After the ceremony, we walked the river's edge, weaving through booths selling books, crafts, and mementos. We even bought a Lewis and Clark board game—a Trivial Pursuit–style journey that felt like history slipping from the clouds into our hands.

OFF BY A DAY, OFF BY A MILE

After lunch, we turned north toward Leavenworth, Kansas—another community on the bicentennial map. The short drive carried the scent of grilled food and a light lift of hope.

It didn't last.

What I'd imagined as a gathering of period craftsmen, reenactors, and storytelling turned out to be something else: a classic "Small Town, USA" Fourth—rows of country crafts, state-fair food stalls, a car show. Nostalgic, yes. But not the thread we'd come for. At the renovated riverfront, we discovered the reason: the Lewis and Clark events had taken place the day before. We walked the shaded trail, found a gazebo, and let disappointment cool. Then we headed back to Platte City to regroup, dry out, and get ready for the evening's dinner in Atchison—hoping it would bring us back into rhythm with the trail.

AN EXTRA GILL OF GRATITUDE

A Journey Fourth: Taste of the Trail was held in Atchison, the last stop on our Fourth of July arc. We cleaned up, traded shorts for something more fitting, and drove the 30 minutes north. After one wrong turn, we found the small conference center.

With two adult beverages in hand, we wandered the reception. In one corner, Michael Haynes's paintings commemorated scenes from the expedition. We talked with him for several minutes; rather than a painting—where would we hang it?—we chose a set of note cards and a hat. He signed one of our dinner tickets.

Across the room stood Mary Gunderson, author of one of our cookbooks: *The Food Journal of Lewis and Clark: Recipes for an Expedition.* She signed the other dinner ticket. Her reception bites—smoked catfish, fresh fruit, trail-inspired fare—were surprisingly flavorful, which made us all the more excited for the meal.

Inside the banquet hall, the room glowed—branches with tiny lights hung like prairie stars. Dinner was served buffet-style: bison, turkey, corn, and potatoes, all from Gunderson's recipes. We learned that the meal we'd enjoyed at Michie Tavern a year earlier had also come from her book.

After dinner, Gunderson spoke about the foods of the expedition—what they carried, what they hunted, how food shaped survival. Then Dayton Duncan took the stage. He began by again remembering his close friend Stephen Ambrose. The loss still sat with him. That quiet weight seemed to travel with Dayton from event to event.

At the end, we raised a toast—honoring the Corps' "extra gill of whiskey" when they celebrated our nation's 28th birthday on the Missouri in 1804. To our surprise, our cups held real whiskey. As a keepsake, each guest received a small metal cup modeled after the kind the Corps might have used. Our toast may have been barely a shot, but it was enough.

Afterward, we drove around town to get the lay of the land for the next day's celebration, then followed the river. I thought we'd end up at Independence Creek. Instead, the road drew us into the cornfields stretching across the bottomlands north of town.

We pulled onto a quiet gravel road and let the silence settle. Carmen paged through a brochure we'd picked up earlier. It wasn't until we stopped and read together that the full weight of where we were—and whose land we stood on—started to sink in.

GUESTS IN ANOTHER STORY

Somewhere along the trail—perhaps at the opening ceremonies—we'd picked up a slim book called *Native American Resource Handbook*. It offered guidance for visitors to tribal lands and events: how to behave respectfully, what to understand, and how to listen. We were drawn to its quiet authority. It was a reminder that we were guests in someone else's story.

I've long felt a deep compassion for Indigenous peoples and the injustices they endured. That awareness may have started on a family vacation in the 1970s, when we visited Cherokee, North Carolina. One evening, we saw *Unto These Hills*, an outdoor drama that tells the story of the Trail of Tears. I can still feel how it landed—quietly devastating. The title comes from scripture, Psalm 121: "I lift mine eyes unto the hills." My father was an American Baptist minister, and those words carried weight in our home. Sitting on that gravel road with the booklet open, the verse took on a new shape—sorrow, endurance, stolen land. It has stayed with us ever since.

fourteen
Fireworks and Forks in the Road

Wanting to beat the crowds, we rose early and returned to Atchison. As luck would have it, we found an excellent parking spot in a lot just a block from the riverfront park. I was nearly bursting with excitement. I had been looking forward to this event for over two years—ever since I read about it as one of the Signature Events.

The Fourth of July has been one of my favorite holidays since I was a kid in Lebanon, Indiana. The parade marched past our porch, where my siblings and I sold lemonade. When I was old enough, I marched with the Boy Scouts. One year, our float had a Native theme, and I "danced" the route in a handmade bison mask my mom created. The day always ended the same way: The whole town gathered at the American Legion fields to watch fireworks burst over the Indiana night.

And then, many years later—on another Fourth of July—while on a pity-party canoe trip, I had stumbled onto a park on the outskirts of Dayton, Ohio, and discovered a story that led me to Lewis and Clark.

No wonder I'd circled this day on the calendar. It felt like all the versions of me—boy, Scout, husband, seeker—were converging here in Atchison.

We wandered the park to get our bearings and find a good viewing spot for the 10 a.m. boat landing. We were also scoping out where we might sit later for the fireworks.

Eventually, we found a shady patch beneath a massive cottonwood tree near the river's edge. It was the kind of tree that looked like it had seen everything—storms and sunrises, river floods and frontier marches. Its limbs stretched wide like open arms, offering shelter to anyone in need of a pause. We spread our blanket in its dappled shade, as if claiming a pew in nature's quiet cathedral.

The day was already sweltering. I left Carmen to hold our place while I returned to the car for the blanket and a couple of beers. By the time I got back, the crowd had thickened. Even above the noise, I could hear her voice—laughing, chatting easily. Of course, she'd made new friends.

Carmen has that rare gift—not just conversation, but connection. While I had been counting down to this day like a kid before Christmas, she arrived with her usual grace, grounding the morning not in hype but in presence. I spread the blanket beside her and the two local women she'd befriended, and we settled in to wait.

In the distance, we caught sight of the keelboat, followed by two pirogues. They made their way upriver, fighting the powerful current. They fired their guns as they approached the landing, and the crowd erupted with cheers. The reenactors disembarked and marched into town. We fell in behind them, becoming part of the procession. At Atchison's new pavilion, the mayor welcomed the Corps. We stayed for the greetings, then headed to the speaker's tent—Dayton Duncan was scheduled again.

THE HAWK RETURNS

The tent was packed. Dayton's talk was more or less what he'd given the night before, but I didn't mind hearing it again. His voice carried warmth, respect for the past, and love for the story and the people who helped tell it.

He shared a moment from that morning—he'd been invited to board the keelboat and fire the cannon in honor of the day. Just as he said "fire the cannon," a real cannon boomed from the center of the park—perfect timing and completely unplanned. Dayton burst into a laugh, big and unrehearsed, and the crowd laughed with him. The trail has its own rhythm.

After his talk, Carmen said, "You should tell him about the hawk."

I shook my head. "He'll think I'm just some nutjob." I half-laughed.

She didn't push. Seeds, not shoves. The thought kept circling. When the line thinned, we stepped forward and shook his hand. I told him how much his books meant to me and how deeply I admired the way he spoke about Ambrose. Then I shared the story—the hawk we'd seen flying over Monticello during the ceremony the prior January, and how it felt like a messenger.

He didn't laugh. His eyes welled with tears.

"I saw it too," he said softly.

We stood there a moment—suspended in something that didn't need words.

THE FIRST FOURTH... AND OUR SECOND WIND

We hiked to the town center for the Fourth of July picnic. The sun was merciless now, climbing toward 95 with no intention of letting up. We stood in line for food, grateful when Carmen spotted a large tree nearby. She secured a patch of shade while I carried our trays—her gift for seeing solutions in the heat of things.

On our walk back toward the riverfront, Carmen made a beeline for the town fountain and stepped in without hesitation, ankle-deep in cool water. Me? I'm a rule follower. I couldn't bring myself to do it, even if the water looked like salvation. Watching her—barefoot, laughing like a kid—I wished I could let go like that, too.

We returned to the riverfront to stake out our spot for the fireworks and the next event. While I fetched the chairs, she scouted for the perfect view. When I came back, she'd moved upriver, drawn by a better vantage point and the flow of the crowd. We crossed the road, laid out our blanket, and settled into the rhythm of the day.

Beers in hand and chairs planted under a sky wide as memory, we exhaled.

Then it was time for the next chapter.

Clark Remembers the First Fourth was scheduled for 4 p.m. at Independence Creek, where the Corps had camped exactly 200 years earlier. A yellow school bus ferried us and a dozen others toward the site—the kind of ride that makes you feel like a kid again, except now the air was 100 degrees and the nostalgia came with sweat.

We arrived around 2:30, but from the parking lot, it was still a half-mile walk to the encampment. We crossed a narrow footbridge and hiked through tall grasses under relentless sun. Carmen, ever the trouper, didn't complain, but I could tell the heat was getting to her.

At the encampment, we wandered near the reenactors and found the Geological Survey Marker commemorating the 1804 camp. Curious, we climbed the levee, hoping to catch sight of the river. On the other side was not water but corn—miles of it. Two centuries will do that.

We found a spot beneath a shade tree and collapsed onto our blanket. For a while, it was enough—sit, sweat less, be still.

When it came time for Clark's reenactment, we moved closer. The performance area was a full sun trap, not a shadow in sight. After a brief seating kerfuffle that blocked Carmen's view, we shifted to the bleachers and—miracle—found a slight breeze behind them. The play continued; what I remember is Carmen—tough, smart, sweat-soaked, still looking out for me.

THE QUESTION THAT LINGERED

After the performance, we made our way to the buses. The line unraveled; we ended up shoulder to shoulder with two women we'd see again at dinner. Back in town, we beelined to the tavern—ready for food, air-conditioning, and something cold. Miraculously, we scored the last open table. Just as our drinks arrived, I spotted the same two women lingering nearby—tired, hungry.

I offered to share our table. They accepted.

Over dinner, we learned they were best friends. We had assumed—wrongly—that they were a couple. Turns out they were both married, but their husbands didn't share their love for history or travel. "If it's not golf, they're not interested," one of them said with a laugh. So the two of them explored the world together.

We told them about the trail—our year of chasing history and the strange, sacred rhythm we'd found in doing so. We talked about the reenactors, the ceremonies, the coins and pins, and the unplanned moments that leave you changed.

And then, just as I took a sip of beer, one of the women looked up and asked a question—simple, unexpected, devastating.

"So, what will you do when all this Lewis and Clark stuff is over?"

Slam. Her words hit like a canoe paddle to the face. I blinked, stunned—like someone had flipped on a light I wasn't ready to face.

What were we going to do?

This journey, this obsession—it had become the scaffolding of our life together. There wasn't a day I didn't think about the expedition. Not a day I didn't dream about floating a quiet river somewhere, caught between then and now. This wasn't just a road trip. It had become our compass. Our cathedral. Our story.

"Well..." I started. "It's never really over."

It was the only answer I had. And the truest.

Before I could tumble deeper into that sudden sense of loss, Carmen gently saved me—as she so often does. She pointed to the line growing by the door, quietly suggesting it was time to give someone else our table.

We said our goodbyes, left a good tip, and stepped into the golden light of early evening. The heat was finally beginning to break.

We made our way to the car to grab the cooler, but not before one last impulse stop.

I needed to buy a T-shirt.

A what?

Yes, a T-shirt. The tavern sold shirts from Boulevard Brewing Company, and one in particular caught my eye. On the front, it featured a Lewis and Clark–style logo. On the back, in bold white letters, was a single phrase: "To those who make maps, not follow them."

At the time, it felt like a clever turn of phrase. But it lodged deep. Years later, it would follow me into talks and workshops, reshaping how I speak about life, leadership, and legacy.

Because here's a truth no one tells you at the start: The story doesn't end at the Pacific. The real map is the one you draw with your life.

And sometimes, the smallest souvenirs hold the biggest truths.

THE RIVER REMEMBERS

We set up our chairs, fixed our drinks, and settled in to wait. Just below us, the Missouri flowed by—slow and steady, swollen and powerful. The family on our right had also been at Monticello. The wife was the devoted fan; the husband, along for love. Presence counts, even when the itinerary doesn't.

As the sky darkened, the river disappeared into shadow. Large video screens flickered across the park. We couldn't see them from our vantage point, and the crowd noise swallowed most of the sound. We caught a few bits and pieces.

We were glad we'd seen the opening ceremonies, because here at the closing, we were mostly on our own.

And then—finally—the fireworks began.

Precision and color burst over the river, blooms lighting the sky and water at once—red, gold, silver, white. Reflections danced across the current like visible prayers. For a moment, time folded in on itself. Past, present, possibility blurred into one.

We sat in silence, awed.

Neither of us could remember a more spectacular Fourth of July—not just for the fireworks, but for everything the day had held. The history. The heat. The questions. The laughter. The ache of the unexpected. And the quiet comfort of knowing we'd done it together.

It was an etched-in-the-heart kind of day—one of those rare, uncharted moments that never really leaves you.

EXACTLY AS IT SHOULD BE

The following day, it was time to head home—nine hours back to Indiana. But we weren't in a hurry. We rarely were when the trail was still whispering.

Our first detour was to the village of Arrow Rock. The town had grown up along the Missouri and was said to be near one of the Corps' original campsites. We left the interstate and followed back roads that wound like tributaries to a Lewis and Clark Historical Site. When we arrived, we found that it had been converted into a campground.

Still curious, we wandered. On the far side of the park, a break in the trees opened to the Missouri River valley—broad, quiet, timeless. In the distance, the river wound through the green, moving steadily on. We stood for a while, just watching.

Farther up the road, a small visitor center and museum welcomed us. We told the woman behind the desk about our journey, and she showed us a local map and invited us to explore. Again, I was struck by how much meaning hides in tucked-away places. The stories may be modest, the exhibits simple—but the impact is real. Like the river, history often speaks softly and never stops speaking.

In town, the historic tavern was closed for the holiday, so we drove to the river overlook. The river had vanished behind summer's green—hidden, elusive. We were grateful we'd found that opening earlier.

Following the curator's advice, we drove to a nearby wildlife refuge. A sign promised a short three-quarter-mile trail to the river's edge. The heat was blistering, the deer flies relentless. We pushed through to a tangle of driftwood—evidence of the river's last tantrum—and just beyond it, the muddy Missouri flowed: wild, unruly, relentless. Exactly as it should be.

We lingered, then turned back, hiked to the car, and continued the slow, steady journey home.

THE SECOND QUESTION (WHISPERED OVER WINE)

Several miles later, we decided to investigate the Katy Trail. Our guidebook recommended Rocheport as an excellent spot to view the river, so we left the highway again and headed into town. We found the trail easily—a whole community had sprung up around it: a restaurant, a bike shop, a museum.

But... no river.

We debated walking the trail, but couldn't tell how far it was to the water. The heat made the decision easier—we passed.

On our way back to the highway, a small vineyard advertised on a billboard tempted one last detour.

We were rewarded instantly.

The A-frame wine café's back deck perched nearly 300 feet above the Missouri River, with a wide-open view up and down the valley. This was the picture from the guidebook. This was what we'd been seeking all along.

We found a picnic table near the edge, ordered a glass of wine to share, and soaked it in. Far below, the Katy Trail curved along the riverbank. From up there, we could see exactly where we'd stood minutes earlier, debating whether to keep walking. I was so glad we hadn't, so glad we'd found this place.

From that vantage point, the river looked peaceful. Patient. Perspective-giving.

Eventually, we had to leave—reality waited on the horizon.

Somewhere along the drive, Carmen broke the silence with the second big question of the weekend.

"You know what we should do?" she said, light but purposeful.

I glanced over. "What?"

"We should buy a motorhome."

I blinked. "You mean an RV? Like... buy one—not rent?"

She nodded, already leaning in to the idea. "Yes. A motorhome. We could leave it at different points along the trail so we wouldn't have to drive the whole distance each time. Fly in, get in our motorhome, go to the next event, leave it somewhere else, and fly home."

She made it sound so easy. So logical. So completely Carmen.

Carmen is one of the most intelligent and articulate people I've ever met. She can speak confidently on everything from public policy to dirigibles, and she's precise with language. She'd remind you that all motorhomes are RVs, but not all RVs are motorhomes—just like all blimps are dirigibles, but not all dirigibles are blimps.

Me? When it comes to motorhomes, I'm more like Cousin Eddie from Christmas Vacation: "Oh, that there? That's an Arrrrr Vee."

I smiled at the thought. It sounded like a great plan. But what did I know about motorhomes? What did either of us know?

Little did I realize what my brilliant wife was already cooking up in her head.

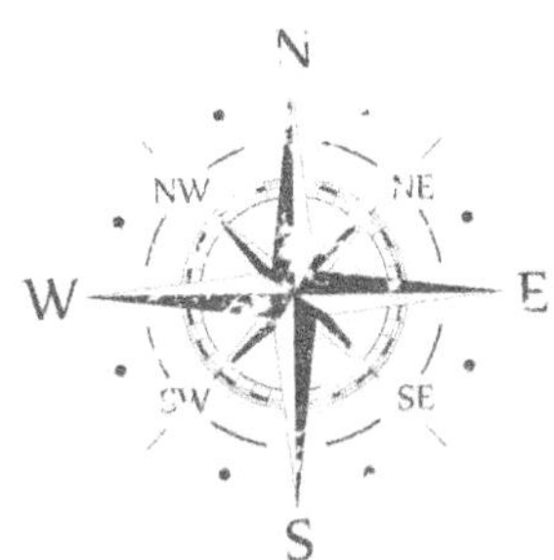

The Shakedown Cruise

To: Bismarck, North Dakota, via Omaha
October 2004

We had the map, the motorhome, and the memories—
now it was time to see if everything would hold together.

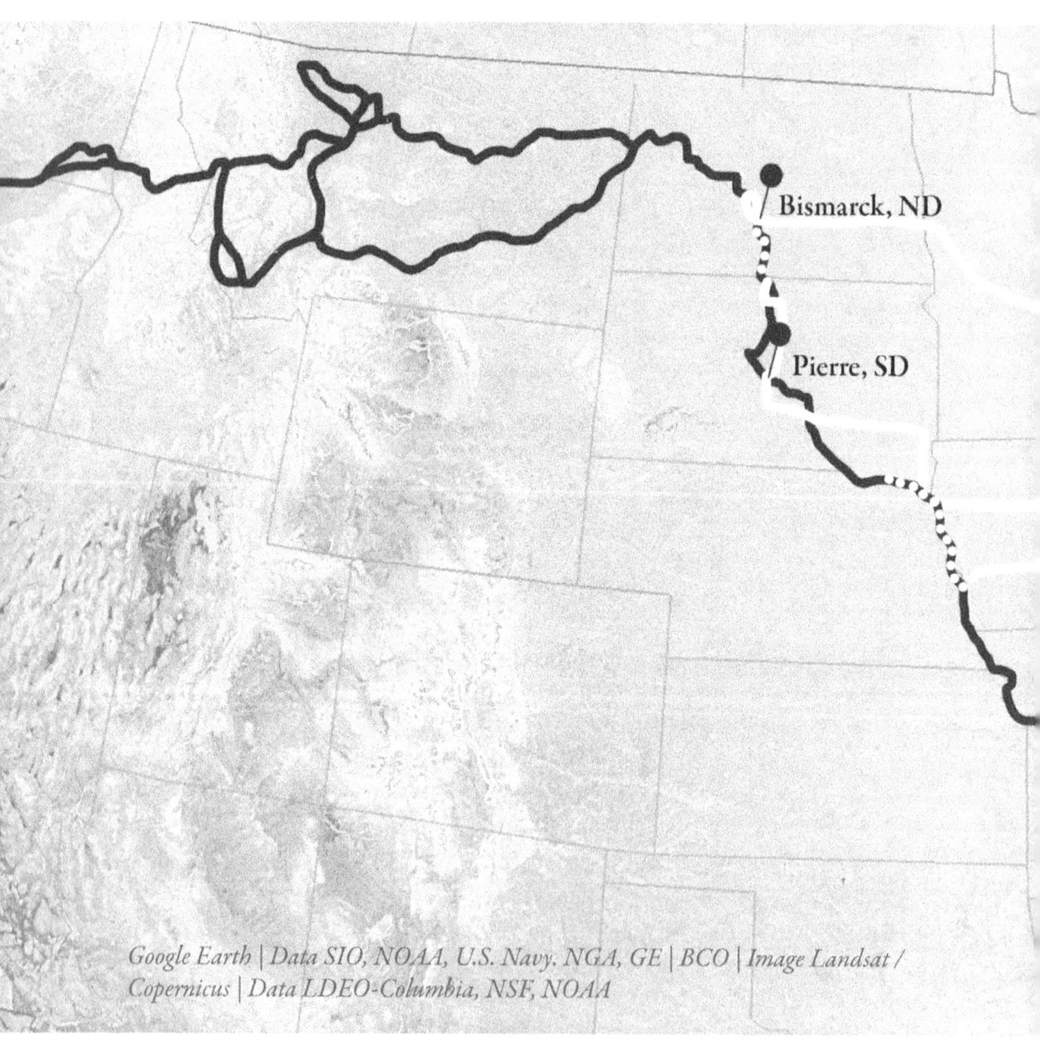

Google Earth | Data SIO, NOAA, U.S. Navy, NGA, GE | BCO | Image Landsat /
Copernicus | Data LDEO-Columbia, NSF, NOAA

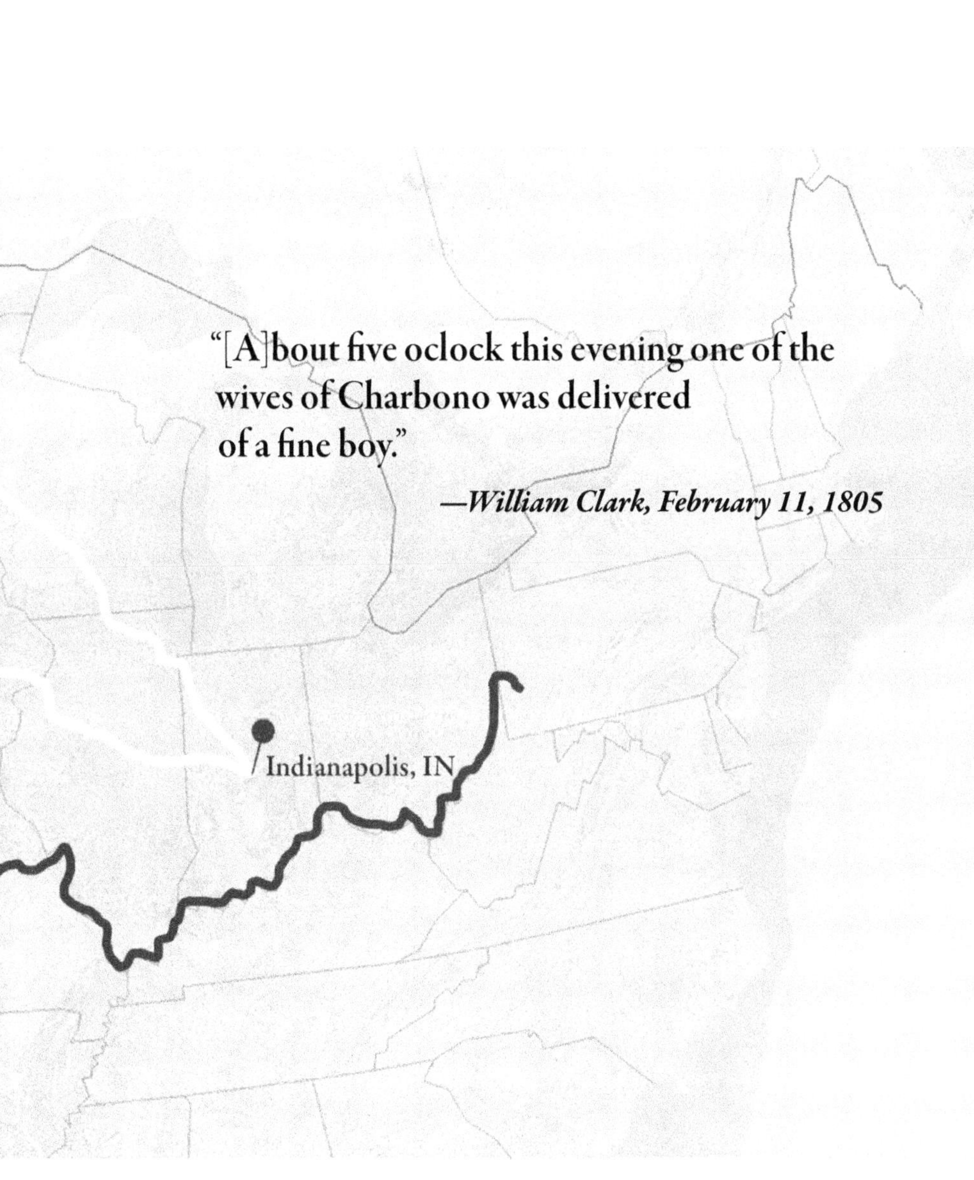

"[A]bout five oclock this evening one of the wives of Charbono was delivered of a fine boy."

—William Clark, February 11, 1805

Indianapolis, IN

fifteen

Shakedown Begins

A few weeks later, I was sitting in my office when Carmen called. She had been researching RVs—excuse me, *motorhomes*—and had narrowed it down to two options.

Of course she had.

"Can you get out of work early so we can go look at them?"

Of course I could!

Several hours later, we signed the papers on a B Touring Cruiser. It was a cross between a Class B and a Class C—built on a Ford E350 truck chassis. Big enough to stretch out in, small enough to thread through the mountain passes we dreamed of. It felt like the next phase of our journey had already begun.

We'd learned back in March—during a visit to Camp Dubois—that the original Corps of Discovery spent the winter of 1803–1804 in training. They practiced navigation, loaded and unloaded boats, and prepared for the unknown. They may have called them shakedown cruises.

Instead of a victory lap, we planned a shakedown cruise or two—to see if the house we'd just put on wheels could carry the life we were building. We needed time to learn how to actually use our new Arrrrr Vee.

And boy, did we ever learn.

Gray tank. Black tank. Pilot lights. A fridge that cools by burning propane. Backing up. Leveling. Every task a new dialect to learn—and fast.

Our first campground had back-in sites only—no pull-throughs. This meant I had to reverse the house on wheels into a narrow spot using only the side mirrors. Want a test of your marriage? Try backing up a motorhome for the first time while your spouse stands behind you, waving directions that are the mirror image of reality.

No automatic levelers. Just plastic ramps, ready to shoot out if you overshot. And every site had a wooden deck inches from where you needed to stop—as if daring you to miss.

To make matters worse, veteran RVers love watching rookies fumble with their rigs. It's their favorite pastime. Finally, one guy—clearly a seasoned pro—walked over and asked, "Want me to back it in for you?"

Heck yes.

I had no pride left. Within minutes, he had it parked half an inch from the deck and perfectly level.

The first CC and 7 tasted really good that night.

A SECOND BIG DECISION

All this was happening in the summer of 2004—and then we made another big decision.

We sold our house.

Well, Carmen's house.

Carmen and her first husband had bought that house together in 1990. It was their first home. It was the house where Carmen and her husband brought home their dogs, Guinness and Watney. When her dad, Jim, was transferred to an office a hundred miles from his home, he often stayed at Carmen's to save time on the commute. He would spend hours on the back patio smoking his cigars and "watching" the dogs. It was the house where her husband told her he wanted a divorce, while her dad was dying of cancer.

Afterward, it became her refuge. Her friends would come over, and they'd drink wine, watch movies, laugh, cry, and begin again. It was a house of survival and reinvention.

It was the house where the vet came one day to help Guinness cross the rainbow bridge.

It was the house Carmen still lived in when we reconnected in 1998. The house I moved into in April 2001... and had never left.

That spring of 2001, Carmen had knee surgery. Taking care of herself—and Watney the dog—was nearly impossible. I started coming over every day to help. Then I started spending the night. I only returned to my apartment on the days when Brad, my teenage son, was with me.

Eventually, we knew it was time to disclose our relationship at work. The leadership was supportive, but they also took steps to maintain our professional separation. Carmen was passed over for a promotion soon after. She resigned gracefully.

This time, the goodbye party was hers. We gathered at our usual spot—the Fox and Hound: friends, colleagues, laughter, and drinks. I waited until one of her good friends arrived… then I nodded to the hostess.

"Pretty Girl" by Eric Clapton began to play over the speakers.

Carmen looked up, instantly knowing something was up.

The hostess brought a bouquet—a "floral tribute," as Carmen and her girlfriends called them.

Carmen opened the card. I dropped to one knee.

As she read, I spoke the words aloud:

> I give to you my life
> You make my life whole
> I give to you my soul
> And ask you to be my wife

Through tears, she cried "Yes! Yes! Yes!"

We kissed like no other kiss in all of time. We were crying. Everyone was crying.

So, no—I never moved out. And I was about to see another incredible part of Carmen.

Brad began staying with us during my parenting time. Carmen made sure he felt welcome. We rearranged the guest room—it became his room. She invited his friends over. She cooked excellent meals when his girlfriend came to visit. She even decided to quit smoking—for me, but also for Brad. She wanted to be a positive influence in his life.

That house became our house.

That Thanksgiving, we invited both our families to dinner. Before the meal, we asked everyone to look under their plates. There, they found the invitation to our wedding—just two days away.

Our house.

We painted fences. We planted flowers. We sat on the patio and watched the sun set over the pond. We laughed. We dreamed. We grieved. We entered the lottery for the first Lewis and Clark Bicentennial Event.

We began building something permanent.

But now, Carmen was ready. Sitting on our back patio one summer night, the moon casting a glow across her face, she asked me quietly, "Does it bother you that we live in this house? The house I shared with my ex? Do you feel the ghosts?"

I laughed. "Only when I called the Chinese takeout place and they asked, 'Mr. Hillenburg, would you like the usual?' before I said a word."

She smiled, but asked again, more seriously.

"This feels like our home to me," I said. "Because you made it that way."

"I think," she said, "we should find one that's ours."

In one year, we took a Mediterranean cruise, crossed two continents, bought a motorhome, chased Signature Events, made memories—and chose to sell a past to build a future. We sold her house, lived with my parents for a few weeks, and then bought a new one together.

Like the Corps, every new phase came with new tools, new skills, new trust—a different kind of expedition—powered by curiosity, courage, and commitment.

UNPACKED BOXES, UNFINISHED STORIES

Two weeks after moving in—boxes still stacked, walls still bare—we pointed the motorhome west for The Circle of Cultures: Time of Renewal and Exchange, commemorating the Corps' winter among the Mandan and Hidatsa. We had several meaningful stops planned along the 1,300-mile drive.

Ever since reading the *Native American Resource Handbook* in Atchison, we had been thinking differently. We wanted to deepen our understanding—not only of the Indigenous peoples Lewis and Clark encountered, but also of the Indigenous experience as it exists today. This trip would give us that opportunity.

We decided to pick up where we'd left off in July, following the trail northward. Our first stop was Council Bluffs, Iowa—just across the Missouri River from Omaha, Nebraska. Tracing that stretch in the atlas, we named where we were headed—Otoe-Missouria and Omaha homelands—and reminded ourselves to show up curious and listen first.

Back in August, we had missed the First Tribal Council Signature Event near Fort Calhoun, Nebraska, which extended into Council Bluffs and Sioux City, both in Iowa. That event commemorated the first formal meeting between Captains Lewis and Clark and the Otoe-Missouria in late July and early August 1804. The council took place beneath a large oak tree overlooking the river—a site later named Council Bluff, from which the city would eventually take its name.

We had also missed The Oceti Sakowin Experience: Remembering and Educating, held in Oacoma and Chamberlain, South Dakota, focused on the Seven Council Fires of the Dakota, Nakota, and Lakota Nations.

At the time, we were only beginning to grasp how layered Native perspectives are. Missing those events felt like more than a scheduling miss; it felt like a lost chance to listen—and to be uncomfortable, if that was the price of learning. As our journey continued, curiosity was evolving into responsibility. We wanted to make up for missed chances and tell a fuller story.

sixteen

Where the Spirits Dwell

The next morning dawned gray and chilly. Our first stop was the Western Historic Trails Center. Just outside the building stood a sandstone mural that told the story of America's westward expansion. We both agreed it was pretty cool—but what we were really eager for was a walk along the Missouri River Bottoms Trail and the chance to reconnect with our dear Missouri River for the first time in months.

Carmen looked adorable in her hiking boots, jeans, black long-sleeved top, and her "cow vest." She would probably kill me for calling it that, but it was white wool with big black splotches. (Think early 2000s Gateway computer boxes, like a Holstein.)

The river did not disappoint. Though the morning was cloudy, it reflected the trees on the opposite bank with quiet clarity. A light fog trailed downstream like a veil, softening the edges of the world. As we hiked back to the motorhome, we turned for one last view—the trail carpeted in yellow leaves, the river slowly swallowed by the lifting haze.

Our next stop—before crossing our (now) favorite river—was the Lewis and Clark Monument Park. The centerpiece is two large, curved granite stones etched with imagery commemorating the Corps of Discovery's first council with Native leaders. The mural depicts what Lewis called the "Maha," though we now understand that to mean the Omaha people. The formal council honored here, however, was with the Otoe-Missouria—and it happened across the river, upstream.

Names blur; stories overlap. What mattered for us in that moment was the beginning of dialogue—imperfect, incomplete, but a beginning.

We stood at the overlook for a long time. The Missouri valley stretched wide before us, a soft palette of golds and browns. Omaha's skyline rose across the water, softened by distance and haze. In seeing both sides of the river at once, we were reminded that history isn't always where you expect it to be, but sometimes it still manages to find you.

A LESSON IN IMPROVISATION

We arrived at Fort Calhoun with high hopes and low expectations for weather—but not for access. The visitor center was locked. My bad—again. We walked the tallgrass to the bronze council group—Lewis, Clark, and an Otoe leader in a ring of wind. We read every plaque. We tried to feel the ground tell its version.

When we got back, a parks department truck pulled in. Carmen did Carmen. Doors opened.

The visitor center was small and thoughtful. Pins acquired.

Fort Atkinson sits just beyond town, a reconstruction with honest bones. We wandered the blockhouses, bakery, and barracks, then hiked down to the sculpture at the estimated council site—concentric rings like a compass; within them, a pipe and a plume, dialogue signaled in metal. If Monticello's small brass compass pointed us forward, this one pulled us back—toward the exchange that began here.

Eventually, we climbed back aboard our wheeled keelboat and headed toward Sioux City—no idea what was around the bend, ready anyway.

ONLY ONE MAN DIED

Near present-day Sioux City, Sergeant Charles Floyd—the only member of the Corps to die during the expedition—fell ill and died days later of what Lewis called "bilious colic," likely a burst appendix. We toured the retired-steamboat museum named for Sergeant Floyd, then climbed to the obelisk on the bluff—wind, river, silence.

As we pulled away, I said, "The book is called *Only One Man Died*. But the Blackfeet remember two of their own. We tend to leave that out."

"In Montana?" Carmen asked.

"North of Great Falls. Maybe next year we'll learn more."

A DETOUR OF THE SPIRIT

We crossed the river heading west, then turned north toward Ponca State Park. I'm almost sure we made the drive to the Tri-State Overlook, where you can see South Dakota as well as Nebraska and Iowa. I remember winding park roads, the climb and descent, the fog—or was it rain? Maybe we didn't get out of the motorhome. Perhaps we were catching our breath. Even if we never stood at the rail, the shape of that hill stayed with me like a half-remembered chorus.

Driving west across northeastern Nebraska on our way to Gavins Point Dam, I told Carmen the story of the captains hearing about a mysterious hill rising from the Dakota prairie—sacred ground many local nations approached with caution. Spirit Mound. Little devils, the stories warned. Eighteen inches tall, sharp voices, armed and dangerous.

"What?" Carmen snapped her head toward me, grinning. "You're taking us to a dam tour instead of Spirit Mound? That surprises me."

I laughed sheepishly. "I wasn't sure we had the time. I really wanted to see Ponca, and there aren't many places to cross the river."

"How far is it?"

"I don't know."

With that, my navigator—my Sacagawea, my Lewis—pulled the atlas into her lap, flipped to South Dakota, and traced a finger along the routes like she was tuning an instrument. We made a new plan: Hit the dam's visitor center, cross into Yankton, loop back east to Vermillion for the mound, then head north to I-90 and make up time. From here on out, the Missouri braided itself into a chain of man-made lakes; we'd learn to read the crossings like commas in a long sentence.

North out of Vermillion on SD-19, Spirit Mound lifted from the patchwork of corn and soy like a question being asked out loud. Even from a distance, it had presence—not dramatic, just certain.

We parked the motorhome and set out on the narrow path through restored prairie, a ribbon cut through waist-high grass that ticked at our knees. Grasshoppers skittered ahead of our boots. The wind moved like water. Every few yards, we looked back to watch the motorhome fall smaller against the fields, our strange little keelboat beached on an ocean of gold.

At the summit, the world opened. Miles of fields, grain elevators pricking the horizon, clouds lying low like a second ground. The view had changed since the Corps climbed here, but the feeling hadn't. It still asked you to be small and awake at the same time.

Near the crest, we noticed a few small prayer bundles—"fetish sacks," as we would later learn—resting against the earth, the way you leave a conversation mid-sentence knowing it will continue without you. We didn't touch them. We just stood. The wind carried a sound that wasn't quite silence.

I didn't have a theology to explain what I felt. It wasn't religion in the way I grew up; it was older, nearer to bone. Reverence that arrives before you name it. Carmen slid her hand into mine, and for a while we didn't speak. If the veil between worlds thins anywhere, it's on hills like this— where a story is both a place and a presence.

Back at the trailhead, the light had warmed, brushing the prairie in gold. We turned toward the motorhome—the keelboat on wheels—and I realized we hadn't just ticked a box. We had honored a place. We had listened.

AS THE LIGHT FADES, THE RIVER REMEMBERS

We aimed west for Chamberlain, where an interpretive center sits high on a bluff above the river, crowned by a towering tipi-inspired frame. I-90 crests the hill and dives for the water like a kid sprinting for a swimming hole. Even if you don't stop, the view reaches up and grabs you by the collar.

Inside the Lewis and Clark Welcome Center, we wandered through exhibits hoping to understand more about the Oceti Sakowin Experience we'd missed—what it tried to surface, where it fell short, and how the Lakota, Dakota, and Nakota carry their stories forward now. Maybe we were road-weary. Maybe Spirit Mound had raised the bar. Nothing quite stuck. Sometimes the river keeps the thing you're after until you're ready for it.

We crossed the bridge and tried a scenic route along the west bank toward Pierre. The map promised a closer dance with the water, but a few miles in, the pavement loosened into gravel—the kind meant for ox carts and patient souls. The motorhome rattled like a drawer of utensils. We looked at each other, weighed daylight against adventure, and turned back toward asphalt.

Sometimes the road you want isn't the road you get. And sometimes the sacred shows up in the recalibration—the choice to listen to time, to machine, to the narrow band of light left in the day.

We chased that light north and reached the confluence of the Bad River and the Missouri just as the sun slipped away, leaving a bruise of purple and gold across the water. The park itself was simple: a few interpretive signs, a short path, and benches tucked under cottonwoods. It didn't need more. The story was already written in the meeting of those two waters.

We read the markers about the encounter here—the Corps and the Lakota (Teton Sioux), tension stacked on misunderstanding, a standoff that could have unraveled the whole expedition. The words carried weight in the dimming air. To our left, the Bad slid in with its own color, its own current; straight ahead, the Missouri received it and kept going. Conflict once. Confluence now.

We lingered until the shapes softened. Carmen stood at the bank with her hands in her pockets, the wind tugging at her sleeves. I framed her in silhouette and pressed the shutter. You can't see her face in that photo, but you can feel the belonging. Like she's a note the river was waiting to hear again.

We didn't say much while walking back to the rig. Some places don't need words, and some moments scold you if you add them.

Night had settled by the time we found the highway again. After a few hours, hunger snuck up on us. We pulled into a truck stop, fired the generator, reheated leftovers, raised the antenna, and watched an episode of *The West Wing* with semis idling outside our windows. It was nothing and everything—plastic forks, blanket over Carmen's knees, the hum of our little house working precisely as it should. Contentment can be a quiet thing.

At some point in the darkness, we crossed into North Dakota. Near midnight, we rolled into Prairie Knights Casino and RV Park, the lot mostly empty, pole lights humming, the casino's neon down the hill. Park. Level. Plug in. Collapse. Through the window screen came the cottonwoods whispering and, beyond them, the river telling its endless story—steady, unseen, close enough to touch if you listened hard enough. Sleep found us fast.

seventeen

Echoes on the Prairie

We pulled out early under a low, pewter sky and followed a ribbon of asphalt called Highway 1806—a number that felt like a wink from the trail itself. The wind pushed at the motorhome, and every so often, the clouds tore just enough to show a lighter gray behind the first one. The river was never far, even when we couldn't see it. You learn to read the land: Cottonwoods gather where water lingers; the horizon opens when a channel wants room.

Somewhere in the planning, I had circled Fort Yates with a simple note: Sitting Bull's grave. Detour-worthy, we agreed. The town was quiet when we rolled in. Not Sunday-morning quiet—more like a weekday afternoon that had run out of errands. The only gas station was shuttered. We drove a grid of streets looking for a marker, a sign, something that would tell two respectful strangers how to pay our respects. Nothing. No arrow, no plaque, no fence line with a gate. Just a stillness that bordered on private.

We idled a minute at a four-way stop, wipers ticking time. Carmen scanned the empty sidewalks and said, softly, "Maybe it isn't ours to find today."

We sat in that for a breath. There are graves the world insists you visit—bus tours, gift shops, a scenic turnout for your grief. And then there are graves the world guards, where memory is a living thing kept by the people who belong to it. We turned back toward Highway 1806, the motorhome

125

humming, each of us a little quieter than before. Not finding him felt... right, somehow. A reminder that reverence can also sound like leaving something alone.

North again, the road lifted toward Fort Abraham Lincoln. Rain stitched the windshield, and the fog hugged the slope as we climbed to the plateau. You can feel the layered history before you see a single sign: the rounded backs of earth lodges rise from the grass, and beyond them the straight lines of a fort that came later, imposed on a village that had already been here for generations. On-a-Slant Village—Mandan ground—carrying centuries of winters and weddings and children and trade, long before uniforms and guidons.

We started in the village. The reconstructed lodges felt honest—timbers sunk deep, ribs bending toward a smoke hole, earth packed tight against the weather. Inside, the air was warmer, the light softer, as if voices still knew how to live here. Carmen touched the doorframe and whispered "Home," like a word trying out its echo.

Up the rise, the fort waited—blockhouses squared to the wind, clapboard and command. A guide welcomed us and stepped straight into character, dated to the very morning the 7th Cavalry rode out under the command of General Custer. For an hour, we were led through rooms where trunks were half-packed and confidence felt inevitable—destiny rehearsed in the mirror. Knowing the end made the performance ache. The guide spoke of orders and glory; the village below held a longer story: survival, sovereignty, a future that refused to disappear.

Standing at the edge of the parade ground, we could see both histories at once—the curve of the lodges and the angles of the fort, one nested inside the other like truths that refuse to be told separately. We didn't have language big enough for that contrast, so we let the wind carry some of it for us.

Back in the motorhome, we drove into the town of Mandan for a couple of small museums before crossing the river. Pieces clicked into place: maps we'd seen in March, beadwork that moved like water when light found it, names we were finally learning to say out loud. The sky began to lift at the edges.

HOOKUPS AND HINDSIGHT

From Mandan, it was a short run to Bismarck, and then a few miles south to General Sibley Campground, down in the bottomlands where the cottonwoods gather. The season was nearly over. Power was on; water and sewer were already shut for the winter. We made a mental note to ask more questions before we pulled in anywhere new.

It didn't matter much that night. The hush was its own kind of hospitality. We couldn't see the river from our site, but we could feel where it was—the way the air cooled differently, the way the trees listened. We leveled, plugged in, and stood for a minute under a sky finally giving up its rain. The Missouri was near. Waiting... again.

eighteen
Ghosts and Gas Stations

We had arrived in Bismarck a day or two before the Signature Event, so the next morning we boarded our motorhome and headed north to find Fort Mandan. Ironically, the fort is located in *Washburn*, not forty miles to the south in *Mandan*. The day was gray, windy, cold, and rainy—but not even the biting North Dakota wind could deter us. We followed the Missouri River as it carved its way northward, the sky hanging low and heavy above the landscape.

We stopped to visit the Double Ditch Village Historic Site. When Lewis and Clark passed this place in 1804, the Mandan village was already deserted—abandoned in the aftermath of smallpox and other devastating epidemics. Today, the outlines of the old earth lodges remain visible as subtle impressions in the earth, their stories whispered by the wind.

As we walked the path through the ghost of the village, an eagle soared above us, circling high in the air currents rolling off the river bluffs. It felt like an unspoken blessing.

And yet, there was something else in the air, too—something weightier.

This place, long abandoned before Lewis and Clark ever set foot nearby, carried the imprint of sorrow. A smallpox epidemic had ravaged the Mandan and Hidatsa, sweeping through these communities with a violence greater than any weapon. It struck not during a battle or skirmish, but through blankets and breath—brought not by the Corps of Discovery, but by the waves of traders and contact that preceded them.

It was a sobering reminder that the westward movement of this country didn't begin with Lewis and Clark. The groundwork—the fur trading, the disease, the disruption—had already started to chip away at Native lifeways. And what would follow in the Corps' wake would not be an era of mutual understanding, but of displacement, broken treaties, and grief. As much as we admired the courage of the expedition, we couldn't ignore the cost.

There on the trail, with the eagle overhead and the wind rising from the valley, we stood still for a moment—almost in mourning. The river had carried many stories to this place. Some of them were ours. But some—maybe the most important—were not.

Just outside Washburn, we stopped at the North Dakota Lewis and Clark Interpretive Center, which housed an impressive exhibit on the Corps' winter among the Mandan. The displays were well done—thoughtful, detailed, and respectful. From there, we drove a few more miles up the road to Fort Mandan itself.

Another small museum at the site told the story of the fort's construction and offered insight into what life was like during that long, frigid winter of 1804–1805. Outside, a short path led us to the full-scale replica of the fort. The rain had eased, but the cold remained. We hustled along the trail, breath curling in the air, shoulders hunched against the wind.

Inside the fort, reenactors greeted us and described the layout—officers' quarters, storage areas, bunks, and the gathering spaces that had once echoed with laughter, stories, and strategic planning. You could almost feel the fire in the hearth and the tension of the unknown to come.

Back in our motorhome, we made an impromptu decision. Instead of heading back the way we came, we turned left at the fork near the fort, hoping to catch a closer glimpse of the river. The road soon ended in a turnaround, but what a reward—before us was the Missouri, no longer obscured by trees or buildings. It was broad and brown, flowing with quiet authority past our parked vessel. We sat in silence, letting the river fill our view. It moved with the power of time itself—unchanged, unstoppable.

OF BUFFALO HIDES AND EARTH LODGES

After a quick lunch, we crossed the Missouri once more and began heading west toward the Knife River Indian Villages—home of Sacagawea. She was likely sixteen or seventeen when the Corps met her in the winter of 1804–05 near present-day Stanton, North Dakota. A Shoshone girl kidnapped as a child and living among the Hidatsa, she entered their story already displaced. In February 1805, she gave birth to Jean Baptiste, carrying him on her back as the expedition pushed west. Even her name remains unsettled—Sacagawea, Sakakawea, Sacajawea—a reminder that her life moved between languages. A teenager. A mother. A bridge between worlds.

We had first learned about this sacred place through Gerard Baker. He had shared the story of the night he and Dayton Duncan camped in the replica earth lodge at the Villages. Dayton, ever the historian, wanted to experience a North Dakota winter night the way Lewis and Clark had. Gerard obliged—sort of. When bedtime came, he handed Dayton a single bison hide to fend off the minus-30-degree chill, then unrolled his own high-tech, Arctic-rated down sleeping bag. The way Gerard told it, Dayton never quite forgave him. The skies were ominous as we arrived. Hoping to beat the rain, we went straight to the lodge. Stepping inside felt like entering another time. The thick earthen walls muted the wind, and the air held the faint scent of wood, earth, and something older. We lingered there for a while, letting the quiet of the space settle around us.

The Hidatsa earth lodges were unlike anything we'd ever seen up close— massive domed structures built to endure brutal North Dakota winters and shelter entire families, even generations. They began with massive cottonwood timbers, buried deep into the ground and bent inward toward a central smoke hole. Cross-beams supported the dome, and the whole thing was packed with a thick, insulating mixture of earth and prairie grasses. Over time, the structure became part of the landscape—alive with weather, seasons, and stories.

Inside, the space felt quiet and sacred. The circular floor plan radiated outward from a central fire pit, with raised platforms for sleeping, storage areas for corn and tools, and alcoves that offered both privacy and togetherness. I imagined the warmth, the laughter, the generations who had lived here before. Families. Children. Horses, even. It felt vast and intimate all at once—big enough for a community, yet still deeply personal.

For a few minutes, we stood inside, silent, listening to the wind outside and sensing how the earth seemed to hold the memory of all that had passed here.

Then the rain came.

By the time we darted back down the path to the visitor center, the wind had kicked up hard, driving sheets of rain sideways as we scrambled inside, soaked but laughing. We wandered through the small museum, drying off and taking in the exhibits. There, among artifacts and stories, we found Sacagawea again—not as a quiet side character or guide, but as a woman of the Knife River villages. A mother. A translator. A survivor. A bridge between worlds.

JUST TOP IT OFF, HE SAID...

Soon, the rain let up, and we dashed back to the RV. Our next stop was Cross Ranch State Park, where we planned to camp for the night before returning to Bismarck. The forecast called for near-freezing temperatures, so I wanted to make sure we had a full tank of gas. While the motorhome's furnace ran on propane, the generator—needed to power the furnace blower—ran on gas from the engine's tank. And our salesman had warned us: The generator had a built-in safety mechanism. If the gas level dropped below a quarter tank, the generator would shut off automatically. It was meant to ensure you didn't drain your tank dry and wake up stuck.

So we pulled into a small roadside station in Stanton—the kind of place that doubles as a feed store and triples as the community gossip post. It was the only fuel stop for miles. The wind was howling as I jumped out to pump gas, zipping my coat and bracing myself against the gusts.

A few minutes in, I heard a piercing alarm—and at the exact moment, Carmen's scream. She burst out of the door, frantic.

"It's not fire!" she yelled. "I don't see fire—no smoke—but the alarm's going off!"

I leapt up the steps and into a wall of shrieking—the carbon monoxide detector. I fumbled with the instruction book, my hands shaking more from adrenaline than cold. Finally, I found the right button to silence the chaos. We checked everything—no smell of gas, no smoke, no sign of trouble.

Relieved, I stepped back outside to finish fueling up. Not 60 seconds later, the alarm went off again.

Lesson learned. We surmised that, on a windy day, the swirling fumes from pumping gas into an RV with a carbon monoxide detector positioned low and near the fuel intake could trigger a full-blown alarm. And the kind of alarm you never forget.

I finished filling up and moved our house on wheels away from the pump before heading inside to pay. We climbed back in, both of us jumpy as cats, nerves still rattling.

As we drove off toward Cross Ranch, I glanced at Carmen—her hair a little windblown, her eyes still wide. She looked over at me, half-laughing, half-scolding.

"You just had to top off the tank."

As we entered the park, night was falling. We were going to have to park the RV in the dark. Wow, we were learning all kinds of lessons that day! We found our site with little problem, and using a combination of flashlights, RV lights, and a little blind luck, we backed the RV into the snug space among the trees.

The wind had finally calmed. The stars were beginning to prick through the inky sky, and the scent of pine and riverbank hung in the cold night air. Carmen clicked on the furnace and unpacked our usual nightcaps—CC and 7s in plastic cups—and we toasted another unforgettable day on the trail.

Tired but content, we crawled into bed, the faint hum of the heater our only soundtrack. Somewhere nearby, the Missouri rolled on in darkness, steady and unseen—just as it always had. And somehow, even out here in the chill of the unknown, it felt like we were home.

nineteen

The River Remembers

We awoke the next morning to find a delicate layer of frost coating the picnic tables, the grass, and the windows of our tin can on wheels. But inside? Toasty warm. Our little house on wheels had done its job.

We made our way to the University of Mary, where the Signature Event was already underway. The day's schedule included a series of "lectures," but that word doesn't do them justice. They were performances. Stories brought to life.

We watched Daniel Slosberg channel Pierre Cruzatte, fiddle in hand, telling his stories through music and movement. Cruzatte, the half-blind French fiddler and expert riverman, was both comic and tragic—a figure of resilience, joy, and occasional chaos. Spoiler alert: A year and a half later, he'd accidentally shoot Lewis in the buttocks (and yes, it's impossible to say that without channeling Forrest Gump).

Then came Amy Mossett as Sacagawea. Barely 17. A girl and a mother. A translator, a guide, a survivor. Her story—told with such grace and power—hit deep. Carmen and I barely spoke as we watched. It was as though Sacagawea had stepped out of the shadows of history and into the room.

We finished the day with Arch Ellwein as Sergeant John Ordway. His delivery was deadpan and deeply human, filled with wit and weary wisdom. Ordway's journal entries—so often overlooked—had been brought vividly to life.

After such a meaningful afternoon, we were already thinking ahead to the evening. Our dinner experience in Atchison had been unforgettable, and we weren't about to miss the Bismarck edition. I'd managed to track down tickets in advance.

UNINVITED BUT UNFORGETTABLE

Before dinner, we attended the play *Edge of the Unknown*. It was told through the memories of William Clark as he processes his emotions upon hearing of Meriwether Lewis's death in 1809. His memories bring him back to the winter of 1804 and Fort Mandan. Through his musings, we gain insight into the relationship between Lewis and Clark, as well as the cultures they encountered among the Mandans that winter. It was poignant.

When we arrived at the dinner, there was a lot of confusion. We realized we were the only ones there who did not know anyone. It seems like we had somehow crashed the dinner for the organizing committee.

We had the good fortune to be seated with a group who were visiting from upriver and who were organizing the Signature Event at Williston the following year.

Dinner conversation ran the gamut, but I bet they'll never forget Carmen.

About midway through the meal, she leaned over and whispered, "Do you think I should tell them?"

"Tell them what?" I asked.

"That I think Lewis may have been in love with Clark."

I shrugged. "Go for it."

She turned back to the table and, with that unmistakable twinkle in her eye, captured everyone's attention. Calmly, confidently, she laid out her theory: that Meriwether Lewis died from unrequited love—for William Clark.

There was a beat of stunned silence, forks frozen midair. Then someone chuckled. A few nodded thoughtfully. One woman leaned in and said, "Well, I've never not believed that." The rest of the table buzzed with speculation, and just like that, Carmen had turned a polite committee dinner into a late-night college seminar.

As we walked out that evening, someone from another table called after us, "Hey! Let us know when the book comes out!" Carmen just smiled. She had dropped her theory like a stone in the water—and the ripples were still spreading.

THE LONG ROAD HOME (AND THE LONGER ONE THROUGH CHICAGO)

Over the next two days, we attended a half dozen more lectures, each offering a unique perspective on the expedition. We prioritized those that helped deepen our understanding of the Indigenous peoples' experience, like Brian Bitner's detailed explanation in "The Building of the Earthlodges." Another highlight was Keith Bear's "Flute Workshop," where he shared the cultural and spiritual significance of the flute among the Mandan and Hidatsa peoples—how they were crafted, what they symbolized, and how their sound carried meaning far beyond melody.

The closing ceremonies on Sunday, October 31, were a fitting end to this remarkable chapter of our journey. The parking lots were jammed. Of course, traveling in our Arrrrr Vee, we were directed to the "special" lot across campus. At least the sun made a rare appearance that day, though the walk was still a brisk one.

Before the ceremony, we attended one final lecture: "Selected & Implanted by Nature"—a tribute to Stephen Ambrose, delivered by his daughter, Stephenie Ambrose Tubbs. It was a heartfelt remembrance of a man whose passion for telling this story had inspired so many—including us.

Afterward, we began the long drive home. We pulled onto I-94 and aimed east, planning to drive until we dropped. The plan was simple: Stop at a rest area, fire up the generator, sleep a few hours, and repeat the process until we reached Indiana.

The trip itself was uneventful—just long. But we did learn another thing about RVs: no matter how solid they seem, they rattle. Not all the time, of course—just when crossing a bridge. Or approaching a bridge. Or leaving a bridge. Or during road construction. Lesson number 179: Do not drive through Chicago in an RV. Between the endless bridges and the perpetual construction, it's a symphony of squeaks, bangs, and cabinet door slaps. For 90 straight minutes, our tiny house on wheels sounded like it was trying to shake itself apart.

Moments Along the Trail
Photo Gallery

1. We headed east to explore the West.

2. Monticello—the spark that lit the map.

3. Here, the story ended for Lewis—and changed for us.

4. The old road still carries a whisper.

5. Paying homage to the Lizard King.

6. *Under stone and story at Les Invalides.*

7. *Drums at the river's edge, a statue learning to listen.*

8. *The send-off, under canvas and flags.*

9. *Carmen beside the bronze—still choosing forward.*

10. *First touch, long river.*

11. On the bluff above the river, we dreamed of a home on wheels.

12. "A Journey Fourth" came around the bend and into our lives.

13. Carmen in the cow vest—joy at the river's edge.

14. We climbed the rumor and listened for truth.

Leg 8

15. *At the divide, we said proceed on.*

16. *White Cliffs— first camp, first hush.*

17. *We looked for a museum and found a dig.*

18. *Cold rain, full hearts—still saying yes.*

19. *Three generations bearing flags—we entered listening.*

20. *In a chapel of wood and window, the mountains did the preaching.*

21. *At the meeting of waters, we learned to become one.*

22. *Flags rising under the Arch—we stood to listen.*

23. *Angela's Ark—a boat, a blessing, a thread of home.*

24. *At the place where the journey downriver began.*

25. The museum was closed; the vault opened.

26. We ended where his river began.

27. *Our keelboat on wheels.*

Don't Forget the Coke Money

To: The White Cliffs, Great Falls, Montana; and Lemhi Pass, Idaho
June–July 2005

We came for history. We found something more.

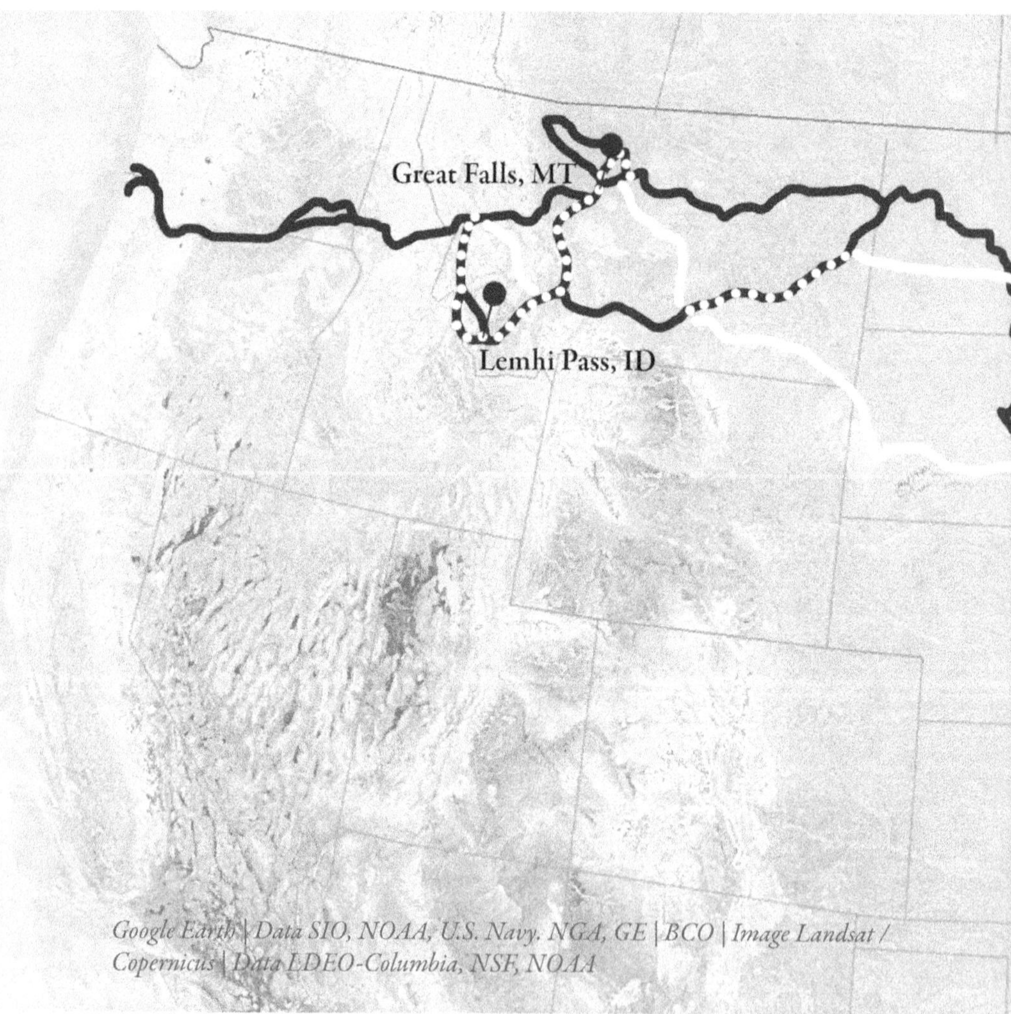

Google Earth | Data SIO, NOAA, U.S. Navy, NGA, GE | BCO | Image Landsat / Copernicus | Data LDEO-Columbia, NSF, NOAA

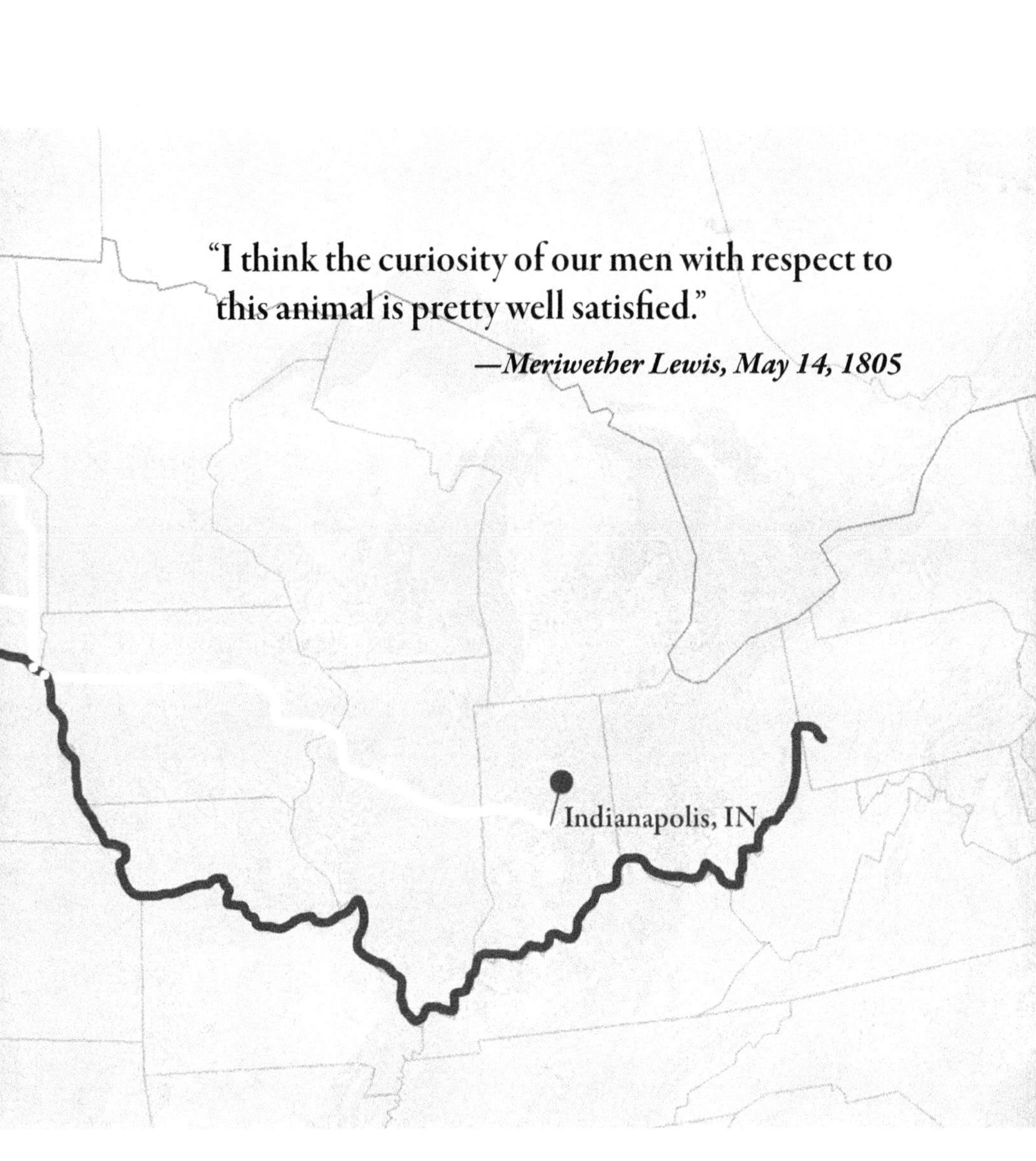

"I think the curiosity of our men with respect to this animal is pretty well satisfied."
—Meriwether Lewis, May 14, 1805
Indianapolis, IN

twenty

The Road to Her

Somewhere between the smell of propane, the scratch of a rock riff on satellite radio, and Carmen thumbing through her trusty atlas, the 2005 road trip finally began. We were on the road to Great Falls, Montana, and the Explore! The Big Sky Signature Event. The event would commemorate their arduous portage around the falls and mark our second Fourth of July west of the Mississippi.

The storm of the spring months had left us tired—but ready. Ready to leave behind calendars, contractors, and conference calls. Ready to be anonymous on the open highway. Ready for another chapter of the Lewis and Clark Trail—as participants in a story still unfolding.

We had maps—digital and paper. We had playlists. We had snacks. We had each other. And we had the Missouri River waiting for us out there, somewhere to the northwest. The river kept teaching us the same lesson— go slower, go deeper, skip the shiny detours.

The map listed a hundred side trips. The compass—hers and mine— pointed northwest.

On the longer legs, we give ourselves permission to add a few waypoints that aren't strictly Lewis and Clark—stops that say "since we're here." It's our way of traveling with the map and the moment: Mount Rushmore, Little Bighorn Battlefield, a turn through Deadwood and Lead, and the odd roadside pull-off that becomes a story. Those detours don't distract from the trail; they widen it.

We left Indianapolis in late June and headed toward Montana—but not through Chicago! We headed northwest through Illinois; crossed the Mississippi River outside of Davenport, Iowa; shot up I-380 through Cedar Rapids; and got on I-90 heading west. We crossed into South Dakota near Sioux City and continued west.

It took over two days of driving along the red asphalt interstate (Yes, red! Who knew asphalt in South Dakota was *red*?) before we came upon the Missouri River for the first time in almost eight months.

Traveling by motorhome is a unique experience. Think about it. You have everything at your fingertips: food, drink, refrigerator, bathroom, couch, bed—everything! We took turns driving and only stopped for gas. Hungry? Fix some sandwiches and keep moving. Thirsty? Grab something cold out of the fridge (I can neither confirm nor deny that on occasion, I asked Carmen to "beer me"). Tired? Lie down on the couch or the bed and take a nap.

On this trip, we had two new pieces of technology with us. The first was a Garmin GPS we borrowed from Tom. He loved gadgets. GPSs were a new thing, and it was fun to know exactly where we were at any given moment. Carmen still preferred her trusty atlas, and I preferred my Streets & Trips printouts. Still, it was cool.

The other new device we had was a Sirius XM satellite radio. Again, kind of a new thing. No more trying to tune in radio stations. No more static as you drive out of range. No more FM DJs (no offense, DJs). No more annoying commercials. Just rock and roll! In those days, the Sirius radio could be plugged into a boombox, or when traveling, it could broadcast to your FM radio. High tech!

Two days, a few thousand "Visit Wall Drug" signs, and one RV stocked to the roof—we were all in.

We loved playing Name That Tune or Rock Genealogy as the miles clicked away. I was the champion of Name That Tune in our family... as long as it was rock. There was this one time, however—one time. And my dear, lovely, adorable wife will never let me forget when I called out "Bob Seger" when, in fact, it was Steve Winwood or, more specifically, Traffic.

Ugh! How could I mess *that* up? I was also pretty good at Rock Genealogy, which wasn't much of a game. It was more of an opportunity for me to show off my genius of who played in what band and which band or bands they came from. Heck, I became a Rolling Stones fan because guitarist Ronnie Wood left the Faces to join the Rolling Stones. Uh, Rod Stewart was also in the Faces. Before the Faces, both Stewart and Wood played in one of the incarnations of the Jeff Beck Group. OK, I will stop now.

While we drove, we talked. Oh, and did we talk! You can't lock yourself inside a tin can hurtling down the highway at 70 miles an hour for hours on end without learning something new about each other. Even after five years together and three years married, we still considered ourselves newlyweds. Conversations flowed easily, looping from the kids—my sons, her stepsons, Jeremy and Brad—to my parents; her mom, Judy; and Judy's husband, Dave. We talked about work, politics (we were aligned, thank goodness), and life.

At one point, as the South Dakota sun poured through the windshield and turned Carmen's hair into strands of liquid gold, I stole a glance at her and smiled.

"Do you know what I regret?" I asked.

She turned, amused, that knowing smile curling at the corner of her mouth. "What do you regret?"

"I wish I'd gone to Indiana University instead of Indiana State. I don't know how, in that mass of students, but I think I would've found you sooner."

She didn't say anything right away. She just reached for my hand and held it.

Back in high school, the only thing I ever wanted to be was a rock star. I didn't think much about college—or life beyond the next gig. I met my first wife in the summer of '74. She had just graduated from high school and would be heading to Ball State that fall. Me? I was about to start my junior year of high school. When she transferred to a school closer to home after her freshman year, we were already making plans for our future: love, marriage, the whole package.

As for my college decision, well... it was less strategy and more of a cop-out. I was at a meeting of the Indiana Baptist Youth Foundation, and the leader asked each of us to introduce ourselves and say where we were going to school. One by one, the teens to my right said: "I'm Lisa, and I'm going to Indiana State to major in music." "I'm Glenn, Indiana State, music." "I'm Terry..." You get the idea.

When it was my turn, I didn't miss a beat. "I'm Jeff, and I'm going to Indiana State to major in music."

Boom. Decision made.

Heck, I figured I wouldn't need the degree anyway. I was going to be a rock star.

As we continued west, we intersected our trail from the previous fall at Chamberlain, South Dakota. Remember the humongous concrete tipi and the combination travel plaza and interpretive center? We stopped again to gaze at the river before continuing west, crossing it and leaving it to continue its winding trail north to Bismarck, then turning west and back south again to Great Falls. We wouldn't see the river again until Fort Benton, Montana, still several days ahead.

VISIT WALL DRUG!

We had seen the signs for hundreds of miles: "Free Ice Water!" "Home-made Donuts!" "5¢ Coffee!" "See the Jackalope!" And, of course, "Visit Wall Drug!" At first, we laughed. Then we started counting. Then we started anticipating.

By the time we pulled into the tiny town of Wall, South Dakota, we were already under its spell.

Wall is a town that feels like it grew up around a single establishment. Wall Drug is the epicenter—a souvenir stand that expanded until it seemed to swallow Main Street whole. Shops and side alleys and sculptures and Western dioramas spill outward from its doors. There are racks of cowboy hats, shelves of jewelry marketed as Native-inspired—but clearly mass-produced—endless rows of leather goods, and more T-shirts than one could reasonably justify owning. And the people—goodness, the people. RVers like us, bikers in leather vests, young families corralling kids with ice cream cones already dripping down their arms. We all wandered through the maze of shops, part theme park, part time capsule.

Of course, we got ice cream—how could we not? We sat outside on a carved wooden bench near a life-sized bucking bronco statue, soaking in the scene. Carmen, stylish as ever, somehow made licking a double scoop look elegant. I, on the other hand, was trying to eat mine before it melted all over my river shorts. We people-watched; we giggled; we pointed out some of the more outrageous souvenirs. We even considered buying matching cowboy hats... briefly.

Wall Drug wasn't on our original itinerary, but that's the thing about road trips—you don't always find the magic in the places you plan for. Sometimes it's the places that bill themselves with 200 billboards that surprise you the most.

After one last loop through the maze of shops and a quick stop to fill up our water bottles (free, of course), we climbed back into the RV and headed west again, full of sugar and smiles.

Sometimes, you pull off the road for kitsch—and leave with something closer to joy.

Soon after we got up to speed on I-90, I stole another glance at Carmen.

"Hey, I want to continue our conversation. How did you end up at IU?" I asked.

"Honestly? My first choice? I was going to be like Joni Mitchell, you know—a house, two cats, a yard," she said with a little grin, her voice half-singing the line. "I even had a boyfriend with a 12-string guitar. I was set."

I smiled. That sounded exactly like her.

"But I knew my parents wanted me to go to school. I wanted to go to Michigan, but they both said no to out-of-state tuition after paying for four years of private school at the Academy. I didn't want to go to Purdue—too many kids from home were headed there. A bunch of my friends were going to IU, so... IU for me."

She paused, gazing out the window for a moment, the prairie stretching endlessly in every direction.

"Remind me of the name of the Academy?" I asked.

"ICA—Immaculate Conception Academy in Oldenburg, Indiana," she answered. "The college transition wasn't hard. I'd already spent four years away at the Academy. I think I was ready for a place that felt a little bigger, a little more alive. And I fell in love—with Bloomington, with campus life. I made some great friends. Lifelong friends. You know that." I did. I'd come to know those friends, too—each one a thread in the fabric of Carmen's life that had quietly become part of mine.

twenty-one
Where Memory Rides the Wind

That night, we stayed at the 7th Ranch RV Camp, just south of the Little Bighorn Battlefield National Monument. Nestled amid rolling hills and open prairie, it was a quiet spot—simple, rustic, and hauntingly close to hallowed ground. This is Apsáalooke (Crow) and Lakota/Northern Cheyenne country—their story runs under every boot print here.

There was a stillness in the air, the kind that settles when you know you're on the edge of something important.

It had been several months since we visited Fort Lincoln. We had stood on the very parade grounds where Custer and the 7th Cavalry had set off to confront the Lakota and Northern Cheyenne. Now we were tracing that arc to its tragic conclusion: the Battle of the Little Bighorn.

We arrived at the memorial just as it opened. To orient ourselves, we stepped inside the visitor center and watched a short film recounting the days leading up to the battle. It presented both perspectives—the U.S. military strategy and the Indigenous resistance—and helped frame the conflict's chaotic terrain. Watching the dramatization unfold, Carmen reached for my hand. We didn't speak. There wasn't much to say.

Leaving the center, we followed the path uphill to the memorial dedicated to the 7th Cavalry. Marble markers dotted the hillside—each one placed where a soldier had fallen. They weren't lined in ranks or rows, but scattered, almost desperate. There was something jarring about their placement. This wasn't Arlington. This was raw, real, and final.

As we crested the hill, the land opened up before us. We stood at the overlook, gazing out toward the Little Bighorn River. With a bit of imagination, we could picture the vast encampment of Sitting Bull, Crazy Horse, and the thousands who had gathered on the plains below. In that moment, it became clear: This place was a crossroads of sovereignty, resistance, and consequence.

We continued to the Native American Memorial—a graceful circle of stone and steel, cut open to the sky. The memorial features a prominent bronze sculpture of three Native warriors and a woman handing a shield to them. It includes interpretive panels and inscriptions that honor the collective memory and perspectives of the Indigenous nations involved in the battle, such as the Lakota, Cheyenne, Arapaho, Crow, and Arikara. Their presence balanced the story and, at last, gave voice to the other side of the fight. The art was striking, the message clear: This place holds not one memory, but many. And not all of them were mourned equally. It felt like standing in a story that had waited too long to be told.

In a contemplative silence, we wandered through the adjacent National Cemetery. Soldiers from the Indian Wars, the Civil War, World Wars I and II, and beyond lie buried here. Row upon row of markers, each one its own story. The weight of all those lives—across time, across causes—was humbling.

As we walked back toward the parking lot, a small stone marker near the roadside caught our eye. It read simply "7th Cavalry Horse Cemetery." We paused, a little surprised. Carmen stepped closer, reading the inscription aloud. She didn't say anything at first—just stood quietly. Then she reached out and gently brushed the top of the marker. "They didn't ask to be part of this," she said softly. There was something tender in her voice, reverent and sad. These were not war horses in her mind. They were innocent bystanders. Companions. Like her dogs, Watney and Guinness. We lingered there for a moment longer, paying our respects to soldiers and warriors—and to all who had no say in the battles they were caught in.

We left the grounds quietly, our footsteps soft on the gravel, the wind whispering across the grass.

A NAME ETCHED IN STONE

Quietly, we climbed back into the RV and headed toward our next stop: Pompey's Pillar.

We knew there was a Signature Event planned for the site the following summer, but we weren't sure we'd be able to return. So even though "the boys" didn't pass through here until their journey back in 1806, we made it part of our westbound path. The pull of the place was too strong to ignore.

The new interpretive center was still under construction, so we stepped into the older building—picked up our collector pin (of course), browsed the modest displays, and chatted briefly with the staff. We learned we were standing on Apsáalooke (Crow) homelands.

Pompey's Pillar juts abruptly from the flatlands on the south side of the Yellowstone River, just east of Billings, Montana. William Clark named it after Sacagawea's infant son, Jean Baptiste Charbonneau, whom he affectionately called "Little Pomp." And it was here, on this solitary sandstone outcrop, covering an acre and towering almost 200 feet above the plains, that Clark left behind one of the expedition's only enduring physical signatures—a literal mark on the land.

The name and date he carved in the soft rock are still visible today, now preserved behind a protective glass panel affixed to the cliff face: *Wm. Clark, July 25, 1806.* There's something about seeing it—his actual handwriting etched into stone—that stops you cold. It's proof. Not a journal entry or a monument or a reenactment, but the real hand of Clark, inscribed into the bones of the earth.

To stand there—to place your feet where his once stood, to look out over the river and the plains as he did, to run your eyes along the same ridgeline—stirs something deep inside. It's about history. It's about presence. Connection. It's the electrifying realization that someone from the pages of your books, someone who helped shape the very nation you live in, once stood on this very spot and left behind proof. Not a myth. Not a monument made by someone else later. His actual name, scratched by his own hand into stone that still holds it more than two centuries later.

This is why I love the story. Why I chase the past. It's not to collect facts—it's to collect moments like this. Moments where time folds in on itself and you feel, just for a breath, like you're part of something greater.

Before we made the climb to the top, we walked down to the edge of the Yellowstone River. The current was strong—wide and swift—and the water looked deep, deceptively calm in places, then suddenly agitated by hidden currents. Across the river, a series of dark cliffs rose. It was a striking contrast: the power of the water, the stillness of the rock, the sense of something eternal.

Near the river stood a dugout canoe, carved from a single cottonwood log. I stepped beside it, trying to imagine crawling in and spending hours navigating a river like this one. I'm not a large man, but even I would've felt like a sardine.

Eventually, we began the climb to the top. The decking wound upward through the scrub and prairie grass. About halfway up, Carmen stopped to photograph a patch of prickly pear cactus—the first we had seen on the trip. She became absolutely smitten with the little plants. I can still hear her exclaiming, "They're so *tiny*! Look at those needles!" Dozens of photos later, we resumed the climb.

From the summit, the view was extraordinary. You could see for miles in every direction. The river coiled through the land like a living ribbon. And though we were alone up there, we felt accompanied—by the wind, by the echoes of history, by the mark left behind.

We descended the trail, now shadowed in afternoon light, and returned to the RV. We had considered calling my cousin in Billings, perhaps to stop by for a quick visit. But we were running behind—and Fort Benton still lay far ahead. We decided to press on.

A HAT TIP IN THE RAIN

We headed out of Billings across the heart of Montana. Rather than take the interstate, I chose a series of state highways that promised to shave a few hours off the trip. But this was Montana—big sky country—where the land stretches out in all directions and you can drive for hours without the mountains seeming to get any closer.

We stopped for gas in the small town of Lewistown, Montana (no relation to our hero), then "proceeded on." The highway out of town was even smaller than the one before—the kind with no shoulders, no traffic, and no margin for error.

The first drops of rain began to fall. Then came the clouds. Dark and brooding, they swept in fast. The sky closed down. The road narrowed.

Road Construction Ahead.

The mountains pressed in, and the wipers—though on full speed—couldn't keep up. I slowed to a cautious crawl.

Road Construction Ahead. Use Extreme Caution.

It looked like midnight but was only 2:30 in the afternoon. We hadn't seen another car for over an hour. Carmen and I were on edge—should we stop? There was nowhere *to* stop. No shoulder, no pull-off. Just road, rain, and rising tension.

The cliffs hugged us on the right, a sheer drop lurked to the left, and then we rounded a curve and—

There was no road.

Just a long, muddy stretch where the asphalt had been completely removed. Two hundred yards of nothing but carved-out gravel, dissolving under the deluge. I stopped cold. I couldn't see a safe way forward.

And then, out of the downpour, a pair of headlights cut through the storm. A large pickup rounded the curve from the other direction and came to a halt. Without hesitation, the driver angled his truck to cast his beams across the washed-out roadbed. He flashed his lights and flicked on every auxiliary light he had—flooding the path ahead with light, like a guardian angel in Gore-Tex.

As our wheels jolted up onto the asphalt on the other side, we were side by side with his truck. With no way to speak above the roar of rain, I gave a grateful wave. He tipped his hat, and just like that, we both continued on our separate ways.

Within minutes, the rain tapered off. An hour later, as we crossed the Missouri River into Fort Benton, the clouds parted and the sun broke through—like nothing had happened at all.

Fort Benton is a sleepy little town tucked gently along the banks of the Missouri. Once a bustling hub—first as a riverboat stop, then as a rail stop—it now wears its history quietly. The heart of town is a single row of historic storefronts, a small museum, and a handsomely restored hotel, all nestled close to the river.

We found the RV park and, truth be told, were a little underwhelmed.

While it was clean and tidy, it felt more like parking in someone's oversized gravel driveway than staying at a campground. We climbed back into the RV and went scouting, hoping to find a spot closer to the river—maybe one with a view—no such luck. So back we went, settling into our original site—and, naturally, as we backed in and began hooking up, the rain returned. Of course it did.

Our original plan was to camp here for two nights and then move the RV closer to the outfitters for our three-day canoe trip through the White Cliffs section of the Missouri. But after scouting the outfitters' location and confirming logistics, we devised a new plan: we would leave the RV right where it was, let it wait for us like a loyal friend, while we followed in the wake of Lewis and Clark—by canoe.

twenty-two

Near Misses and True North

Since we didn't have a car, we drove the RV into downtown Fort Benton to visit the museum and explore the area. It was there that we learned the story of Shep—a story that, of course, resonated with Carmen.

Shep was a dog, likely a collie mix. He had been the constant companion of a sheepherder who roamed the hills outside of Fort Benton. The two were inseparable. Wherever the man went, Shep followed.

Until one day... the man passed away.

A wagon came and carried his body to town. Shep, faithful as ever, followed. At the train station, the man's casket was loaded aboard a train bound for the East. Shep stood on the platform, watching. Waiting.

As the train pulled away, he wandered off. But the next day, when the train returned, Shep was there—watching each passenger disembark, hoping his human had returned. When no one came, he wandered off again.

Day after day. Week after week. Month after month. Year after year.

For five and a half years, Shep met the train. He waited until he couldn't.

By January 1942, Shep was aging. His hearing wasn't what it used to be. One icy morning, the train arrived—he likely didn't realize how close it was until it was too late. He tried to move, but his body didn't respond as quickly as it once had. He slipped. And the train took the rest.

The entire town turned out for Shep's funeral. The Great Northern Railroad built a monument in his honor.

As we finished reading the story, I turned to Carmen. Tears welled in her beautiful blue eyes. She reached for a tissue and gently dabbed at them as they ran down her cheeks.

I knew she was thinking not only of Shep, but of Watney and Guinness—our faithful companions now resting beyond their own final crossings.

We walked back to the RV in silence, hearts full. Then we pointed our wheels toward Highway 87 and the next stop on our trail: Decision Point.

FORKS IN RIVERS, FORKS IN LIFE

In 1805, Lewis and Clark and their crew came upon a confluence of two rivers. The prior winter, they had spent hours gathering information about the journey ahead from the Mandan and Hidatsa chiefs. They had told them about the great Yellowstone River, they had told them about the incredible game that would surround them, they had warned them about the great bears (grizzlies), and they had told them about the waterfall they would encounter. What they had not told them was that a river flowed into the Missouri in this area. Confused and exhausted, the Corps halted at what is now known as Decision Point.

As Carmen and I stood on a bluff between the two rivers, we tried to imagine the Corps. Which branch should they take? Which one would lead to the falls and, consequently, to the mountains? Even though it was late June, the captains knew if they chose the wrong branch, it would doom the expedition to failure. They would not be able to cross the Rockies this season, and spending another winter on the plains felt daunting.

In a remarkable display of leadership, they paused here for nine days to gather information, discuss the options with the men, and reach a decision. Thirty-one men pointed west. Two captains pointed south. They chose the south fork—history tells us it was the right choice—and in doing so named the unexpected northern river the Marias. Soon, they would stand in awe before the Great Falls of the Missouri.

We didn't know what the future held—who does, really? We had already experienced so much as newlyweds in our mid-forties. We had lived our lives separately, and now we were living our lives together. We had made a significant life decision to sell Carmen's house and buy one of our own. Was it the right choice? Would we find the falls as Lewis and Clark did? Having made the decision, we could only proceed on.

WHAT COULD POSSIBLY GO WRONG?

We walked back to our RV and headed back to Fort Benton. The next day would be a moment two and a half years in the making. We were going to canoe for three days on the Missouri River, following in the footsteps, er, uh, paddle strokes of the expedition.

When we returned to our campsite, I began unpacking our canoe and camping gear so everything would be ready for the next morning, when our outfitter would pick us up. There's something about preparing for a canoe trip that puts me in a certain mood. It takes me back in time. I'm an outdoorsman, an adventurer; I'm in a simpler time. The aroma of campfires past emanates from the canvas gear. The smell of fire. The smell of burnt canvas... *What? That's not right.*

The further I dug into our gear carrier, the stronger the odor became. When I removed our canvas canoe seats, instead of looking at the bottom of our carrier, I was looking at the gravel lot through a huge hole melted in the vinyl carrier. I turned the canoe seat over to find it charred, the canvas burned away, and the cushion exposed. What the hell? "Carmen!" I yelled.

"Oh my God," she exclaimed when I showed her the seat. "We could have died!"

Our gear carrier was one of those that attaches to a rack mounted on the receiver hitch of a vehicle. The exhaust from the RV had roasted our gear carrier. Had I packed our propane on the left instead of the right, there might have been a pretty big explosion. RV Lesson 180: Heat maps matter—know where your exhaust points. We would have to travel the rest of the trip with our camping gear inside the RV.

Still not over the fright of the possibility, we needed to prepare for the next day, and we needed to eat. That night, we learned something else. The mosquitoes were *vultures*. I tried to grill out for dinner, but could barely dash out of the RV and flip the burgers before being eaten alive. Camping? *We were going camping, in a tent?*

twenty-three
Where the River Speaks—and a Coke Costs 20 Bucks

I had been anticipating this canoe trip since I read about the White Cliffs in the summer of 2000. I was like a kid at Christmas as we went to bed that night. The hours crawled by. Every hour, I looked at the clock, and only five minutes had passed. Finally, 5:58, 5:59, 6:00—time to get up. Almost falling over Carmen, I threw open the RV door to bask in the warmth of the rising sun and watch it rise, a fireball over the mountains to the east. Uh, no. Rain. 40 degrees. Gray. Clouds. Rain. Dammit.

"It will clear up," Carmen said, forcing bravery.

We began packing up our gear and realized we had not brought rain gear. After a frantic call to our outfitter, he promised to throw in a couple of rain suits with the gear he was providing.

The rain had stopped for the moment, and we needed ice for the coolers, so rather than move the RV, I decided to walk up the road to buy a few bags. As you can probably guess, about the time I bought the bags of ice and headed the half mile back, it started to pour!

I arrived back at the RV looking like a drowned rat. I don't know what I was fighting more: my own disappointment or the fear that we were about to embark on a trip that Carmen would hate and be miserable on. I sank into a sullen depression.

We loaded our gear into the outfitter's van and headed off to Coal

Banks, the start of our trip. We were canoeing about 70 miles from Coal Banks to Judith Landing. During these three days, we would not see roads, bridges, or many people. This was the first canoe trip we had been on that required checking in with the Bureau of Land Management (BLM), so if we didn't show up at the other end, they would know where to look for us. As the agent reminded us, this was also a "carry out what you carry in" area—including what you eat, if you catch my drift. I couldn't believe my Carmen was doing all this—for me!

We bundled up in our attractive blue rubberized ponchos and rain pants and loaded the canoe. The outfitter must have asked us a dozen times if we were sure we wanted to go. Maybe it was the look in our eyes as rain dripped off our noses. Each time, I glanced at Carmen. Each time, she answered "Yes!" Finally, he explained where he would meet us in three days. "You can't miss it," he said. "It's the first bridge you come to. There will be a campground on this side of the bridge. There is a BLM trailer, but it may not be staffed. There is also a little country store. "Camp there, and I will pick you up."

With that, we pushed off into the brown, strong current.

We proceeded on.

A GRANDFATHER, A TREE, AND A CAMPSITE WORTH FIGHTING FOR

Before long, the rain let up, and the clouds began to lift. As we settled into the rhythm of the river, a calm came over me. The stress of the morning—the forgotten rain gear, the ice-soaked walk, the rising worry that Carmen might hate this entire experience—started to melt away. With each paddle stroke, the current seemed to carry my anxiety downstream. There's something about a river that knows how to settle your soul. The sound of the water lapping against the canoe, the soft rustle of wind through the cottonwoods, Carmen in front of me—present, quiet, steady—all of it wrapped around me like a blanket. Out there, far from cell service, traffic, or expectations, I found my peace again. It's always been that way with rivers. They don't ask questions or demand anything. They just invite you to follow, to trust, to breathe.

The wind was at our backs, and the current was strong. Even without paddling, we were drifting along at nearly seven miles per hour.

Which only made me marvel all the more: Years ago, I was planning to *canoe UP* this river?

Our destination for the day was a designated campground near a landmark called Hole in the Wall. While campsites weren't strictly required, you did need to avoid private land. The designated areas made that simpler.

As we rounded a bend, we saw the first site on river right. We fought our way through the whitecaps—whipped up by wind—and landed. There were three primitive shelters: little more than wooden lean-tos. We were alone, but each shelter was filled with gear. Clearly, other campers had already claimed them.

It wasn't what we'd imagined. We weren't looking for a sleepaway camp experience. We wanted wild, not communal.

So we climbed back into the canoe and proceeded on.

Soon we neared the Hole in the Wall itself, and Carmen spotted it: a massive tree rooted in a wide, flat meadow beside the river. I checked the map—public land. We pulled over and claimed it as our own.

Setting up camp in the wind was a chore, but on the plus side? No mosquito could fly in this weather.

That evening, nature rewarded us. As the sun set behind us, it lit up the cliff face, casting golden hues across the Hole in the Wall, a natural window cut through the stone, framing the darkening sky to the east. We were basking in the glow when a man and two teenage girls hiked by. He paused, introduced himself, and explained that the girls were his granddaughters. They were returning from their climb up to the hole.

They were from the shelter camp upstream. The man was kind enough, but the girls? All slumped shoulders and sighs. Clearly, this was not their idea of a summer highlight.

We smiled, waved, and bid them goodnight. They scurried off down the trail.

We stayed behind, wrapped in a peace of our own making, watching the shadows stretch across the cliffs and feeling the wind soften—just slightly—as if the river was saying "You made it."

Over the last several years of canoeing together, we had developed a bit of a tradition—maybe even a ritual. We read to each other as we floated downriver. I always tried to find a book that matched the water beneath our boat. It had begun on our overnight trip along the Wabash back in

Indiana, three or four years earlier, when we read *Ouabache Adventure: Canoeing the Wabash* aloud as we paddled. There's just something about hearing a river's story while you're floating in it.

For this journey, I couldn't very well pack all 13 volumes of *The Journals of Lewis and Clark*—though I might have tried, had Carmen not stopped me. However, I did bring along *Scenes of Visionary Enchantment* by Dayton Duncan. We decided we'd save it for each night at camp. We didn't want to miss any of our own "scenes of visionary enchantment" while our heads were buried in a book.

That night, after dinner and after the sun lit up the cliffs behind us in that final golden glow, we climbed into our tent. The wind still rattled the fabric from time to time, but inside, wrapped in sleeping bags and the smell of river and canvas, we were warm. Carmen unzipped the side pocket of the pack and pulled out the book. Her voice was soft and steady as she began to read from Dayton's words—about this river, these cliffs, this journey. We were surrounded by the same silence Lewis and Clark must have known. The light from our small lantern danced across the nylon walls, and for a little while, time bent. It felt as if we were not simply reading history—we were part of it.

She read aloud Lewis's own words from May 31, 1805: "As we passed on it seemed as if those scenes of visionary inchantment would never have an end; for here it is too that nature presents to the view of the traveler vast ranges of walls of tolerable workmanship, so perfect indeed are those walls that I should have thought that nature had attempted here to rival the human art of masonry had I not recollected that she had first began her work."

Hearing those words, written over two centuries ago, while nestled in the very landscape they described, was profoundly moving. It was as if time had folded in on itself, connecting us directly to the explorers' awe and wonder. In that moment, the river, the cliffs, and the history converged, enveloping us in a shared sense of discovery and enchantment.

We drifted off that night to the sound of wind in the cottonwoods and the soft rustle of the river against the bank—our tent held firm in the wide-armed shadow of that old tree. We zipped our two sleeping bags together to form one large enough for both of us. Hey, we *were* basically newlyweds! The stars came out one by one, unbothered by city lights, and the last thing I remember was Carmen's hand finding mine tucked inside the sleeping bag.

By morning, the wind had calmed. The sky, so moody the day before, now stretched clear and endless above us. We brewed coffee on our little camp stove, packed up our gear, and prepared for day two on the river—still unsure what we would encounter, but certain we were exactly where we were supposed to be.

There's a rhythm to river travel, especially when you're miles from anything resembling a road. The river moves forward, and so do you. But the thing no one tells you—at least not in the outfitter's manual—is that the real journey happens inside you. Day two began not with rapids or cliffs or breathtaking scenery, but with an awkward encounter. That same group of campers—grandpa, the girls, and a woman we assumed was grandma—floated by as we made breakfast. Not a smile. Not a nod. Not a wave. Just blank stares and the steady dip of paddles. Carmen and I exchanged a glance. "Well," I muttered, "guess they're in a hurry to get to the next weird encounter."

We were in no hurry.

We packed up, loaded the canoe, and pushed off. Sunshine! Bright, beautiful sunshine. The wind had quieted, though the river still moved with strength and purpose. Within minutes, we entered the White Cliffs region—and everything changed.

It was like drifting into a dream.

Towering white bluffs rose from the water's edge, their faces smooth and pale as bone, sculpted by centuries of wind and rain into spires and towers and bridges in the sky. Some stood like cathedrals, others like castles. The names whispered by travelers before us—Citadel, Eagle, Shepherds—did their best to capture it, but even those fell short.

Two centuries ago, Meriwether Lewis passed through this very place and called it "a scene of visionary enchantment." I looked over at Carmen, her hair catching the sunlight like threads of gold beneath her wide-brimmed hat, and I knew exactly what he meant.

In that stretch of river, time seemed to pause. We floated in silence, carried by the current, surrounded by an ancient hush. The cliffs appeared to watch us pass—sentinels of stone, bearing witness to every soul who had ever dared this journey.

It was as if we were the only two people in the world.

For a few sacred miles, Lewis and Clark's journey folded into ours.

As we rounded a bend, a lone wolf high in the canyon began to howl. The sound echoed down the walls and across the water. It was chilling. And beautiful. We scanned the cliffs with binoculars, trying to spot him. He saw us—we felt it—but we never saw him.

Several Lewis and Clark points of interest were marked on our map, but one we especially wanted to see was Slaughter River (now Arrow Creek). According to the journals, across the river from the mouth of the creek was a large cliff. When the Corps passed this way in 1805, they discovered dozens of bison carcasses floating in the river at the base of the cliff. They assumed it had been a pishkun—a cliff used by Indigenous peoples to stampede bison to their deaths. While experts now debate whether this site was actually used for that purpose, the story remains.

As we floated past the cliff and the mouth of the creek, we laughed at the irony: A dozen head of cattle were cooling themselves in the water. No stampede necessary.

A little later, we pulled off at a site marked as one of the Lewis and Clark campsites. It was nearing lunchtime, and we planned to stop for a quick bite and explore. But once again—guess who was already there? Gramps and the gang.

Not to be deterred, we began unloading anyway. As luck would have it, they were packing up just as we climbed the bank. One of the women, probably Grandpa's wife, asked where we planned to camp that night. Carmen told her the river mile we had marked. The woman got weirdly territorial. "Well, that's where we're planning to camp," she said firmly. "And it's a very small site."

These people were just... odd.

After they left, we enjoyed our picnic and took some time to explore. It was peaceful again. We wandered the site, imagining it filled with some 30 members of the Corps, gathered around a fire, cooking their evening meal, preparing for the next leg of their journey.

A BRIDGE TOO SOON

As the afternoon passed, so did the miles. Before long, we were approaching the site where we had hoped to camp—and yes, Gramps and company were already there. Not thinking twice, we proceeded on in search of another spot.

And proceeded.

And proceeded.

And proceeded.

Unfortunately, there was no large tree and inviting meadow like the night before. In fact, the further we paddled, the more barren the riverbank became. It wasn't long before we spotted the bridge—our take-out point.

We've always believed the best way to end a canoe trip is by wishing it were longer, not by dragging your paddle through water you're desperate to be done with. But here we were: 70 miles behind us in just two days, and still hours of daylight ahead. Disappointed, we began scanning for the campground.

We finally spied it on river left, near the mouth of a small creek. What we didn't see was a way to get up the bank—it rose a good eight or nine feet above the river. There was no tie-off, no trail, and certainly no easy scramble up. The bridge our outfitter had described stood in the distance. We floated past, defeated.

Just beyond the bridge, we found—of all things—a boat ramp.

We pulled out and looked around. The air was still. Not a soul in sight. We knocked on the door of the BLM trailer. Nothing. It was nothing like what we had imagined. We're from Indiana; when someone says there's a campground, we expect people.

Still somewhat bewildered, we walked over to the tiny country store— amazed it even existed out here. It couldn't possibly do more than 10 bucks in business a month. Outside, a young woman sat cross-legged on a picnic table while two little girls played in the dirt beneath her feet.

"Is that the only campground around here?" we asked, pointing back upriver.

She nodded. "That's the only one."

Our shoulders sank. "It's about a half mile... and we've got 400 pounds of gear." Ok. Maybe I was exaggerating the distance and the weight of our gear… but not by much.

Without hesitation, she said, "You can borrow my truck. It's right there. Keys are in it."

We weren't in Indiana anymore.

Gratefully, we climbed into the dusty, dented Dodge pickup, tossed our gear in the back, and bumped down the road to the campground. We picked a site right on the river—it wasn't hard, as we were the only ones there—unloaded, and returned the truck.

I told Carmen to give the woman 20 bucks for the favor while I carried the canoe from the boat ramp to our campsite.

By the time I got to the site, Carmen was already there. "She wouldn't take it," she said. "Said it was no big deal—just glad she could help."

Finally, Carmen had given up, bought a Coke, handed the woman a $20, and said, "Keep the change. Take your girls to McDonald's."

McDonald's. Yeah—probably a hundred miles from here. But at least she took it.

That evening, wrapped in fleece and the comfort of shared silence, we sat by the fire—the only humans for miles. The deer stepped gently to the river's edge, the current whispered past our camp, and the sun painted the cliffs in shades of amber and gold. It was one of those moments that required nothing more and offered nothing less than peace.

No schedule. No cell phones. No noise.

Just the sound of crackling wood and Carmen's hand in mine.

We didn't talk much. The river spoke for us.

And in that hush between day and night, as the last glow slipped behind the bluffs, I remember thinking, *This is it. This is why we came.*

THE WOMAN ON THE SIGN

The next morning, we had several hours to kill before our driver picked us up, so we decided to hike over and see the mouth of the Judith River. Clark named this river after "the girl back home." The river enters the Missouri from the south, but there was a small interpretive site on our side of the river. We had seen hundreds of these now-familiar sites: small patches of ground with one or two National Park signs describing the events that had occurred there.

We had no idea that this little brown sign in the middle of nowhere was about to deliver one of the most surreal, incredible twists of our entire journey. This one had a sign we had not seen before. It was a sign for Undaunted Stewardship... a play on the Stephen Ambrose book *Undaunted Courage*. It described the not-for-profit organization that is working with ranchers throughout Montana to set aside portions of their land as interpretive sites, just like this one. So, geeks like us could drive for thousands of miles, paddle for dozens more, and stand here and say, "Oh wow, they slept on this blade of grass!"

But it was the picture that really caught our attention. There on the sign was a picture of a vast herd of cattle and two people on horseback corralling them. A young man and a young woman. The woman? It was Amy Wortman. She owned a 40,000-acre ranch. It was on her ranch that we were standing. It was on her ranch that we camped the night before. It was on her ranch that the country store stood. Did I mention that in her spare time, she also ran a small country store near the BLM trailer at the Judith Landing take-out? Yes, the picture on the sign was none other than the young lady who had loaned us her truck. And we tipped her 20 bucks! To this day, we wonder if she laughs about the irony as much as we do.

Later, we told the story to our outfitter as he drove us back to Fort Benton and our RV. His round-trip that day to pick us up was over 300 miles. I think he laughed about our story the entire trip. Big Sky indeed!

What were the odds? We'd driven for days, paddled through wind and rain, and landed—quite literally—at the feet of a woman who had already shaped our story without us even knowing it.

Carmen was the one who saw the good in her. Who felt comfortable asking for help. Who handed her that $20 and said, "Take your girls to McDonald's." It was kindness—it was Carmen's way. She noticed people. She felt them.

And here she was again, noticing. Pointing at the sign. Laughing first. Reminding me that the map is never the whole journey. That sometimes, the most uncharted moment of all is the one you never saw coming—but your heart recognizes it just the same.

twenty-four

Barney, Bottle Rockets, and an Early Goodbye

We spent one more night in Fort Benton and then headed off toward Great Falls for the Signature Event. We had reserved a rental car so we could attend the events and tour the area without having to pack up the RV every day. We made our way to the Great Falls Airport to pick up the car. We discovered the airport was small. Officially, it is classified as a non-hub; it receives little air traffic. What that meant to us was that the rental car counter was not staffed. We had to call the agent. He would then hop in his car, drive to the airport, and hand us our rental car.

After what seemed like hours, but was probably only 45 minutes, he arrived. He walked us to our car, a bright purple PT Cruiser. OMG, no chance of blending in with this ride. With limited options—no options— we headed across town to the KOA with me driving the rental car and Carmen maneuvering the RV.

The KOA was one of the largest—and busiest—we'd stayed in so far. Apparently, Fourth of July weekend draws a crowd. By the time we were set up and settled in, we were too tired to cook, so we climbed into Barney—our bright purple PT Cruiser—and went in search of something simple and satisfying.

As we drove through town, Carmen was the first to say it: "It's not what I expected." I nodded. After the sacred hush of the White Cliffs, Great Falls felt louder, harder, more practical than poetic. We had come hoping to feel the footsteps of the Corps—but here, the echoes seemed fainter. Maybe we were just tired. Or perhaps we were learning that not every place along the trail would sing in the same key.

OF SPRINGS AND TINY RIVERS

The next morning, we followed our usual strategy—explore first, event later—and made our way to the Lewis and Clark Trail Heritage Foundation and Museum. From the outside, it's modest, even easy to miss. But stepping inside felt like entering a sanctuary for trail lovers. The building is ingeniously set into the riverbank, so when you walk through the front doors, you're arriving on the second floor from the riverside—almost like the river is holding it up.

The exhibits were thoughtful and rich with detail, clearly curated by people who cared deeply about the story. There was a reverence here. And yes, I lingered too long in the gift shop and walked out with more books than I needed and exactly as many as I wanted.

Afterward, we took the paved trail that winds along the Missouri toward Giant Springs Park. The walk was peaceful, lined with native flowers and shaded by shrubs that felt like they belonged. And the springs? Just as the journals promised—an eruption of crystal-clear water, bubbling straight from the earth. The spring (Roe River) is often cited as one of the world's shortest rivers, flowing only a few hundred feet before joining the Missouri. But what it lacked in distance, it made up for in wonder.

We stood at the water's edge, watching the current swirl and bubble in impossible shades of turquoise and green. Carmen slipped her hand into mine and whispered, "It feels like it should be sacred, doesn't it?"

I nodded. It did. It was. There was something ancient here—something pure. For a moment, we didn't speak. We just stood there, side by side, mesmerized by the way the light danced on the surface, how the spring fed into the river that had drawn us both in—centuries after it first drew Lewis and Clark.

Springs that feed a river flowing through Apsáalooke and Niitsitapi homelands—water remembers what maps forget.

We paused at the interpretive center to cool off and sip a Coke before hiking back to the museum and Barney. Then it was off to tour the falls.

THE BEAUTY BENEATH THE DAMS

Of all the thousands of miles we traveled and all the sights we had seen, this was one of the most disappointing—and sobering. When Lewis first saw the falls, he could barely find words to capture their beauty. To his surprise, there wasn't just one but five separate falls. Today, only four remain—one lies forever underwater, drowned by the reservoir formed by a dam. And the others? While still impressive, they're now framed with dams, concrete, and power lines. It was almost impossible to take a photo without wires in the frame or a turbine in the background.

I had even read that the electric company planned to release more water over the Great Falls in honor of the Signature Event. A noble gesture, but it still felt like trying to glimpse the past through a chain-link fence.

Still, the power was there. The roar. The mist. The sense of wonder that Lewis must have felt. You just had to squint a little harder to see it.

Carmen stood beside me, her arm looped through mine as we looked down at the water rushing through the dam gates. "Do you think they were disappointed?" she asked softly. "Lewis and Clark, I mean. After all they went through to get here—what if it didn't live up to the stories?"

I smiled. "I think they were too exhausted to be disappointed. I think the disappointment came later, when they discovered five falls, not one."

We laughed, but it was a quiet kind of laugh—reverent, almost.

A breeze lifted the edge of Carmen's hair, and for a second I saw her the way I had earlier, standing at the edge of Giant Springs, the morning sun catching her face just right, her eyes reflecting that same clear water. That moment had stayed with me all day; something about it felt timeless, like we'd tapped into a current older than either of us, something still flowing just beneath the surface.

This place wasn't what we imagined—but it didn't have to be. We were here. Together. That was the magic.

We stood for a long while in silence, letting the river say what words couldn't.

That evening, we returned to the KOA and learned another lesson about the Fourth of July—namely, that some lessons go unlearned.

Despite the printed rule—NO FIREWORKS—the KOA had apparently decided to suspend common sense in the name of patriotism. Nothing quite says "celebrating our freedom" like launching flaming projectiles into a forest of fiberglass, propane, and vinyl siding.

As night fell, the campground lit up—literally. The pops and bangs echoed off the RVs like we were in a war zone. Carmen and I sat outside for a while, sipping our drinks, trying to laugh it off. "You'd think a campground full of mobile gas tanks wouldn't encourage explosives," I said.

"Maybe it's a natural selection thing," she replied, deadpan.

By morning, our roof looked like the launch pad for a small-scale missile test. I climbed up there, grumbling as I cleared off the remnants of bottle rockets and singed cardboard tubes.

When I stopped by the front office to ask if they might reconsider the policy for future years, the staff smiled politely and nodded. The kind of nod that says "We will absolutely do nothing with your suggestion."

Still, we had survived the night. And with any luck, the next day we'd find a quieter place to celebrate the Fourth.

IN SEARCH OF SOMETHING MORE

The next morning, the Signature Event's opening ceremony was held at Riverside Park near the Heritage Trail Museum. We had driven past it the day before in our unmistakable Barneymobile, so we knew right where to go.

Like the other events we'd attended, the ceremony was well-organized, heartfelt, and deeply respectful. The planning committees had clearly poured themselves into every detail, and we were grateful. But something was shifting in us. We were starting to understand that what moved us most wasn't the speeches or the ceremonial fanfare—it was the quiet. The solitude. The sense of sacred ground beneath our feet.

It wasn't a criticism. It was just clarity. Our journey had become less about history as performance and more about presence. We were chasing the echoes in the land itself—the soft places where time folds in on itself. And in Great Falls, despite all its historical importance, that feeling was harder to find. Maybe it was the modern sprawl, or the noise, or just the contrast with the days we'd just spent in the White Cliffs. But the connection here felt different. Less spiritual, more structural. Still meaningful, but not in the same way.

THE HEALING SPRING

After the ceremony, we craved a quieter kind of connection—something off the beaten path, still echoing with footsteps from long ago. We crossed to the other side of the Missouri and made our way toward the trail that leads to Sulphur Spring. This was where, according to Lewis's journal, the young woman who had guided them so faithfully fell ill, and he offered her sulfur water from the spring.

The trailhead wasn't exactly picturesque—just a gravel lot near a humming electrical substation—but by now we knew that uncharted moments often come in plain wrapping. Still tired, Carmen decided to wait in the car. Sometimes your body says "Not today," and you listen.

So I hiked alone.

The trail was quiet, just wind, the rhythmic crunch of gravel beneath my boots, and the flutter of a bird in the brush. Soon, the modern world thinned. I could see it: Sacagawea weakened and pale from the journey. Lewis kneels by the sulfur spring, its scent sharp and earthy, a tin cup in his hand. He lifts the cup and offers it as a gesture of care. She accepts it with that slight nod of gratitude she was known for—perhaps not understanding the words, but knowing the intention.

I reached the spring and crouched beside it, watching water bubble up from the earth as it had for centuries. I cupped my hand and took a sip. The taste was unmistakable—mineral-y, sulfurous, strange. As it hit my tongue, I could hear Lewis's line in my head from June 16, 1805: "I caused her to drink the mineral water ... now the pulse had become regular ... a gentle perspiration had taken place ... and she feels herself much freeer [sic] from pain." And for a breath, around this little spring, fear loosened its grip.

From where I stood, I could see the mouth of Belt Creek—the beginning of the Grand Portage, 18 miles of dragging boats and supplies around the falls that gave Great Falls its name. Eighteen miles of grit and determination, of backs breaking and spirits tested.

I turned back toward the trail, already rehearsing how I'd tell it to Carmen. As the wind moved through the grass, I could almost hear Sacagawea's breath, steadier now.

Healing.

THE GRAND PORTAGE

The next morning, we set out to follow the route of the Grand Portage. No, there isn't a marked hiking trail—at least not in the way you'd hope—but there are a couple of historic sites scattered along the roughly 18-mile route. Our first stop was at the top of the hill above the river where Lewis and Clark staged their gear before hauling it around the falls. We parked the car and walked down to a nearby creek, trying to see the landscape as the Corps might have seen it—less parking lot, more wilderness. It wasn't hard to imagine the sheer magnitude of the challenge they faced.

Of course, where they had grit and grit alone, we had air-conditioning. From there, we hopped into our purple PT Cruiser and followed the route as closely as modern roads would allow, tracing the Corps' path across the Montana plains. It wasn't until that morning that we realized just how close we had been camping to the original trail. In fact, directly across from the entrance to our campground stood a route marker—right there the entire time—quietly noting where the Corps had passed through town.

As we drove along the portage route in our PT Cruiser, we found ourselves repeatedly stunned. The modern roads followed the undulating terrain of the plains, dipping in and out of ravines that looked innocent enough from the comfort of a car. But the deeper we drove into this landscape, the more impossible the feat of the Grand Portage began to feel.

It was one thing to read about hauling boats overland. It was quite another to see the ravines they had crossed, to feel the incline as our engine strained to climb out of them. A dugout canoe could weigh about a ton—empty. The Corps had loaded it with gear and provisions, then dragged it mile after mile across these ridges and gullies using makeshift wheels and sheer will. Carmen and I looked at each other in disbelief. How? Just... how?

And then, layered into this already unimaginable story, came the quieter moment—the kind of detail we now cherished the most. At one point during the portage, a sudden thunderstorm had flooded one of these very ravines. Torrents of water rushed down, sweeping gear and supplies in every direction. Clark even lost his compass in the sudden flood; they recovered it the next day. Clark's compass, perhaps the very compass we had stood in front of just two and a half years earlier at Monticello—now here in spirit, a tether between centuries.

We sat in the car for a long moment after driving through that ravine, letting the weight of it all settle over us. The physicality of the portage, the quiet courage of Sacagawea, the sheer improbability of their success—it gave the next stretch of our day a sense of reverence.

Eventually, we continued to the far end of the route, where a preserved overlook marked the location of the Upper Portage Camp. Below us, just as the Corps once stood, we gazed down at the Missouri. Nestled along its bank was a recreated encampment of reenactors, canvas tents arranged in careful order.

We wandered into the camp, hoping for familiar faces—"our boys" from St. Charles. But these reenactors were local, sanctioned for the Signature Event. Though their uniforms were crisp and their stories rehearsed, the camp didn't carry the same magic. Perhaps it was unfair, but once you've shared a fire and laughter with someone who's paddled and marched their way across history, the bar is set high.

Still, history had one more surprise for us.

As we strolled through the camp, something caught our eye near the edge of the trail—a tiny mound of dirt that seemed to shiver ever so slightly. We paused, watching. And then, as if summoned by curiosity, the mound of earth pushed upward, a hole appeared, and a tiny nose emerged. A prairie dog? A gopher? We weren't sure. But in that moment, the ancient land reached up to greet us.

Later, we headed out to the fairgrounds for the event's exhibits, vendor booths, and Indigenous peoples' art show. The artwork was stunning— moving, textured, alive—fine art, not the arts and crafts we thought we would find. Still, we didn't leave empty-handed. We stumbled across a booth for Two Chicks Winery and, true to form, made sure to buy a couple of bottles. That kind of history, we could afford.

On the way back to the RV, we took a short detour through the western edge of Great Falls, tracing the Corps' final steps through this rugged country. This was the site of one of their most crushing setbacks—the failure of Lewis's experimental iron boat. After dragging a canoe-shaped metal frame for months across brutal terrain and assembling it near White Bear Island, they discovered, heartbreakingly, that it simply wouldn't float. The hides meant to waterproof it shrank and leaked, and the entire contraption—two years in the making—was abandoned. White Bear Island, now mostly submerged beneath the modern river, had been a staging ground for the final push, a place where hope and exhaustion collided. Today, it's more memory than map, its name surviving in journal entries and ghosted impressions in the landscape.

We didn't make it all the way to Canoe Camp—the place upstream where, humbled but unbroken, they set to work hollowing out dugouts from cottonwoods. I would've liked to see it. But even from a distance, the story lingered in the dry air. Failure. Adaptation. Persistence. The idea that when something you've invested your soul in doesn't work, you carve a new path forward—literally. It's one of the most human chapters in the expedition. One I'm still learning from.

THE GREAT ESCAPE

That evening, the hailstorm of bottle rockets only escalated. The next day was the Fourth of July, and we had initially planned to stay for the parade. But over a couple of glasses of Two Chicks wine, we chose a quieter path— an early morning drive through downtown to admire the old buildings and bid adieu to Barney, then back on the road in our keelboat on wheels.

Great Falls hadn't moved us the way other places had. But not every bend in the river needs to shimmer. Some simply carry you forward, reminding you that the journey is made of more than high points and revelations; it also holds quiet turns and subtle transitions. And sometimes, it's only in looking back that you realize what a place gave you.

twenty-five
What She Saw in Their Eyes

As we drove south out of Great Falls, it felt strange to be heading in that direction. After all, the Corps was seeking the Northwest Passage—not a route that led them south. But rivers don't care much for straight lines or manifest intentions. The Missouri curved that way, and so did we.

Not far from town, we spotted a small herd of antelope grazing in the morning sun. We slowed to watch them for a moment—elegant, alert, almost curious. It felt like the land itself was beginning to shift, pulling us further into the past.

Our destination was Ulm Pishkun inside the First Peoples Buffalo Jump State Park, where towering cliffs once served as sacred hunting grounds for the region's Native peoples. At Ulm Pishkun—on Amskapi Piikani (Blackfeet) ground—the cliff tells the hunting story before the signs do.

At the interpretive center, we learned how bison were driven over these cliffs in coordinated hunts—how the people used every part of the animal, not out of scarcity but out of reverence. They gave thanks to the bison with prayer and ritual, honoring the life that sustained theirs.

We moved quietly through the museum, taking in the exhibits. At one point, Carmen stopped. Dead still. I looked over to find her staring at a black-and-white photograph hanging on the wall.

A group of Native women sat before sewing machines. Their clothes were identical—prim pioneer dresses. Their faces were not. Not one smile. Eyes dulled, expressionless. Erased.

Carmen stood frozen, transfixed. Then, in a voice so soft I could barely hear her, she whispered, "Look what we have done to them."

She didn't say another word for a long while. That photograph... it stayed with her. It still does.

Eventually, we stepped outside. There was a trail that climbed the cliff face to the top of the pishkun, but we chose to drive. At the summit, we found a prairie dog town stretching out across the grasses, their chatter echoing like tiny sentinels. We walked the edge of the cliff, peering down at the path the bison once took—and the people who orchestrated the hunt with such precision and respect.

Leaving the park, we climbed steadily into the mountains. The terrain grew rugged. We pulled off at an overlook and gazed down at the river, now far below. A group of rafters drifted through the current, laughing and splashing. From our perch, we could barely make them out. From theirs, I doubt they knew we were there.

It was one of those moments where time folds over on itself—when you see the river as memory, witness, and mirror.

WHERE THE EAGLE KNOWS THE WAY

We continued south to the Gates of the Mountains, a stretch of the river named by Lewis himself. As they passed through this towering canyon, the captains believed they were finally entering the true mountains of the West. Today, the canyon is only accessible by water—or by a long, rugged hike through steep rock formations. We opted to play tourist and purchased tickets for the tour boat that ferries sightseers into the canyon.

Our guide was full of character and clearly at home in his element. Even if it was the thousandth time he'd given the tour, his enthusiasm never waned. The boat moved slowly north, riding the current into the canyon. Near the northernmost point of the route is the formation that gave the Gates their name.

As the boat turned, we saw what Lewis and Clark saw: the grand illusion. Facing south, the river appears to dead-end into a solid wall of limestone. But as the boat draws nearer, the cliff seems to part—towering stone walls opening like gates, revealing a narrow channel between them. It's a striking visual trick, one that stirred the imagination of the Corps two centuries ago—and still stirs the imagination today.

Though the canyon is now partially inundated by Holter Dam, and we floated 25 or 30 feet above where the expedition would have traveled, the sense of awe remains. The gates still open. The spirit still rises.

On our return to the marina—and to our RV—we were greeted by a bald eagle soaring high overhead, gliding effortlessly through the crystal-clear Montana sky. It seemed to be saying, *These are my hills, this is my river, this is my sky*, as we floated under the arching wings.

UNDER THE SURFACE: WHAT THE RIVERS REMEMBER

We climbed back into our keelboat on wheels, still buzzing from the magic of the Gates. As we turned onto the highway, a flash of movement under the overpass caught our eye. There, tucked neatly in the shadowed corner, stood a mountain goat. Unbothered. Unmoved. He stared at us with the calm authority of someone who belonged there far more than we did. *What are you looking at, buddy?* his eyes seemed to ask. Or maybe he was waiting for us to ask directions.

We left our new friend behind and headed to York's Islands. Clark named this cluster of islands in the Missouri for York, the man he kept as a slave—his companion, servant, and, in many ways, equal during the journey. As we had already learned, even our heroes sometimes carry contradictions. After the expedition, York had hoped for freedom or at least to return to Louisville and his wife. Instead, Clark demanded that he remain in servitude in St. Louis.

As we approached a pull-off near the river, Carmen was quiet. I could tell she was deep in thought, as she so often was in places like this.

"It's all here," she said softly, "the beauty, the heartbreak, the layers."

I nodded. "The story we've been following is about discovery. It's about reckoning."

We stepped out into the stillness, drawn to the water. The sun bore down, the sky wide and high above us, clouds casting slow-moving shadows. The river shimmered, its surface alive with light. And then, just like that, the damn mosquitoes found us.

We managed one photo before scrambling back to the safety of our rolling refuge.

We kept our fingers crossed that our next stop—Three Forks—would be skeeter-free. That is where the Jefferson, Madison, and Gallatin Rivers come together to form the Missouri. When the Corps arrived there, they named the rivers after the president, the secretary of state, and the treasury secretary—leaders of their young government. And then they had to choose. As we stood at the edge of the confluence, it was easy to imagine them weighing the possibilities, reading the terrain, deciding which way to go.

"They followed the Jefferson," I said, watching the water split and merge in front of us. "Thought it looked most likely to take them toward the mountains."

Carmen nodded, gazing out across the broad sweep of the river. "And Sacagawea," she said, "she recognized this place, didn't she?"

"She did," I replied. "She had been here before. This was where she was taken from her people, just a young girl."

Carmen didn't say anything at first. Then she said quietly, "It must've been like a wound reopening—coming back here."

"But maybe also a sign," I added, "that they were on the right path."

We stood for a long time, listening to the soft rush of water, letting the moment settle in. So much of this journey was like that—places that held memory like a bruise, places that opened up new questions even as they offered answers.

Soon after, we dipped our hands in each river—one for Jefferson, one for Madison, one for Gallatin—just because it felt like something we ought to do. A simple act. A quiet tribute.

And then it was time to continue west. The next chapter of the expedition—and ours—would take us over the Continental Divide.

A PAUSE BEFORE THE PASS

We left Three Forks behind us and, in a way, stepped back into the future—turning west onto I-90 toward Butte. After days of tracing ancient waterways and standing in sacred places, the hum of the interstate felt jarring, almost too fast for the pace our hearts had settled into. But the journey wasn't over—not by a long shot.

We had arranged to rent a Jeep Wrangler for the next two days. Taking our RV across Lemhi Pass would've been more of a thrill ride than a history trip, and not in a good way. The Jeep was the perfect compromise—sturdy, nimble, ready for the road less paved.

After picking up the keys, we headed to the Three Rivers RV Camp to get some rest before we tackled the mountains. Tomorrow, we'd climb higher still, into the heart of the divide—chasing footsteps, and maybe catching a few of our own.

twenty-six

All She Wanted Was a Shower

We set off the next morning, leaving the RV behind for a couple of days while we tackled the mountains. The sky was a flawless Montana blue, hardly a cloud in sight. We were excited—maybe a little giddy—knowing we'd spend the day tracing Sacagawea's memories and Lewis and Clark's fading footsteps.

Our first stop was in Twin Bridges. Carmen had found a note about a statue there—Sacagawea and Seaman. A woman and a dog? Of course, we were going to stop. We walked quietly around the bronze figures. Sacagawea stood tall and purposeful, her son on her back. Seaman sat at her feet, ears alert, ready for anything. Behind them stood a tipi—not part of the statue, but carrying a message just the same. Carmen stepped up the stone steps toward Sacagawea. She whispered something and gently brushed her fingers across the statue's shoulder. A thank-you, maybe.

From there, we passed Beaverhead Rock—another "recognition moment" for Sacagawea. She remembered the outcrop from her childhood and told the captains that her people—the Shoshone—were near. To the untrained eye, it might not look like much—just another dramatic rock formation—but to her, it was memory made manifest. We pulled over and stared, trying to see it through her eyes. I suppose that after thousands of miles on foot and by boat, in the July and August heat, and after a gill or two of whiskey, the rock would look like a swimming beaver.

We continued southwest through Dillon and found our way to Clark's

Lookout. It's a small park today—just a quiet patch of land overlooking the Beaverhead River—but the marker is powerful. On August 13, 1805, Clark climbed a rocky outcropping and used his compass to shoot bearings. He wanted to be sure they were still heading in the right direction. I climbed to the top, paused, and pointed—just like the silhouettes on the Lewis and Clark Trail markers. One foot in mystery, one in determination.

A short drive brought us to Camp Fortunate—now submerged beneath the Clark Canyon Reservoir. Lewis and Clark had paused here, hopeful they'd soon encounter the Shoshone (Newe, as they would call themselves). They knew they couldn't go much farther without horses to carry their supplies over the looming mountains. It was a place filled with anticipation. But the hoped-for reunion still lay on the other side of the Continental Divide.

After a quiet walk along the interpretive site, we continued toward Bannack, now a ghost town preserved in sun and silence. I love westerns—Clint Eastwood, The Man with No Name, Josey Wales, *Pale Rider*. I couldn't pass up a chance to walk the streets of a real ghost town. And it was right on the way.

Then traffic stopped. *Traffic?* We hadn't seen another car since leaving Dillon. But here, in front of us, a line of vehicles sat still. Construction.

After waiting what felt like an hour, we passed through and headed to Bannack. We wandered through the old buildings—weathered clapboard siding, rusted signs, echoes of stories long gone. Carmen lingered in the old schoolhouse, running her fingers along a dusty window frame. I could see her imagining the women and children who once lived and learned there. Life was isolating, layered, complex.

Finally, we made our way toward Lemhi Pass.

WHERE THE RIVER BEGINS

We climbed higher and higher, the road narrowing as the hills folded tighter around us. As we approached the pass, we fell into silence. There's something reverent about Lemhi. Something that slows your breath. A stone marker identifies the Continental Divide. Nearby, a spring emerges from the rocks. That spring flows down the mountainside, its waters eventually joining the Missouri River—the longest and most powerful river in North America. We both stood astride it—one foot on each side of that invisible seam in the continent—just as the Corps had done.

About a quarter of a mile up from the spring, and I do mean, *up,* Lewis had what Carmen and I call his "oh, shit" moment. He crossed the ridge and looked out, not onto a single mountain range, but onto range after range after range. In that instant, his dream of a Northwest Passage died. But they still had to find the Shoshone. Still had to trade for horses. So… they proceeded on. So did we.

Back in the Jeep, we rolled westward, wondering what might have been going through Lewis's mind. At the first creek west of the divide, we stopped. I crouched down and drank from the cool, clear water—the first taste of the Columbia watershed.

We were in Agaidika (Lemhi Shoshone) country now; memory meets map up here.

Around the next bend, we were stopped again. Not by traffic—but by a lone black steer standing squarely in the road. He stared at us, unimpressed. I eased the Jeep around him, and we moved on.

We came to the grassy plain where Lewis finally encountered members of the Shoshone Nation. The captains sat in a circle with the chief and his advisors. Communication was a challenge. English to French, French to Mandan, Mandan to Shoshone—and back again. Sacagawea served as interpreter, linking the Mandan-to-Shoshone strands.

Midway through the conversation, she stood, crossed the circle, threw her arms around the chief, and began to sob. In what might be the most remarkable coincidence in American history, the chief—Cameahwait—was her brother. He had been with her the day she was kidnapped. She'd feared he was dead. He'd survived, grown up, and become chief.

They got the horses.

We climbed back into the Jeep and headed for Salmon, Idaho, and our hotel along the Salmon River. As we entered the town, we were greeted by another statue of Seaman, standing guard atop a cluster of rocks. A little further along stood Sacagawea, her son nestled in her arms.

Quite the welcome.

WHERE THE RIVER WAS THE ONLY REFUGE

Carmen had this night highlighted on her calendar: a hotel! A hotel with a real bath and a real shower. A hotel with a real bed. After almost two weeks in the RV and in a tent, she was ready.

Before heading to the hotel, we decided to play tourist and explore Main Street. We stopped in at the Lemhi County Historical Museum, where the docent charmed us with her knowledge and pride in the town's history.

Salmon, Idaho, is a river town—split by the Salmon River, nicknamed the "River of No Return" by early settlers. Lewis and Clark had scouted the Salmon as a possible route to the Columbia River, but the daunting rapids and 5,000-foot cliffs forced them to rethink. Today, thousands come to Salmon each year to raft those same waters—though dynamite has tamed the worst of the rapids. Like much of the West, the discovery of gold changed everything. Later, the damming of the Columbia and Snake Rivers decimated the salmon runs that once filled these waters.

When we told the docent where we were staying, she smiled and said, "Oh, that's one of the nicest places in town." Great expectations!

We grabbed an early dinner at a local restaurant. Carmen, being Carmen, tried to strike up a conversation with the waitress.

"We've never been to Idaho," she said brightly. "What's it famous for—besides potatoes, of course?"

The waitress looked confused.

"Potatoes?" she asked.

"You know... Idaho potatoes?" Carmen prodded, her eyes sparkling.

When her question was met with a blank stare, Carmen gave a small laugh. "Never mind. I think we're ready to order."

Afterward, we headed to our hotel to check in.

Carmen slid the key into the door, pushed it open—and reality collided with expectations. The room reeked. The air was thick and damp, somehow even more humid than outside. The Berber carpet was stained with coffee, food, and God knows what else. Bugs crawled along the walls. Some flew.

I turned on my heel and marched to the office.

The guy behind the counter could not have cared less.

I demanded a refund.

"Look," he said, "I don't care if you stay here or not. I'm not giving you your money back."

With nowhere else to go, we decided to make the most of it. Carmen refused to unpack her suitcase. When she inspected the bathroom, she whirled around and said, "There is no way I'm taking a shower in there. There's a spider the size of my hand!"

It wasn't quite that large—maybe the size of a 50-cent piece—but still.

I made us a cocktail, and we headed out to the Salmon River.

If the hotel had one redeeming quality, it was the river. Step out the back door, and a path leads straight to the water. Borrowing from Amy Wortman's playbook, we perched on top of a picnic table, sipping our drinks and staring out at the river in silence.

I didn't know if Carmen was more grossed out by the room or pissed at me for not doing better research. In my defense, the museum docent had said it was one of the nicest places in town—which didn't say much for the competition.

I stared at the water. It calmed me, as rivers always do.

A river is an excellent metaphor for life: always moving, always changing. The past is past—the future unknown. Water flows. Life flows.

As dusk descended, so did the mosquitoes. We retreated to the room— no less humid despite cranking the air conditioner to the max. We laid towels across the bed and slept on top of them, not daring to let the bed linens touch our skin.

twenty-seven

Carmen, Idaho, and No Rest
for These Travelers

We were up before dawn, eager to shake the proverbial sand from our sandals—and get back on the trail. We paused to view the confluence of the Lemhi and Salmon Rivers. I can never pass up a good confluence! A few miles later, we rolled through the town of Carmen, Idaho. Of course, we stopped. How could we not? We snapped pictures of the Carmen Creek sign and the tiny Carmen Post Office. My Sacagawea, Carmen, grinned as she stood beneath the sign bearing her name.

We made several stops that morning, pulling off the road to photograph the awe-inspiring landscape—Tower Rock, a bald eagle perched on its nest, overlooks of the Salmon River cutting through sheer rock walls. We stood at the spot where Clark realized they could not navigate the Salmon. The cliffs were too steep, the rapids too wild. They had no choice but to abandon their boats and proceed on horseback. We, however, proceeded by Jeep.

Near the Idaho–Montana border, we detoured east to the Big Hole National Battlefield. The land was quiet, but the weight of history was not. Clark and a portion of the expedition, including Sacagawea and Jean Baptiste, had passed through this very place in 1806, weeks after leaving Niimiipuu villages. Their time with the Niimiipuu had forged a lasting friendship. But 70 years later, Big Hole bore witness to tragedy—an ambush, a two-day battle, and the death of dozens of Niimiipuu, many of them women and children. We watched a short film at the visitor center and learned about Chief Joseph, a Niimiipuu leader who resisted forced removal to a reservation. He survived the Battle of the Big Hole, and less than two months later—after a 1,600-mile flight toward Canada—he surrendered near the Bear Paw Mountains with the words, "I will fight no more forever."

The memorial outside was haunting. A dozen lodge poles stood in the meadow, arranged like the skeletons of lost homes. Carmen and I stood in silence. It was not the first time, nor would it be the last, that we shed a tear for the Indigenous peoples whose stories are etched into this land.

We climbed back into the Jeep and proceeded on. Soon, we passed back into Montana through Lost Trail Pass, the high, winding route that challenged even the Corps of Discovery. The road descended into the Bitterroot Valley—a place so serene, so golden with light, we found ourselves whispering again. It was easy to imagine the brief respite the Corps must have felt in this valley before facing the towering Bitterroot Mountains once more.

We arrived at Traveler's Rest State Park, the site of the Corps' final camp before tackling the Lolo Trail. For almost two centuries, the exact location had been unknown. Early interpretations of Clark's maps had suggested the site was east of the highway, but recent research has suggested otherwise. A local historian, parsing the journals, argued the true site lay west of the road. Miraculously, the pasture he pinpointed had never been plowed. Testing revealed a rectangular area high in mercury—traces of the Corps' medicinal pills. It was their latrine. Using Army standards from the time, researchers then located the kitchen area, and further on, signs of the blacksmith's forge.

Carmen and I just shook our heads in amazement. History, literally unearthed beneath our feet.

We wandered through the park, dipped our hands into Lolo Creek, and stood for a long time beside the gentle waters. This was one of those sacred moments. The kind that lingers.

Reluctantly, we turned toward the road. The Corps would proceed over the Lolo Trail into the unknown.

The map said we could keep going. The compass—hers, mine, the river's—said we'd gone deep enough... for now.

Missoula came and went. So did the interstate. Our RV was right where we'd left it at Three Forks RV Park, patiently waiting to carry us home. We had traveled 530 miles in two days on a route that carved an oval through Montana and Idaho. We would be coming back!

WHAT THE WIND WHISPERS WHEN YOU LISTEN

The next morning, we were up again at the crack of dawn. The journey home lay ahead of us—more than 24 hours of driving—but first, we had to head west to go east. With Carmen behind the wheel of our trusty RV, we returned the Jeep to the Butte airport and began the long, winding road back to Indiana.

We had no set plans for where we'd stop. That's the beauty of traveling in an RV—freedom. When we got tired, we could pull into a rest stop, a truck stop, or, yes, even a Walmart parking lot. One of us would drive until the other took over. No flights to catch. No check-in times. Just the open road and the rhythm of the miles.

We made two deliberate stops. The first was in Bozeman, Montana, where we visited a statue of Sacagawea. Carmen stood quietly, gazing at the sculpture of that young mother, interpreter, guide. It wasn't lost on me that she saw a part of herself in Sacagawea. The strength, the intuition, the gentle resilience. I saw it, too.

The second stop came many miles later—an overlook of Theodore Roosevelt National Park in North Dakota. The Badlands stretched out below us, wild and weathered. I didn't know it then, but nearly a decade later, I'd find myself immersed in Roosevelt's life as part of an executive coaching journey. I'd write about it and call the series The Roosevelt River. But that day, I stood still and took in the land he loved. It reminded me how the hardest places often shape the strongest people.

The hours rolled on, punctuated by laughter, by memory, by miles of unfiltered conversation. We reminisced about the trip, made half-serious plans for the next one, and fell deeper into a rhythm that was ours alone. With every mile, I fell more in love with my Sacagawea. She was my interpreter. She was my guide. She was my partner on this journey and all the journeys to come.

Soon, we were closing in on the final stretch. Remembering RV lesson 179—Never, ever drive through Chicago in an RV—we turned south at Sioux Falls and wound our way through Iowa and Illinois, making our way back home to Indiana.

The miles fell away behind us, but the memories stayed close. We talked and laughed and reminisced about the rivers we'd followed and the places we'd stood, exactly two centuries after Lewis and Clark had passed through. And we dreamed—about the next road, the next chapter, the next uncharted moment.

In the quiet miles between dusk and dawn, I realized the greatest discovery wasn't in the rivers we followed, but in the woman who chose to walk beside me.

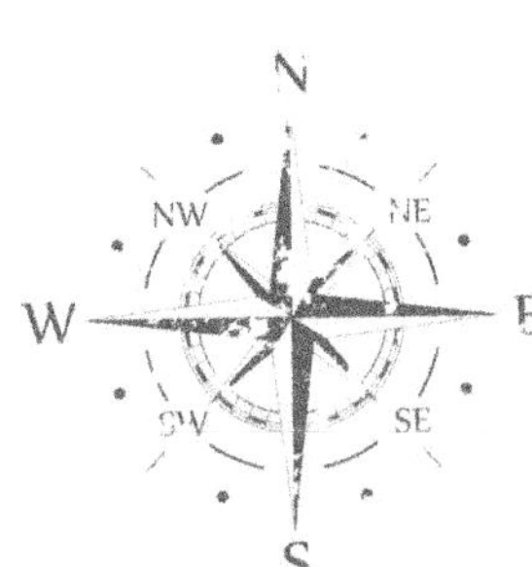

LEG 9

The Joy Was Us

To: Astoria, Oregon
November 2005

After all those miles, all those maps and guesses, it wasn't the ocean that took our breath—it was standing there together, knowing we'd made it.

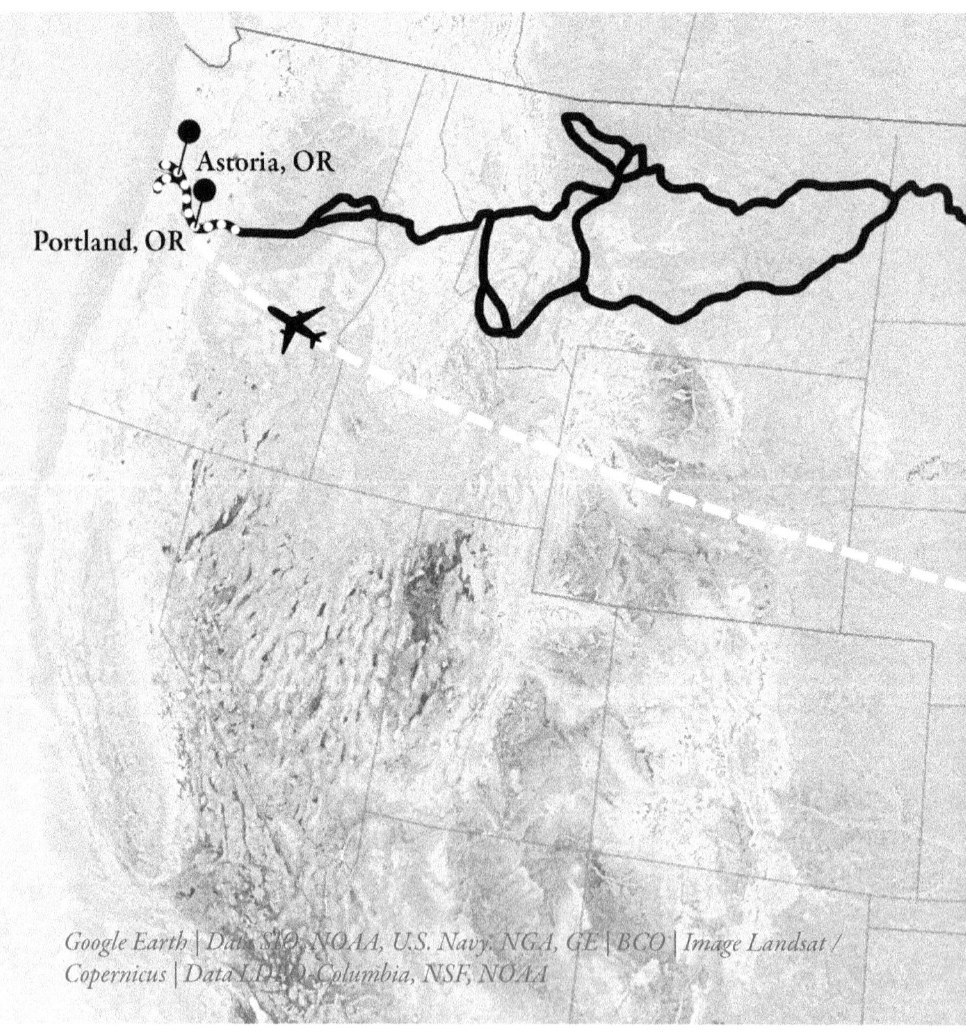

Google Earth | Data SIO, NOAA, U.S. Navy, NGA, GE | BCO | Image Landsat /
Copernicus | Data LDEO-Columbia, NSF, NOAA

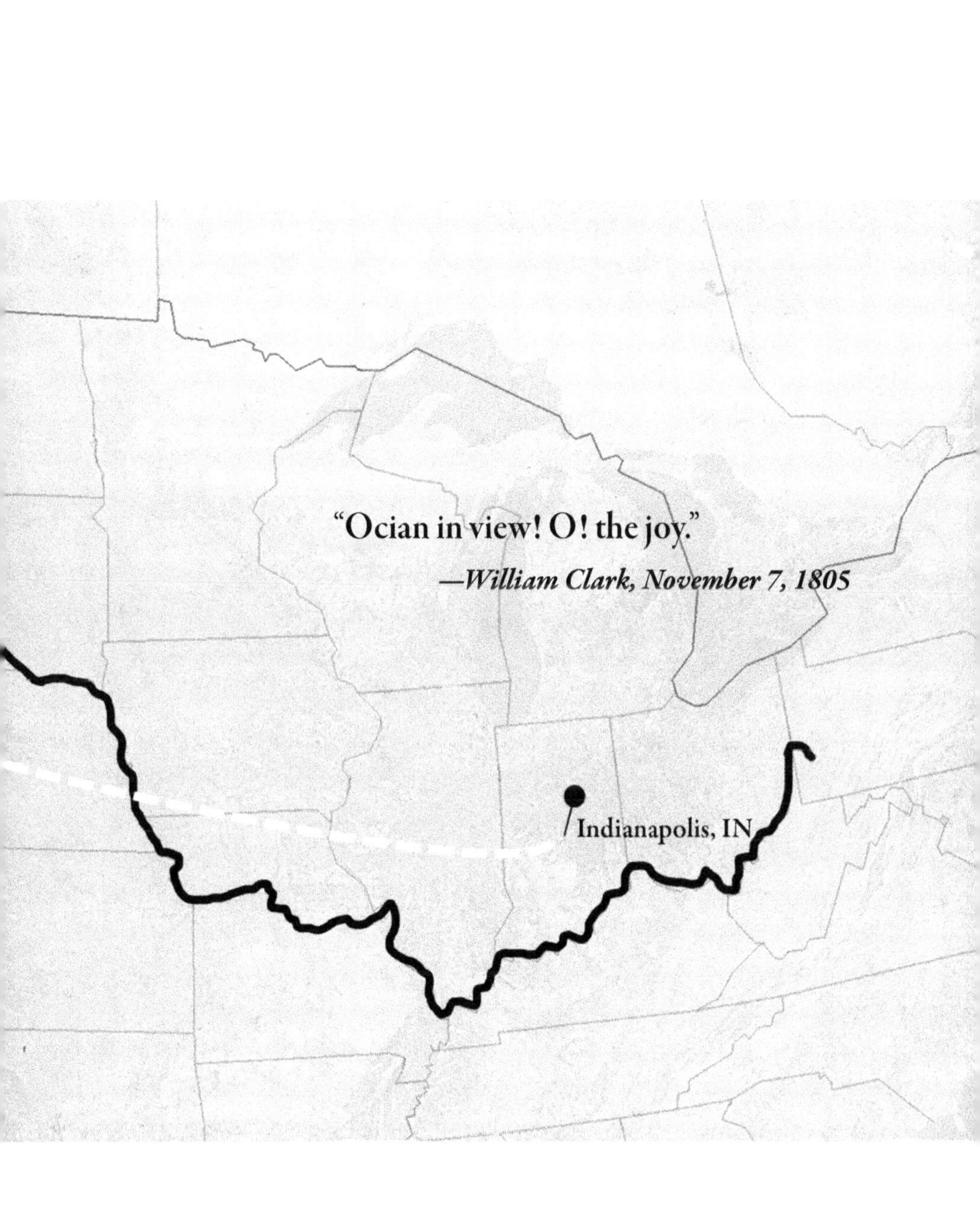

"Ocian in view! O! the joy."
—William Clark, November 7, 1805
Indianapolis, IN

twenty-eight
The River Is Calling Us... Again

That fall, our life settled into a quieter rhythm. Carmen finished sculpting the view from the new deck; the pond became her canvas. Brad painted his face for IU and showed up on the Assembly Hall screen during a Hoosier home game; Jeremy called Carmen—first and instinctively—when his cat, Alex, was dying, and she made room for his grief the way she always does. We took the RV to Green Lake, Wisconsin—holy ground in my family—and I watched Carmen and my mom walk those paths like they'd always been hers, too. We swapped one season's errands and small-town festivals for evenings at home, learning that "home" was less an address and more the way we looked at the same horizon.

Then a headline stopped us: Fort Clatsop had burned. The capstone we'd imagined was gone. We looked at each other across the kitchen and knew—the river was calling again. With our fourth anniversary on the horizon and the ocean at the far end of the map, we packed for Astoria's Signature Event—Destination: The Pacific.

EAST TO GO WEST: WHERE RIVERS SHIFT AND STORIES SURFACE

We decided to fly to Portland instead of trying to cross the mountains in our motorhome during the winter. I know... Lewis and Clark did it on horseback, and we had 350 horses under the hood—but they nearly died in the attempt. I wasn't about to tempt fate two centuries later.

We planned to drive east out of Portland to The Dalles, where we could cross the Columbia and head back west on Washington 14. That route, at least on paper, had more accessible Lewis and Clark sites. And paper was all we had to go on—no travel blogs, no Instagram reels, just guidebooks and good guesses.

One of those guidebooks led me to a few rustic cabins along the river in a small town called Stevenson, Washington. From there, we could make our way to Astoria. Long before online reservations became ubiquitous, I picked up the phone and called. The woman who answered sounded kind, but hesitant—like she was trying to spare us from a mistake.

"You know, there will be train noises. They go by here all night long," she said gently, almost apologetically.

"That's OK," I said, determined. "We're sound sleepers. We just want a river view."

With that, our plans were made.

On November 9, we boarded our Delta flight through Minneapolis to Portland. After several years of traveling to Paris every two weeks, I had accumulated enough miles to achieve Grand Poobah status—business class seats, airport lounges, early boarding. I was secretly proud to pamper my princess a bit, especially after the hotel debacle in Salmon the previous summer.

We landed in Portland, snagged our rental car, and headed east to go west. Our first stop was going to be the Columbia Gorge Discovery Center and Museum in The Dalles, about 90 minutes away. I'd done some research about Lewis and Clark's journey through the region, but the gorge itself was still a mystery to me.

"Hey, there was a sign for a Lewis and Clark site," Carmen said, looking out the window as we zipped along I-84.

"Yeah," I replied, slipping into tour guide mode, "but it looked like just a campground. Maybe we'll stop there next time."

A few miles later, we entered the Gorge Scenic Area. A sign for Rooster Rock State Park flashed by—and beneath it: "Clothing Optional Beach." Carmen burst out laughing and told me about a Key West sunbathing miscue years earlier—a mother shielding her little boy's eyes while Carmen, blissful and oblivious, had picked the wrong stretch of sand. We laughed, kept rolling east to go west.

Just then, we caught a glimpse of something rising out of the mist ahead—Multnomah Falls. We hadn't planned to stop, but the falls had other ideas.

Towering 600 feet above us, the cascade fell in two elegant stages: first into a high mountain pool, then tumbling again before the water flowed under the highway and into the Columbia. We stood in the mist, awestruck. The roar of the water echoed through the gorge like some ancient voice still speaking. It was spectacular.

That uncharted moment put us behind schedule, but we didn't care. We drove on toward the town of Hood River, with snowcapped Mount Hood watching over us like a sentinel. Just past Hood River, the rainforest vanished, and the land turned to high plains desert almost instantly—a different world on the same drive.

We pulled into the Discovery Center early in the afternoon. The museum was split between exhibits about the gorge and our heroes, Lewis and Clark. A full-scale dugout canoe—similar to what the Corps used— spanned the center of one room. Despite the sign inviting visitors to climb in, Carmen and I looked at each other and said "Nope!" There was no way we'd fit.

In the gorge section, our excitement dimmed. Many of the sights that Lewis and Clark had recorded—Celilo Falls, the Grand Chute, the Narrows—were gone, drowned beneath the still waters behind a series of dams. The mighty Columbia looked more like a lake than a river.

We stood at the windows in silence, watching the slow, heavy water drift by.

We couldn't help but think about Woody Guthrie and the songs he wrote about the dams and the river, songs we'd heard since we were kids. We were fans of Woody's son, Arlo—and in a way, Arlo had become part of our story too. Long before Carmen and I ever traveled together, long before this journey west, it was Arlo's storytelling that calmed my boys in the back seat on a chaotic Thanksgiving drive. And years later, when Carmen handed me her own copy of *Alice's Restaurant*, I knew—this was someone who got me. Someone who heard more than the song—they heard the story, a shared language, hidden in lyrics.

Climbing back into the car, I said, "Remember that commercial in the seventies? The Native American in the canoe, watching trash float in the river, then a single tear runs down his cheek?"

Carmen nodded.

"We didn't know then what we know now about that ad," I said quietly, "but the sadness still feels true."

We looked out across the backwater behind The Dalles Dam. "I know this isn't trash," Carmen said, "but it makes me sad just the same."

We crossed the river and turned west to Stevenson and our riverfront log cabin. It was small—just a single room with a sitting area, a kitchenette, and a double bed—but it was perfect. A deck on the back overlooked the Columbia, and as we unpacked, Carmen noticed the earplugs on each nightstand.

"Uh... there are earplugs on both sides of the bed. I wonder..."

"She warned me," I chuckled. "Said the trains can be loud. But I'm sure it won't be that bad."

I mixed cocktails, and we took them out to the deck. It was already getting dark at 4:30. The wind rustled through the lodgepole pines. A train chugged along the opposite bank, its whistle echoing mournfully through the gorge.

"See?" I said. "Not bad at all."

A few hours later, we felt like we were sleeping inside a jackhammer. A freight train—this one on our side of the river—barreled past a hundred yards from the cabin, shaking the walls and rattling the bed. We sat bolt upright, reached for the earplugs, and tried to get back to sleep.

Another fine selection of accommodations on our Lewis and Clark Trail adventures—part pilgrimage, part sitcom.

THE NAVEL OF THE WORLD

Dawn broke over the mountains to the east, casting golden light across the deck. I threw a jacket over my pajamas and stepped outside with a cup of coffee in hand. The crisp fall air carried the scent of pine and river.

I settled into one of the plastic deck chairs and opened a new book while Carmen showered and got ready for the day. With our first stop just minutes down the road, we lingered a little longer, watching the river glisten in the morning sun like it had someplace to be.

The Columbia Gorge Interpretive Center, perched on the edge of Stevenson, offered a few rooms dedicated to Lewis and Clark—but most of its stories honored pioneers, settlers, and local industry. It was an eclectic museum in the best way. One entire room housed nearly 4,000 rosaries, the most extensive collection in the world, maybe more than at the Vatican gift shop! Carmen felt drawn to them—perhaps the bead-by-bead cadence she knew from school.

As always, we stopped in the gift shop. That's where we learned the deeper meaning behind the museum's logo—a stylized figure drawn from a petroglyph on a nearby cliff. Her name was Tsagaglalal, or "She Who Watches." The Wishxam people tell of a woman chief who cared deeply for her people. When the trickster Coyote asked if she led them well, she said, "I am teaching them to live well." She wished to watch over them always, and so Coyote turned her into stone. She watches still, over the river and the people.

Carmen fell in love with the story. We bought a pen-and-ink drawing of Tsagaglalal, and in a quiet nod to Carmen's humor, she now watches over our guest bathroom.

With our guardian in tow, we turned west again.

Lewis and Clark, traveling this same stretch of river over 200 years ago, came upon a towering monolith. Clark described it in his journal on November 2, 1805: "A remarkable high rock on the [Starboard] Side about 800 feet high and 400 yds round, the Beaten [Beacon] Rock."

They didn't climb it—but we would.

We parked at the base of the rock, and Carmen paused at an interpretive sign. "Wow... this is actually a plug from an ancient volcano. It's lava." The Cascade peoples called it Che-che-op-tin—the navel of the world.

The name felt right.

A trail, carved into the sheer rock by Henry Biddle in the 1920s, spirals upward with catwalks and railings. We began our ascent, stopping often to rest and take in the view. Partway up, we saw a small plaque honoring Biddle. I looked at it and mused aloud, "Clark chose a *Nicholas* Biddle to publish their journals after Lewis died. I wonder if there's a connection?"

There was. Later, we'd learn that Henry J. Biddle was his descendant—a thread across centuries—two men preserving the same story in different ways.

We paused to catch our breath at one of the switchbacks, leaning against the railing, looking down at the river winding far below. Carmen flashed me that smile—half mischief, half determination—and kept climbing.

I watched her for a moment before following. My amazing wife. Working her way up the side of this rock like it was nothing new. She had canoed with me for three days through the wilderness—a tent, no bed, bathing in the river, sleeping on the ground. She had snorkeled in Fiji and Australia, bungee jumped off a perfectly good bridge in Queenstown, New Zealand, scuba dived in St. Thomas... and now, here she was, scaling Beacon Rock, a lava plug towering nearly 900 feet over the gorge, because—of course—she was always up for the next adventure.

Always in it with both feet—and with her whole heart.

At the top, the view stunned us into silence. The gorge unfurled beneath us, its cliffs and water wrapped in morning mist. To the west and south, it was breathtaking. To the east, the Bonneville Dam cut across the landscape like a scar. Still, in that moment, with the wind whispering through the pines and no sound but our breath, it felt like hallowed ground. Sacred, in a way that words don't easily hold.

When the next group of hikers arrived, we gave up our perch and began the descent. Clark had noted the first signs of tidal water here. Like him, we had farther to go—but we were getting close.

We followed Washington 14, winding through the gorge, the road hugging the curves of the river.

"This would be an incredible motorcycle ride," said Carmen. In a previous life, with a previous boyfriend, she'd ridden hundreds of times on the back of a Harley.

"Wouldn't it, though?" I replied, picturing us winding along the cliffs on the motorcycle I had sold just months before our relationship had blossomed.

We continued to follow the river, turning north near Vancouver, Washington, before heading west at Longview, eventually, leaving the river behind.

At Rosburg we turned south to rejoin the river. The sun was low now, shadows stretching across the forest. The roads narrowed, the trees closed in. It felt like the world was tightening around us, funneling us toward something. We passed a Lewis and Clark marker but didn't stop—light was fading fast, and Pillar Rock still lay ahead.

Through Altoona. Through Carlson Landing. Finally, the Pillar Rock Salmon Cannery.

Before we turned toward the river, the sky gave us a gift. The sunset lit the water like fire. It was here, in this very place, that Clark had written "Ocian in view! O! The joy." He thought he had reached the Pacific. Like us, he was standing at Grays Bay—close, but not quite.

Pillar Rock stood just offshore, mist curling around it. It's adorned now with a light to warn ships, not guide explorers. The clouds rolled in, the hills across the river vanished, and then, just like that... it was dark.

We made our way to the car, stopping long enough to read that Lewis and Clark marker by headlight. The road eventually led us to Highway 101 and across the bridge into Astoria.

We had made it.

After nearly three years of chasing their footsteps, we were here. At the edge of the continent. The Pacific Ocean waited. And so did the next few days—ceremony, memory, and something just beneath the surface that we didn't yet have words for.

But we would.

twenty-nine
Beneath the Surface

The world was cast in shades of gray when we woke. Clouds hung low over the bay, hiding the sun we knew was up there somewhere. Moisture clung to everything—more than fog, not quite rain. It blurred the hills across the water and wrapped the morning in a kind of sacred hush.

It was Veterans Day, November 11, and the official opening of the Signature Event. It would be held at Fort Stevens State Park, overlooking the Pacific and anchored by the remains of a Civil War–era fort. It was a place meant for memory.

Veterans Day and Memorial Day have always held a special place in our hearts. We come from families who served—my grandfather near Soissons in the First World War; Carmen's father, Tom, was in the Army during the Korean War, and Jim, the man who raised her, wore Navy blue in World War II. In the Vietnam era, Carmen wore a POW bracelet for Commander Cole Black until he came home. Maybe that's why the pageantry still brings her to tears, especially when a lone bugler plays "Taps." Pride and sorrow can live in the same chest. That morning, I found myself wondering how to honor a country's sacrifices while holding its wounds in view.

The opening ceremony was held in Fort Stevens, and the program delivered the full measure of ceremony: the Fife and Drum Corps of St. Charles, a flyover by the Oregon and Washington National Guards, a presentation of tribal flags by Native veterans, and a 21-gun salute. But sometimes what stays with you isn't the spectacle. Sometimes it's the simplest truth, spoken without fanfare.

That moment came from Joe Scovell, an elder of the Clatsop–Nehalem Confederated Tribes and a World War II Coast Guard veteran. Carmen felt an immediate connection because of Jim's service. Reading his bio, we discovered another link: He had earned his master's from Butler University, in our own Indianapolis.

He stepped forward to welcome us to this land—his land, the land of his ancestors—and said: "When Lewis and Clark arrived in this area, we had been here for thousands of years. We were not sitting around waiting to be 'discovered.'"

That sentence hit like thunder.

We were not sitting around waiting to be discovered.

The words rang inside us. It shattered the false premise we'd all been taught. Lewis and Clark didn't discover anything. What was here was already known. Already named. Already home to thousands. We had a lot to learn. And on that gray Pacific morning, our hearts were wide open to it.

The replica at Fort Clatsop had burned to the ground just weeks before we arrived, but we went anyway. The air hung at forty-five degrees, damp and insistent, a fine Oregon rain settling into our jackets while water dripped steadily from the Sitka spruce above us. The clearing felt quieter than it should have, the fort reduced to outline and memory. Instead of walls, we found archaeologists kneeling in the mud, brushing history back into view. We stood there longer than we planned, listening as they explained what lay beneath the ash and soil—post holes, fragments, traces of winter. And before we left, we learned about the small ritual of flying a flag over the fort each day, then lowering it and sending it home with someone who wanted to carry a piece of the place with them. At the time, it felt like a charming detail. We didn't yet know it would become something more.

Later that day, we crossed the river into Washington to attend a powerful performance in Ilwaco. Hasan Davis, embodying York, and Amy Mossett, portraying Sacagawea, brought the past to life. They focused on the vote—that remarkable moment in November 1805 when the Corps faced the question of where to spend the winter. We'd seen Davis and

Mossett more than once along the trail. Each time their portrayals brought us to tears.

Should they stay on the north side of the river or explore the south? The captains called for a vote. And in a move unprecedented at the time, everyone voted—including York, a Black man, and Sacagawea, a Native woman. Their voices were heard. Their votes counted. No one knows exactly why the captains included them. Historians still debate it. But that simple act, whether conscious or intuitive, stood in contrast to the norms of the time—and, heartbreakingly, still stands out two centuries later.

Carmen sat with tears in her eyes. Not from pain, but from something more complicated—recognition, sorrow, reverence. Her curiosity about these lives rivaled my own. It was one more reason—number 367,000, by my count—why I loved her so much.

Before returning to Oregon, we visited Dismal Nitch, where the Corps had been pinned for five miserable days by a brutal storm. No shelter. No food. Cold, soaked, and worn down to the bone. It was here, on the edge of despair, that they came so close—and could go no further. Only once the storm passed could they move on to Cape Disappointment.

Ironically, it was named not by the captains but by British explorer John Meares in 1788. He had searched for the fabled River of the West, missed the Columbia's mouth, and named the cape for his failure. The name stuck. Disappointment layered upon disappointment, long before the Corps ever arrived.

As the afternoon waned, we raced the light back to Fort Stevens, hoping to glimpse the Pacific before the sun slipped away. We made it—just barely—to the jetty observation deck. The ocean opened before us, massive and wild. Yes, we'd both seen the Pacific before—San Francisco, Los Angeles, San Diego—but not like this. Not here. Not in this fierce, untamed corner of the continent where the waves roared in.

We made our way to the shipwreck of the *Peter Iredale*, its rusted skeleton half-buried in the sand. There, the sky caught fire. The most spectacular sunset we'd ever seen unfolded in slow motion. I reached for Carmen's hand, and she took it without a word.

We stood together in silence. The surf pounded in our ears. The light turned gold, then blood orange, then was gone. Not a word passed between us. We didn't need words.

This was what we had come for. This moment. This knowing.

"LEWIS AND CLARK. LEWIS AND CLARK"

After a seaside dinner, we ducked into a small Astoria theater for *Simple Salmon Discovers Lewis & Clark*—sharp, silly, exactly right for the day. What stayed wasn't a sketch but a chorus: "Lewis and Clark. Lewis and Clark." We hummed it on the walk to the car, brushed our teeth still grinning, and fell asleep with the refrain looping like a lullaby.

thirty

Where the Rivers Meet

Sunday morning greeted us with yet another world of gray—only colder. Maybe 40 degrees. And yes, it was raining. Drizzle, mostly. The kind that soaks you slowly, deliberately. We were headed to a program called Consider the Columbia, a solemn ceremony to symbolically blend the waters of the Missouri with those of the Columbia. A gesture rich in meaning. And, I suppose, the rain was fitting. The Corps spent 117 days on the coast and recorded only 12 without rain. We were just doing our part.

Did I mention the ceremony was outside? Did I mention it was taking place on the bridge? Did I mention we would be standing on the bridge, in the wind, in the cold, in the rain, halfway across the Columbia River?

Now, I know the Corps endured a lot. But think of my amazing wife for a moment. I have a photo of us freezing on Jefferson's lawn at Monticello—it was eight degrees. I have another of us wilting in Atchison, Kansas, searching desperately for shade when it was 104. And now? There she was, standing in 40-degree drizzle, in the middle of a bridge, hood drawn so tight that only her eyes, nose, and mouth were visible. And what was she doing?

She was laughing. Her eyes were twinkling.

That is my wife. That is my co-captain in this journey called life.

We crowded against the railing with the others as a tugboat emerged from the harbor. The mixing of the waters took place onboard—Missouri meeting Columbia, East merging with West. Each of us was given a small vial of water and sand from both rivers. Together, as the rain traced lines down our cheeks and jackets, we read a Chinook blessing aloud, a responsive reading with a single line repeated, over and over: "Teach us, and show us the Way."

The ceremony stayed with us as we boarded the buses back to the hotel, still holding our vials of river water and sand, still turning over those words in our minds: Teach us, and show us the Way. We were damp, chilled to the bone, and grateful for a chance to dry off and regroup. The rain let up while we changed clothes, but the clouds held their ground, blanketing the day in soft gray.

There was something fitting in that. The sun didn't need to shine. It felt like we were moving through a kind of quiet communion—echoes of the past and promises of the future.

We started at the saltworks, where members of the Corps had spent weeks boiling seawater to extract salt—pivotal for preserving meat through the long winter. A small reconstruction stood by the shore, humble and utilitarian, just a few barrels, a fire pit, and rough fencing. But standing there, with the scent of brine in the air and the low rumble of waves in the distance, we could almost hear the hiss of the fire under kettles, the steady work of men who were trying to survive. It was easy to miss, easy to pass by—but we were learning not to.

From Seaside, we drove to Cannon Beach to visit Haystack Rock, that iconic monolith rising from the surf like a forgotten cathedral. We'd seen photos of it, of course, but being there was different. The tide was out, the beach wide and wet, the sky a soft watercolor of gray and silver. We walked slowly toward the rock, shoes in hand, the cold sand firm beneath our feet. We didn't say much. We just took it in. Carmen paused to watch a gull lift into the wind. I snapped a picture of her, hood half-up, hair blowing. Sacredness doesn't always come with fanfare. Sometimes it just stands there, like a rock, waiting.

We kept driving, following the road as it curved inland and then back out to the sea. Indian Beach sits tucked below Tillamook Head, wild and raw. The trail winds through coastal forest, moss-covered trees giving way to ocean and rock. It was quiet when we arrived. The surf was louder than anything else.

Standing there, it hit me—Clark and his scouting party hadn't driven around the headland like we had. They had hiked up and over it. In January. Through wind and rain and sodden underbrush. Clark later wrote: "I made a very bad march over the worst country I ever saw ... thick brush and fallen timber for nine miles ... raining and snowing and the wind violent."

They were desperate, cold, and running out of food—searching for a whale that had washed ashore. And somewhere near here, Sacagawea insisted on going, insisted on seeing the whale herself. She didn't ask. She insisted. That quiet defiance, that assertion of presence, still moves me.

Carmen and I stood at the edge of the beach, looking up toward the cliffs where the Corps had scrambled. We didn't follow the trail. We didn't need to. Just being there, looking up into that mist-draped forest, was enough to feel the weight of it. Another uncharted moment, waiting quietly to be honored.

We circled back to Cannon Beach one more time, this time not for a destination, but just to be there. We walked along the shoreline until the tide began to return, our footprints disappearing behind us. The wind had picked up, and the waves were more restless now. But it wasn't threatening. It felt alive. Restless like we were.

Our final stop was Seaside again. We needed to exhale. We walked a bit, shared a warm drink, and watched the sky begin to slip toward evening. The day had been long and cold and full, and yet, somehow, it had gone by too fast. These places had been waiting for us. And we had arrived— soaked, curious, reverent.

THE LONG WAY TO THE SEA

We woke to another cloudy sky—no surprise there—but there was a different kind of anticipation in the air. This wasn't a ceremony. It wasn't a lecture or a reenactment to observe. This was a walk. A 6.5-mile hike through forest, across ravines, and all the way to Sunset Beach, where the Pacific meets land with its usual dramatic flair.

The trail, newly dedicated that day, retraced the route the Corps might have taken from Fort Clatsop to the ocean, winding through the ancestral lands of the Clatsop people—lands they walked, hunted, and lived upon long before Lewis and Clark arrived. It was meant to be both a physical journey and a gesture of respect. For me, it was both of those things—and something else, too. It was a chance to walk alone with my thoughts. Something sacred in its own right.

Carmen opted to sit this one out; it was only the second time she "sat one out," and it may have been the last. She would meet me at the end, at the beach. She said it with that smile—the one that's part "you go ahead, I'll be fine" and part "you're gonna owe me for this." Truth was, I missed her the moment I stepped onto the trail. But I knew she'd be there when it mattered most. She always was.

The hike began behind Fort Clatsop—or, rather, behind where it once stood. Reenactors in full Corps dress led the way, Seaman the dog bouncing at their heels, tail high like he owned the trail. A Cub Scout troop followed close behind, their blue uniforms bunched under raincoats, their leaders herding them like happy chaos. I've always had a soft spot for the Cub Scouts—something about that mixture of wide-eyed enthusiasm and untucked shirts. They made the morning feel lighter.

And then there was Sacagawea—a reenactor, walking the entire trail with a baby snug against her back. I didn't catch her name. It didn't matter. Her presence carried weight. Her silence said more than words. In a way, she led us all.

The trail itself was dense and green and quiet in the way only a rainforest can be. Ferns covered the ground like waves, and massive Sitka spruce stretched skyward as if trying to pierce the clouds. The ground rose and fell. We crossed wooden bridges, descended into ravines, climbed back up again. Now and then, I passed small groups or walked alone for stretches, the only sound the crunch of my boots and the soft murmuring of a meandering creek.

Somewhere around mile three, I started thinking about Carmen—missing her, and cataloging what she gives this journey. Smart—she reads people and places and somehow sees around corners. Caring—she makes room for every hurt, human or otherwise. Encourager—she nudges, not pushes, and celebrates every small learning. Beautiful—that smile finds me in storms and in quiet. I swear my pace changed then, like my heart remembered it had somewhere to be.

Eventually, the forest began to thin. The light changed—brighter, somehow, even though the clouds lingered. A golden-brown field of grasses stretched out in front of me, bending in the breeze. Beyond it, the long sweep of Sunset Beach, the Pacific Ocean crashing on the shore, the sky still gray but lit in places, like it couldn't help but smile.

And there she was.

Carmen, standing just past the trailhead, her raincoat unzipped now, her face flushed pink from the wind. She saw me before I saw her, and when I did—I couldn't move fast enough.

I walked straight into her arms and held her like I'd been gone a lot longer than three hours. I had walked through time and terrain and history—but the journey didn't end at the beach. It ended here, with her.

Because this has always been our trail. Our journey. And somehow, she makes every destination feel like arrival.

THE DAY THE SKY FINALLY CLEARED

Miracle of miracles, we woke up to a world bathed in blue. Not a cloud in sight. For the first time all week, the sky seemed to stretch wide open, as if the heavens themselves had decided we'd earned a little sunshine. It felt like a reward. A blessing. A proper send-off.

We had one final stop before beginning our journey home: the Astoria Column.

Perched high on a hill above the city, the 125-foot column tells the story of this place—from the First Peoples to Lewis and Clark, and on to John Jacob Astor's fur trading outpost, just five years after the expedition's return. A mural spirals up the tower, history literally winding toward the sky.

To reach the top, you climb 164 spiral steps—tight, steep, and echoing with footsteps. As we climbed, I was reminded of a tower in Sevilla, Spain, that Carmen and I had visited. Then the higher we climbed, the more I was transported back to my childhood, to the Judson Tower in Green Lake, Wisconsin. My mom always sang "We Are Climbing Judson Tower" to the tune of "Jacob's Ladder." Without thinking, I began singing it again.

Carmen peered at me, a twinkle in her eye and a smile that teased. *If you keep singing that*, her expression said, *you might not make it back down.*

At the top, we stood in silence. Below us, the Astoria Bridge spanned the water like a ribbon of steel. The mouth of the Columbia yawned open into the Pacific. Moisture hung in the air, catching the light just enough to turn the horizon hazy.

"I think I can see Fort Clatsop from here," I said, pointing toward what I believed was the Lewis and Clark River flowing into Youngs Bay.

"Or maybe Youngs River," Carmen offered gently. "I think the fort is five miles south of the bay."

I grinned, defying geography. "I'm sticking with the Lewis and Clark River."

There we were—at the edge of the continent, having followed their trail from Monticello to here. It felt like an ending. We felt triumphant, the way I imagine the Corps must have felt. But just like them, we knew the journey wasn't over. They'd still have to survive the winter, push upriver, recross the Rockies, and travel thousands of miles to return home.

Us? We had to drive to Portland, catch a flight, and be back in Indiana by dinner tomorrow. And yet... our story felt unfinished, too. There were still more adventures planned. More trails to walk. More rivers to follow.

As we turned toward Portland and the airport, the week gathered itself in the rearview: rain threading a blessing across a bridge; the jetty wind at the edge of the continent; a long walk from fort to sea, and the way she was waiting at the end, arms open. We flew home to mark four years of marriage, but the celebration had already happened—in gray light and salt air, in the small, stubborn ways we kept choosing the same horizon. The ocean was the destination. The arrival was us.

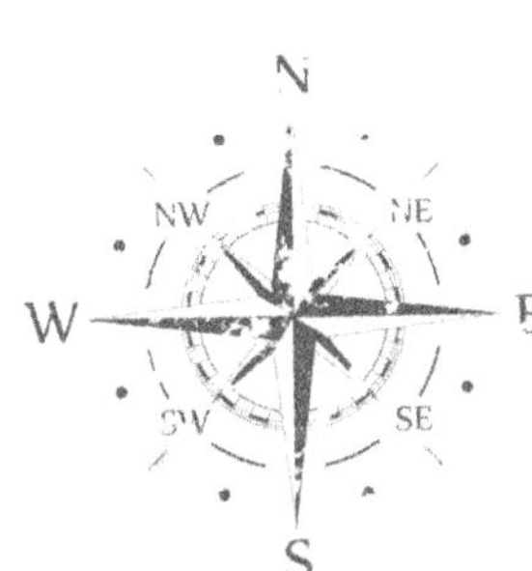

Summer of Peace, Road of Memory

To: Lewiston, Idaho, and Clarkston, Washington
June 2006

*The road taught us that the quietest moments are
often the ones that last the longest.*

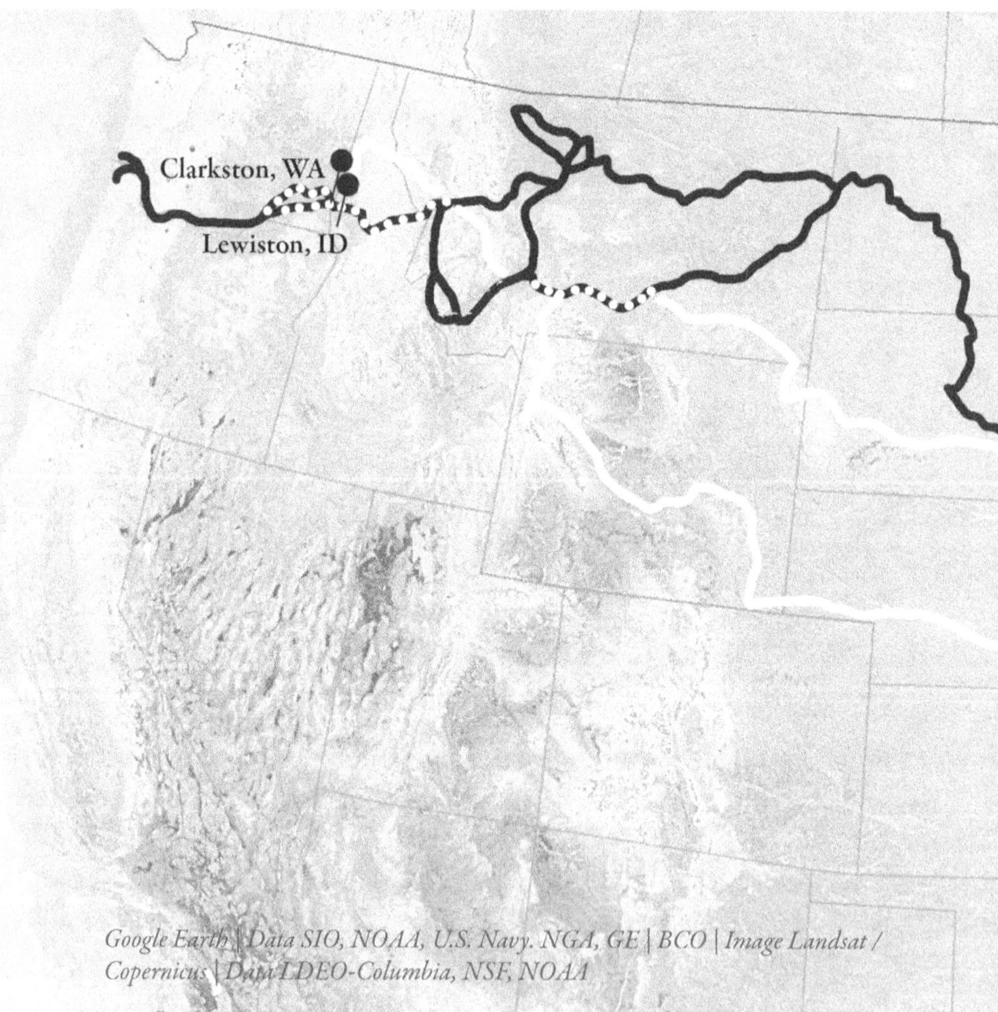

Google Earth | Data SIO, NOAA, U.S. Navy, NGA, GE | BCO | Image Landsat /
Copernicus | Data LDEO-Columbia, NSF, NOAA

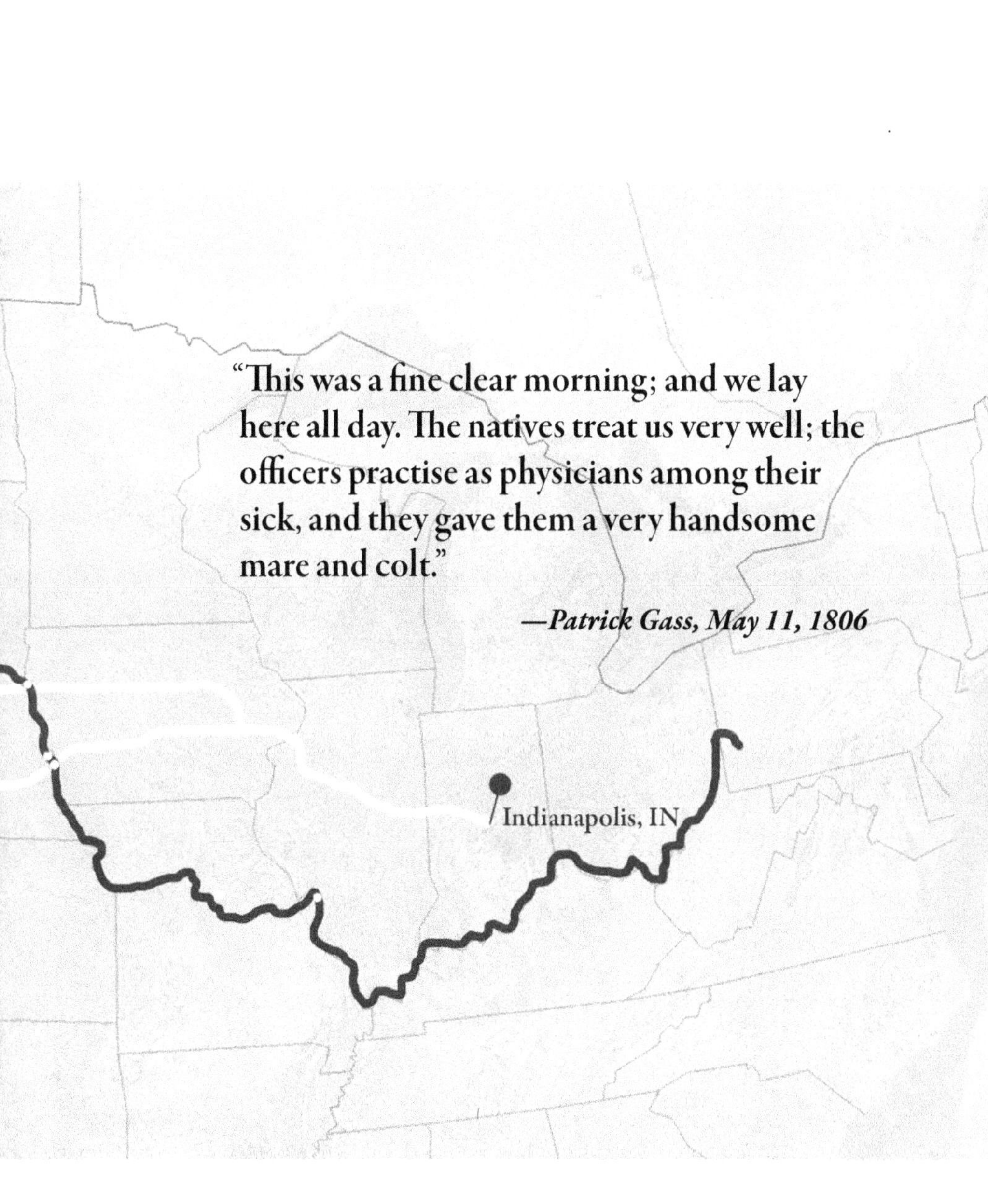

"This was a fine clear morning; and we lay here all day. The natives treat us very well; the officers practise as physicians among their sick, and they gave them a very handsome mare and colt."

—Patrick Gass, May 11, 1806

Indianapolis, IN

thirty-one

Spam: It's What's for Dinner

We returned home from our Astoria trip high on life. What an incredible experience. We jabbered about the Pacific Ocean during the entire flight back to Indiana. The next Signature Event was set for June 2006, but before we hit the trail again, life swept us into a whirlwind back home.

That winter became a hinge. Carmen stepped fully into managing the life we were building, and I stepped away from Thomson toward my first CIO role. We marked the turn with two bright notes—a Christmas week in Paris and Brad's IU graduation—and then pointed the RV west with enough vacation banked to keep following the trail.

MACGYVER AND THE CHEF

We packed up the Arrrrr Vee—and no, that joke never gets old—and hit the road after I got home from the office. Our destination was Lewiston, Idaho, site of the Signature Event titled The Summer of Peace: Among the Niimiipuu. The event wouldn't begin for another week, but we had a major bucket list item to check off first: Yellowstone National Park. And that meant three full days of driving.

We were headed to Lewiston–Clarkston for one reason: to listen. The Summer of Peace wasn't another pin for our map; it was a chance to stand where the Niimiipuu welcomed, taught, and waited with the Corps—and to carry that story home changed. We'd carried the ocean home in our pockets, yes, but here we hoped to carry something harder to hold: humility.

Before the ceremonies, we would follow the side channels—in Wyoming, Tetons to Yellowstone, then east along old names and older homelands—so that when we reached Niimiipuu country, we'd arrive with our ears open. Long Camp, Clearwater, another confluence: names on panels now, but living places still. We came to learn from them.

We were anxious and eager to get to Omaha. We'd driven the route between Indianapolis and Omaha the year before on our way to Great Falls, and the year before that on our way to Bismarck. This was known territory. We were restless for the unknown.

After a quick overnight stop near Davenport, Iowa, we jumped back on I-80 and pushed toward Omaha. We barely blinked as we zipped through town, though we did chuckle about that old Charlie Daniels lyric about heading to LA via Omaha.

The next night, we stayed at a rest stop near Kearney, Nebraska.

We didn't plan to stop at Fort Kearny—at least, I don't remember planning it. But there we were that afternoon, just outside town, driving past one of those brown historical signs that seem to whisper *Come on, just a quick detour*. Carmen glanced over and said, "You wanna go?"

Of course I did.

Fort Kearny told a cleaner story on the sign than the land did. Forts don't just protect; they claim—on Pawnee, Cheyenne, and Lakota homelands. We stood in the grass and listened anyway.

By that afternoon, we were back on the road, heading toward Cheyenne. Another line on the map. Another stretch of sky and silence. Another uncharted moment.

Carmen had been daydreaming quietly for a while—something that always made me smile. We were so comfortable in the silence. Well, the music was playing, but you get my drift. We didn't have to talk. We could just be.

Suddenly, she turned to me, eyes wide.

"Scottsbluff! I didn't know we'd be this close. I used to travel there for work—gosh, it's been 20 years. 1984 or '85."

And just like that, we were in another story.

She lit up as she told it—how she'd worked for the tech company Anacomp after her first job as a staff accountant in North Vernon, Indiana. That's where she met colleagues who became lifelong friends; names like Ruth, John, and Jennie still bring a smile to her face.

Carmen told me about the years she spent living on airplanes: two weeks a month on the road, coast to coast, in a rhythm she likened to that of Lewis and Clark. D.C., Lafayette Parish, Hartford, Harrisburg, Blue Springs, Brewton, Nevada City, Scottsbluff—the list unspooled like a flight board. At Anacomp (the division Lockheed bought in 1989 or '90), she'd land, sit with city and county teams, pull requirements from their workflows, translate them for programmers, then circle back to install and train until the system held.

Then came the winter in Scottsbluff. She flew in during a storm, one of those small airports where you step onto the tarmac and cross to the terminal. A police officer who was the lead on the project she was flying in to tackle waved off the rental counter and drove her to the hotel himself—roads polished to ice, the air never above zero. He later invited her to dinner with his wife and two kids. Warm house, easy talk, snow hard against the windows—and with a little flourish, the main course arrived: Spam. It made her grin. It made me laugh when she told it, too; Sunday lunches at my house were thick slices on floured buns, and I'll admit I still like it. We promised ourselves that next time we were out that way, we'd stop in and say thank you.

We rolled into the Terry Bison Ranch and RV Park that evening, just barely north of the Colorado–Wyoming border. I had picked it so we could finally see bison—real ones. Despite 12 years working for Indiana National Bank, whose mascot was a bison (we even called our running club the Bison Stampeders), I had never seen one in the flesh.

We set up camp and planned to grill steaks—beef, not bison. I worked on the grill outside while Carmen got things going in the kitchenette. It was sunny and warm, but the wind was relentless—gusting so hard it felt like a hurricane. I couldn't keep the grill lit. I used some colorful language.

From inside the RV, Carmen called out, "The refrigerator is beeping!"

Great. The propane pilot light had gone out. RVs are their own strange universe, and apparently, our refrigerator was a delicate flower in the wind. I opened the panel and relit it. A few seconds later—beep. Out again.

I needed a wind block, fast. Channeling my inner MacGyver, I got creative: I stood our little wooden patio table on end, stabilized it with leveling blocks, and built a makeshift barrier. Problem solved… sort of.

"Guess we're cooking indoors tonight," I said.

Carmen took over. Watching her work in that tiny space—confident, calm, creative—I marveled, not for the first time, at just how talented she is. Carmen is more than a great cook—she's a chef. Years ago, she ran a small business called Elegant Creations, baking elaborate cakes for baby showers, weddings, and anniversaries. She once recreated a couple's wedding cake from a single black-and-white photo—for their 50th anniversary. Nailed it.

Later, she helped open an upscale lunch café in Carmel. She did it all—menu planning, shopping, cooking, and presentation. They were hits—places of laughter, clinking silverware, and stories shared over wine spritzers and chilled soup. Her love of cooking and baking came from watching and helping Grandma Delmo when she was a young girl.

That night in the RV, she moved with the same grace. I stood nearby, cocktail in hand, lending a hand when I could. She caught me watching her and smiled—that smile that says *I see you seeing me.*

Tomorrow, we'd see bison.

Tonight, I had everything I needed.

WHERE THE LAND REMEMBERS

The next morning, we actually saw bison.

Off in the distance, in the middle of a field.

We were a little disappointed but eager to press on. This trip wasn't about waiting for wonder—it was about going to find it. Our next overnight stop was Jackson, Wyoming, but we weren't taking the fastest route. We wanted something more scenic, more unknown.

As we drove north on I-25, the landscape began to shift. The plains gave way to rolling hills and rocky outcrops. That's when we saw it—a solitary butte, rising up in the distance like it had been waiting for someone to notice. It wasn't marked, at least not that we could see, and we didn't stop.

But Carmen grabbed the camera and snapped a picture through the RV window, both of us marveling at how it seemed to command the horizon.

I don't know its name. Maybe it has one, maybe not. Maybe it's one of those landmarks locals just nod toward without needing to explain. But for a moment, it was the only thing in the world. Stark, layered, shaped by wind and time—it stood alone and still, while we passed in motion.

As we neared Casper, a sign caught our attention—Ayres Natural Bridge Park. We'd been driving for about two hours and were ready to stretch our legs a bit. Like so many of our best detours, this one wasn't planned. But it didn't disappoint.

Almost as soon as we left I-25, we got our wish: a roadside herd of bison—fenced, yes, but close enough to feel their size in our chests.

Ayres Natural Bridge sits tucked in a red-rock fold near Douglas, a limestone arch carrying La Prele Creek through its shade—one of the rare natural bridges with living water beneath. We spent an hour there, climbing to the top, wading the cold shallows, letting the quiet do its work.

On the walk back, Carmen remembered another sacred stone: Uluru—Ayers Rock—part of an over-the-top 40th birthday trip with Tom that ran from snorkeling in Fiji to bungee jumping in New Zealand to a long Australian loop. She hadn't made the summit. Rain had slicked the rock, and even then it felt wrong to climb; the site is sacred, and climbing has since been closed at the request of the Anangu Traditional Owners. That journey, she said, was where the stories and struggles of Indigenous peoples began to move from "interesting" to "inside." A seed planted, still growing with every stop on our trail.

On the way back to the highway, we saw our bison herd again. This time, a small reddish-brown calf stood near the fence, looking directly at us as we slowed to take a picture. I can still hear Carmen's voice:

"Ohhhh, isn't he cute?"

We left the interstate behind at Casper and headed west toward the Wind River Reservation. About two hours later, after driving through terrain that looked like a movie set from every Western I'd ever watched, we passed through the small town of Jeffrey City—a fitting bookend to the Carmen, Idaho, sign we'd photographed the year before.

We didn't rush our way through the Wind River Reservation. Some places ask you to move slowly. This was one of them. The reservation is home to the Eastern Shoshone and Northern Arapaho tribes—nations of resistance, survival, and quiet resilience.

Just outside Fort Washakie, we pulled off the road to visit a marker we'd read about—a simple stone, set back a bit from the highway, ringed with a low metal fence and red sandstone blocks. The plaque claimed to mark the resting place of Sacagawea. It's not in the cemetery where the more formal monument stands. This one's easier to miss. But somehow, that made it feel more personal. More sacred.

We stood in silence for a while, letting the wind speak for itself. Carmen read every word on the plaque, then took a few steps back and stood with her hands on her hips, scanning the horizon. She always does that when something hits her deep—when the weight of a place settles in.

Of course, there's another story. The more widely accepted historical record states that Sacagawea died in 1812, nearly 2,000 miles east, at Fort Manuel Lisa in present-day South Dakota. According to that version, she died young—maybe 24 or 25—leaving behind her son, Jean Baptiste.

I don't know which is true. Maybe neither. Like so much of history, it depends on who's telling the story. Among her people, she would have been known as Sacajawea—*j*, not *g*, as in SAK-uh-juh-WEE-uh, instead of sah-kah-gah-WAY-uh. But what I do know is this: Standing beside that roadside stone, next to Carmen, with the sun casting long shadows across the grass—I felt something. Not certainty. Not proof. Just... presence.

A few miles later, we pulled into a small roadside trading post. One of those places where the gas pumps are faded, the beadwork is handmade, and you're not sure what door leads to snacks and what door leads to stories. While I wandered the shop, Carmen disappeared down an aisle.

She returned with something small in her hand.

"I want to get this for you," she said.

It was a tiny bison fetish, carved from some kind of white stone—not quite alabaster, not quite marble. But what caught my eye were the ears, inlaid with bright turquoise, glinting like watchful eyes. It stood about an inch and a half tall. Sturdy. Dignified. Like it had always belonged in my hand.

In many Indigenous traditions, a fetish is more than a carving. It's a symbol of protection, spiritual connection, or guidance—believed to hold the spirit of the animal it represents.

"For your desk," she said simply. "To remind you."

She said it like that—like it was obvious. And maybe it was. She didn't say what it was meant to remind me of—the land, the journey, the people we were learning about, the weight of the past, or the promise of the road ahead. Or maybe all of it. Carmen never overexplains her gifts. She just knows.

I still keep that tiny bison on my desk. It watches over me while I write, while I work, while I remember.

The afternoon was slipping away, and we still had three hours of road ahead. We passed by Crowheart Butte, close enough to snap a picture, but not to stop. The terrain around us rose and folded like ancient cloth. One moment, we were watching the mountains rise; the next, they were all around us.

We'd entered the Shoshone National Forest. The highway followed the land's curves. Towering pines reached toward the sky. Massive stone cliffs jutted above the trees. And then—we saw them.

Our first look at the Grand Tetons.

Breathtaking.

They would be our silent sentinels, guiding us down into Jackson and to our campground nestled beside the Snake River.

thirty-two

I Lift Up Mine Eyes

In 2003, when my Granny, Sara Ton, died, I was bequeathed a treasure.

No, not a financial one. Truthfully, the money I inherited from her estate was just enough to buy a simple curio cabinet—the kind you hang on the wall. That cabinet hangs in my office today, and inside is a miniature museum of sorts: coins, bills, stamps, and keepsakes from our many Lewis and Clark adventures. But the real treasure was something far more fragile: a box of her papers—journals, notes, clippings, photographs, and a four-inch-thick, overstuffed scrapbook.

I combed through it like an archaeologist, like the researchers we saw at Fort Clatsop after the fire—carefully, reverently. There were lists of all kinds: U.S. states, presidents, and capitals. I couldn't help but wonder if Granny had been a lifelong *Jeopardy!* fan. Tucked among the pages was a newspaper clipping—a black-and-white photograph of a chapel with a handwritten caption below: The Chapel of the Transfiguration, Grand Teton National Park.

That was it. No date. No notes. No explanation. Just a photo she had cut out and saved.

Curious, I asked my mom why Granny had kept it. She didn't know. I asked my dad—after all, Granny was his mom.

"Probably just a picture she liked. I don't remember ever going there," he said.

Hmm. A mystery. Had she been there once, long ago? I know she and my grandfather had traveled the West in search of work before settling in Lead, South Dakota. But no one could answer the question now. No one alive, anyway.

The Chapel of the Transfiguration—that simple clipping—became the reason we routed through Wyoming on our way to Lewiston, Idaho, instead of the more direct route through Montana. It was the reason we chose this path west.

The drive from our campground to the chapel took less than 20 minutes—barely enough time to finish our to-go coffees. The morning greeted us with fluffy clouds drifting across a powder-blue sky, a breeze soft enough to feel like a welcome. The chapel stood quietly amid tall grass and sage, encircled by a weathered split rail fence. Nearby stood a small interpretive gazebo and a shed. It all felt humble. Grounded. Unassuming. Just like Granny.

The log church was built in 1925, and the Episcopal Church continues to hold services there every Sunday during the summer. My own relationship with the church is, to put it mildly, complicated. I'm a preacher's kid—a PK. Carmen, interestingly enough, is a TK—a teacher's kid. I grew up going to church three or four times a week. But by the time I was a young adult, I was questioning... well, everything. Over the years, I read dozens—hundreds—of books. The ones that resonated most came from John Shelby Spong, an Episcopalian bishop whose theology opened my heart without closing my mind.

After my divorce, I stopped attending church entirely. That was a point of friction with my mother, and years of her telling me why I should go to church—and perhaps my father, too, although he never mentioned it.

Carmen's own spiritual history had its complications. She spent her high school years at a Catholic girls' school, so everyone assumed she was Catholic. But her beliefs align closely with mine—though probably not quite as "new agey." Her spirituality is quieter, steadier, but deep.

When we stepped into the chapel, a silence fell over us. It was quiet—it was still. You could feel the hallowedness of the ground beneath your feet. We both drew in a breath at the same time. Call it what you want—the divine, the sacred, the Spirit—but something holy wrapped its arms around us as we crossed that threshold.

We've been in many churches. Some of the greatest cathedrals in the world, in fact. On our trips to Europe, we'd visited grand sanctuaries across Spain, France, Germany, and Italy. Carmen also studied church architecture while an exchange student in Mexico. The opulence, the grandeur, the sheer labor and wealth poured into those buildings—it was staggering. Palaces built to honor a God whose followers once said, "The God who made the world and everything in it ... does not live in temples made by human hands" (Acts 17:24 NIV). That's irony for the ages.

And yet, in that simple log chapel, we felt closer to the divine than we ever did in the gilded halls of St. Peter's—which, for the record, I wasn't even allowed to enter, because I dared to wear shorts.

At the front of the chapel stood a simple wooden altar, adorned with a modest cross flanked by two vases of fresh flowers. But what transfixed us was what stood behind the altar: a massive plate-glass window, nearly 20 feet wide, framing the Grand Tetons like a painting the earth itself had commissioned.

We stood in reverent silence, unable to look away. Mountains—sharp, snow-dusted, timeless—rose from the valley floor, lit by the morning sun. It was nature as stained glass. A cathedral carved not by human hands but by the slow, unrelenting movement of God's breath through time.

Carmen leaned in and whispered in my ear:

"Can you imagine attending church every week... and this is your view?"

We stayed there for a long moment, the only sound the creak of floorboards beneath our feet. Then, quietly, we stepped back out into the brilliant sunlight of a crisp June morning in Wyoming, grabbing a brochure near the door.

Was it a religious experience? No. It was something more profound. A spiritual moment. A connection across time and mystery.

Maybe Granny had been here. Maybe not.

But somehow, she had marked the way.

WHERE THE EARTH BREATHES

From the moment we left Grand Tetons National Park and entered Yellowstone through the South Entrance, it felt like we were crossing into a different world—one where Earth itself was still being formed.

The road followed the Yellowstone River, which wound its way through towering pine forests. Through the trees, we caught glimpses of snowcapped peaks in the distance, sunlight glinting off distant ridgelines. Carmen was quiet, sipping coffee, taking it all in with the wide-eyed wonder that still melts my heart. I glanced over and smiled. She caught me and smiled back.

"Look at that," she said, pointing out the window. The river carved its way between stands of pines, their green so deep it almost looked painted.

Not long after, we reached Fishing Bridge RV Park, our home for the night. The check-in building was rustic, classic Yellowstone. As I went through the paperwork, Carmen struck up a conversation with the ranger.

"Any bears around here?" she asked, trying to sound casual but already grinning.

The ranger leaned in slightly, voice lowered with a conspiratorial air.

"Actually, yes. We had some rummaging through the campground just last night. So... keep your eyes peeled. You just might get lucky."

Carmen's eyes lit up like a kid at Christmas. She looked at me, triumphant. "You hear that? Bears. Last night!"

We never did see one. Not a single bear. And if you ask her today—two decades later—she'll still roll her eyes and grumble about that ranger's false hope. "I was promised a bear," she'll say, half serious, half smirking.

But the disappointment didn't last long, because Yellowstone had other wonders in store.

After setting up camp, we hit the road again for an afternoon loop. Our first stop was a sulfur spring, bubbling and steaming against a backdrop of bleached earth and yellowed mineral deposits. The air was thick with the smell of sulfur—rotten eggs, Carmen declared cheerfully—and just beyond the spring, we spotted a bison, standing in the grass near the crusted earth. Its fur was matted with white mineral dust, making it look like some prehistoric beast forged in fire and salt.

We watched for a long while as it stood motionless, eyes blinking slowly, steam rising in gentle waves behind it.

Farther down the road, the terrain changed again. The air cooled. Pines gave way to open basins, and we entered the Upper Geyser Basin, home to one of the most famous landmarks in America.

Old Faithful.

Carmen and I stood close, shoulder to shoulder, next to a family with small kids and a ranger answering questions. There's something oddly communal about watching something so ancient and reliable. The crowd buzzed with anticipation.

Then—whoosh.

The geyser erupted, just as promised. A towering column of boiling water and steam burst skyward. The roar was low and primal, almost like the sound of wind in a canyon. For a moment, no one said anything. The water danced in the air, catching sunlight like crystal. Carmen squeezed my hand. I looked over. She was beaming.

"This is incredible," she whispered.

That evening, around our campfire at Fishing Bridge, Carmen pulled out the brochure from the Chapel of the Transfiguration. She began to read it aloud. It was nice to hear the history of the place—but even nicer to listen to her read it. It reminded me of those times on the river, when we'd take turns reading aloud as we drifted downstream.

She paused, then read: "I lift up my eyes to the hills—from where does my help come?" Chills ran down my spine.

Psalm 121. The same scripture quoted in *Unto These Hills*, the outdoor drama that first sparked my interest in the Cherokee Nation—way back in sixth or seventh grade.

Another connection.

thirty-three

Where the River Carved Time

We woke early, wrapped in the deep quiet of Yellowstone morning. Mist hung low over the trees as we pulled out of Fishing Bridge and began our second day of discovery.

Gone were the geysers and sulfur fields of yesterday. Today, it was all about water—crashing, churning, reshaping the land one drop at a time.

Our first stop was Upper Falls.

We stepped out onto the overlook and felt it before we saw it—the low rumble in your chest, the pressure of power. Then, the river. Calm, almost silent as it approached the edge. And then—sudden movement. It dropped violently over the cliff's edge, becoming a curtain of force. The water didn't just fall—it leapt. It threw itself into the canyon below, the mist rising in slow motion like breath exhaled by the earth.

Carmen stood beside me, her arms crossed, her eyes fixed on the drop.

"It's like time slows down at the edge," she said.

She was right. For that moment, it did.

Next came Lower Falls, even more dramatic. We walked to the Brink of the Falls overlook—close enough to feel the spray on our faces, to hear the roar fill the air around us. At the brink, the water almost pauses—like it's holding its breath. Then gravity takes over, and it plunges 308 feet into the canyon, violent and beautiful, defiant and sure.

We didn't speak much there. Sometimes, reverence doesn't need words.

Watching the river plunge over the brink, I found myself thinking back to a very different stretch of this same water. Just a year earlier, Carmen and I stood at Pompey's Pillar, where William Clark carved his name into the stone as he explored the Yellowstone on his return journey east.

And now, here we were again, standing along the Yellowstone, watching it cascade through canyons and centuries. What began for them as discovery had become, for us, something just as powerful: recognition.

The road carried us onward through the Grand Canyon of the Yellowstone—and I don't use *grand* lightly. The walls of the canyon blazed in yellow, rust, and ochre, carved out by centuries of river force. Pines clung to impossible slopes. The sky opened above us, blue and indifferent.

By late afternoon, we'd pushed farther north, finally reaching Mammoth Hot Springs. The formations there felt otherworldly—terraces of mineral and time. Water trickled down limestone ledges in slow ribbons, building and reshaping the landscape even as we watched. It felt like walking on the bones of the planet.

We didn't linger. We had miles to go before reaching Missoula, Montana, that night, but we both paused one last time to look back at the terraces, shimmering in the late light—still no bears.

On the road again, the mountains began to roll past us like memory, each curve taking us farther from Yellowstone but deeper into the story we were writing together—one uncharted moment at a time.

thirty-four

Where the Stories Begin

We left Missoula early, the RV humming along under a morning sky streaked with soft light. Our route would follow the Lolo Trail, or at least come close enough to use wheels and pavement. No horses. No snowshoeing. Just Route 12, curving along the Lochsa River, carrying us west toward Lewiston, Idaho, and the next Signature Event.

Driving the Lolo Trail in an RV isn't exactly how Lewis and Clark did it—but it's as close as we were going to get. The Corps traveled this stretch in 1805, and again in 1806 on their return, crossing some of the most unforgiving terrain of their journey. It nearly broke them. For us, the route was gorgeous—towering pines, rushing water, green hills pressing in on both sides. Even in summer, it felt wild. Untamed. You could almost hear hoofbeats and labored breathing on the wind.

Our first stop was the Powell Ranger Station, just across the border in Idaho. The building itself was modest, with weathered logs and a well-kept flag out front. Inside, we met an older couple who greeted us with warm smiles and stacks of pamphlets.

"We're just volunteers," they said, almost apologetically. "We man the station for you tourists."

We chatted for a while. They had a rhythm about them—playful jabs, knowing glances, a quiet way of working together. Carmen and I exchanged a look.

"That's us in 20 years," she whispered with a smirk.

"Speak for yourself," I replied. "I'll be the guy sleeping in the rocker while you run the place."

We all laughed. But the idea stuck with us. One day, maybe.

From Powell, we made a series of short stops—small signs marking the original trail, sometimes barely noticeable from the road. Carmen would squint out the window and say, "There's one!" and I'd pull over to get a closer look. These weren't grand monuments but simple acknowledgments of footsteps long gone.

We stopped at the DeVoto Memorial Cedar Grove, a hushed stand of ancient trees named after historian Bernard DeVoto. The moment we stepped into the grove, the temperature dropped. The air felt denser. More alive. The sunlight filtered through in quiet shafts. Carmen ran her fingers over the bark of a cedar tree and whispered, "This is what the world used to feel like."

Then came Heart of the Monster, a sacred site for the Niimiipuu, or Nez Perce, as we call them today. The legend tells of the monster slain by Coyote, whose body became the land itself. According to the Niimiipuu, this is where their people began. We stood before the rock formation in silence. We didn't fully understand the story, not in the way the Niimiipuu do. But we understood what it meant to honor the land, to feel the story woven into place.

It struck me then, standing at the base of that ancient stone, how sacred stories rise from the land itself. Just days before, we had stood in a quiet chapel framed by timber and stained pine, staring at the Tetons through a window of stillness. That felt holy. This did too—only this altar was shaped by myth and basalt, a place where a people say they began. But really, both altars were shaped by myth. It's just that one is written into church bulletins, and the other whispered from elder to child. One that the white man calls sacred. The other, he too often calls a legend. But here, in the silence, they felt like the same language.

Next was Weippe Prairie, where Lewis and Clark first encountered the Niimiipuu in 1805. The prairie stretched wide, gold, and open under the sun. It looked peaceful now, but I imagined how exhausted the Corps must have been when they arrived. How unsure. How much they relied on the generosity and guidance of the people they met here. We read every panel, took in every name.

We had first heard the name Niimiipuu back at Big Hole, standing in the wind on that hallowed ground. There, it had been a story of tragedy—an ambush, a battle, lives lost. But here, in the golden quiet of Weippe Prairie, it was something else entirely. This was where Lewis and Clark, more dead than alive after their harrowing crossing of the Bitterroots, met not with resistance but with kindness. The villagers had never seen white men before and were wary, even fearful. It might have ended in violence, if not for an elderly woman named Watkuweis, who stepped forward and said, "These are the people who helped me. Do them no harm." She had been kidnapped in her youth, lived among Native tribes and Canadian traders, and escaped with the help of "friendly whites" to return home with that memory. Her words changed everything.

Same people. Same story. Different chapters. And we were starting to understand just how layered this trail really was.

What followed was a bond of trust and mutual aid. The Niimiipuu welcomed the Corps into their village. They taught them how to speed up the carving of dugout canoes—setting fires on logs and then chipping out the charred wood—and agreed to care for their horses while the Corps traveled downriver to the Pacific.

In 1806, on the Corps' return journey, they again stayed with the Niimiipuu, waiting for the mountain snow to melt. Those weeks—of rest, of cultural exchange, of peace—are what the event we were heading to would honor. And it's why we came.

Finally, as the sun began to shift into late afternoon, we reached Clarkston, Washington, and our home for the next few days—a quiet RV park nestled at the confluence of the Snake and Clearwater Rivers. The light was golden. The water moved slow and deep. We had followed the trail west, and now we were where the rivers meet.

And like Lewis and Clark, we had stories to tell.

thirty-five

Where Paths Converge

After a good night's sleep at our RV site in Clarkston, we hopped in a rental car and headed west. I know, I know—we had just arrived. But sharp readers may recall that back in November, during our trip to Astoria, we had driven east as far as The Dalles. Today's plan? Head west from Clarkston and see just how close we could come to connecting the dots. Maybe not step for step, but close enough to satisfy that shared itch Carmen and I had to stitch the trail together in both directions.

It was gray. Cloud-cover gray. June-in-a-sweater gray. The kind of day where the sky is the same color as the river and everything feels quieter than usual. Carmen threw on one of her long cardigans, I layered up, and off we went.

Our first stop was at Lyons Ferry State Park, where the Palouse River meets the Snake. The Corps called it Drewyer's River—named after George Drouillard (they weren't always the most outstanding spellers), one of their best hunters and scouts. I loved that detail, that human touch. It wasn't "River X" or "Fork Y." It was Drewyer's River. Carmen looked out over the gentle confluence and said, "He must've been something special." He was.

Not far from there, we arrived at Sacajawea State Park, at the confluence of the Snake and Columbia Rivers. There's something deeply grounding about water meeting water. The two great rivers merged here just as two great journeys did—our own, and the one that brought us here.

From there, we drove west toward Hat Rock, crossing back over into Oregon near Umatilla. While we were tracing the expedition's eastward return, our wheels were still rolling westward for a bit longer. Hat Rock is one of the first landmarks Clark described as they made their way home in 1806. A basalt knob rising straight out of the landscape, it looks like something that should have its own story in Native myth. Carmen, of course, couldn't resist a little fun—she threw on a hat with a broad, flat crown and posed beside the formation. "It's me," she laughed. "Hat Rock." The resemblance was uncanny.

But nothing prepared us for Patit Creek. On a quiet hillside just outside Dayton, Washington, we pulled over to see what looked, at first, like shadows frozen in place. Behind a low fence, scattered across the grass, stood a camp scene in silhouette—iron sculptures of the Corps of Discovery, not marching or posing, but preparing camp. Some were gathering supplies. Others were tending to tasks. Sacagawea stood near the edge, Pomp on her back, surveying the scene like a mother who had seen it all before. The figures were arranged with care, as if caught mid-moment.

We stayed behind the fence, which somehow made it more reverent. Carmen stood with her hands on the fence rail, taking it all in. She didn't say much. I watched her face, the way she tilted her head just slightly, absorbing the weight of that place, the silence, the stillness. She didn't just see the history—she felt it.

And I thought, for maybe the hundredth time on this journey: *This is why I love her.*

That evening, back in Clarkston, we walked from the RV park to dinner. The sun was low, casting that golden-hour glow across the river. Carmen looped her arm through mine. We were talking about the drive, the wild beauty of the rivers, the iron sculptures standing watch over Patit Creek—when we noticed something under our feet.

There, embedded in the sidewalk at the marina, was a mural map of the entire Lewis and Clark Trail. Not a sculpture or a plaque—just a simple, hand-drawn path etched into the concrete. It traced the Missouri, the Yellowstone, the Mississippi, and the Ohio all the way to Pittsburgh. We paused for a long time, following the trail with our eyes, retracing it with our fingers.

"Look," Carmen said, pointing. "Falls of the Ohio. Cincinnati. St. Louis. Great Falls..."

We were standing where they stood. Or near enough. And now, we'd walked enough of this trail ourselves that we didn't need the legend to follow it. We knew where we were.

I snapped a picture—of the map, of her, of the sky going soft behind the hills. We smiled at each other, not saying much. But the ground beneath our feet had just whispered another reminder: This journey was still unfolding.

That night, back at the RV, the air was cool and quiet. We sat outside under a sky slowly losing its light, the hum of the rivers just a few hundred yards away. Carmen sipped her wine. I stared into the trees across the water.

I started to say something and then stopped.

She looked over. "What?" she asked softly.

"I was just thinking... I'm happiest when I'm on a river," I said. "But a close second is when I'm surrounded by mountains."

She nodded, knowingly. "And yet," I added, with a chuckle, "I live in flat-as-a-pancake Indiana."

She smiled at me over the rim of her glass. "Well, maybe that's why we chase these places."

Maybe it is. Maybe that's why the river stirs something in me, and the mountains feel like old friends. Maybe that's why this journey matters so much. Because it lets me step into those spaces that feel sacred—not because they're in a church or framed by stained glass, but because they remind me of who I am. Of what still moves me.

The rivers, the mountains... and this woman beside me.

Tomorrow, the ceremonies would begin. But tonight, the trail whispered a quiet truth: Sometimes, to feel most at home, you have to leave home far behind.

thirty-six
In the Heart of the Summer of Peace

The next day dawned—sort of. The sky was gray, the air heavy with drizzle, and rain fell in that quiet, persistent way that feels less like weather and more like a mood. The opening ceremonies for the Signature Event were being held outdoors near the visitor center of the Nez Perce National Historical Park. Of all the ceremonies we had attended so far on our journey, we were looking forward to this one the most.

Because this time, the Niimiipuu would not be a footnote here. They wouldn't be a side tent or a silent presence. They would be front and center.

Like many Indigenous peoples, the Niimiipuu are more widely known by a name given to them by outsiders. "Nez Perce" comes from French traders and means "pierced nose," a reference to nose ornaments worn by a small band within the larger nation. The name endured, even though they call themselves *Niimiipuu*—"The People." The program began, as most had, with the presentation of the colors—but even this was different here. The flags were carried not by military personnel in modern uniforms, but by Niimiipuu veterans dressed in traditional regalia. There was pride in their steps, a rhythm in the ground beneath us, and something in the air that felt old, sacred, and new all at once.

What followed was unlike anything we had seen: a horse regalia parade, set to the steady heartbeat of the Niimiipuu Nation Drummers; a vibrant welcome dance performed by the Niimiipuu dancers, full of color and story and joy; and finally, a circle dance, in which we all participated—visitors, locals, tribal members, volunteers. Strangers joined hands and moved as one.

We fully immersed ourselves in the moment. We danced. We listened. We felt.

I glanced at Carmen, and her eyes were already fixed on the dancers—soft, bright, and shimmering. The circle dance had moved something in her. I saw it in the way she held herself, the way she swayed just slightly, still in rhythm even after the music had stopped.

"That felt different," she said, not quite whispering.

I nodded. "Because it was."

But what caught our attention most was the Invitation to the Healing Conference. We'd heard about it in passing, but now we were listening closely. It would span two days during the Signature Event and culminate in the Healing Ceremony on Friday evening—held on a part of the Nez Perce Reservation that was not typically open to the public.

As soon as the invitation was offered, we looked at each other and nodded. No discussion necessary. We were going to the ceremony.

Later, as we walked back toward the car in the misty rain, she reached for my hand without saying a word. I didn't need her to. I could feel the weight of it—the meaning, the reverence.

We weren't just learning history out here. We were being invited into something much older, much deeper.

And she was walking beside me. She was helping me feel it. Name it. Carry it.

This is why I call her my co-captain. Not because she shares the road, but because she shares the heart of the journey.

We weren't going to miss that Healing Ceremony.

Not for anything.

WHERE THE RIVERS MEET

After the ceremony, we made our way to the confluence of the Snake and Clearwater Rivers. The rivers met here long before Lewis and Clark ever did. Long before the names Clearwater and Snake were printed on maps. And long before we knew to call this trip a pilgrimage. We were drawn to this spot by something we couldn't quite name—but would recognize when we saw it.

The sculpture stood quietly among trees and flowers, as if it had grown there. The Tsceminicum Sculpture was named after the ancient village that once occupied this sacred ground. It didn't shout. It didn't dazzle. It invited.

At first glance, it looked like a woman sitting on the Earth—calm, grounded, her long hair flowing back like it had caught the wind. But as you walked along the curve of the sculpture, you realized: She was the Earth. Her back and hair flowed seamlessly into the mountains, rivers, and forests that rose from her bronze form. Animals emerged from the textures—herons, bears, deer, salmon. You had to look closely; the stories were tucked into every curve and fold. You could see the land—and the life it holds.

Carmen slowly walked the length of the sculpture, hand brushing lightly against the surface. She paused by the heron and again at the salmon, her fingers tracing their outlines like reading Braille. I watched her take it in. That's one of the things I love most about her: She doesn't just visit places; she lets them leave a mark.

When she reached the heron, she lingered longer than anywhere else.

"Of course," I said quietly. "There you are."

The heron has followed us for years. On nearly every river we've paddled, one appears—just ahead, just off to the side. Always leading, always watching. Some people have guardian angels. We have a heron. To find one here, carved in bronze beside the rivers we'd followed west, was no coincidence. It was a reminder: You're on the right path. Keep going.

That stuck with me. Here we were, at the confluence of two rivers—and, in some ways, at the confluence of stories. Sacagawea's story. The story of the Niimiipuu. The story of a people still here, still watching, still telling. And now ours, too.

We lingered longer than we'd planned. The wind stirred the leaves. The rivers moved beside us. The bronze glowed warm in the morning light, like it knew we had come to listen.

On our way back from the sculpture at the confluence, we came across a simple historical marker tucked along a quiet stretch of trail. It read: "Lewis and Clark camped on the north bank of Lewis's (Snake) River, October 10, 1805."

We stood there a moment, rereading it, then looked out across the water—trying to get our bearings. We realized our RV was parked just across the river from where we stood.

Carmen let out a small laugh. "So... we might have slept where they camped?"

It was a surreal thought. We hadn't sought it out. We didn't make a pilgrimage to this specific point. But somehow, the trail had brought us here—right back to the ground where the Corps of Discovery lay their heads 200 years ago.

Not a grand destination. Not a dramatic overlook. Just a bend in the river. A place to pause, regroup, and press on.

RHYTHMS ETCHED IN STONE

After reading the marker and laughing about our accidental campsite on Lewis and Clark's "north bank," we took one last look at the river and crossed the bridge into Washington. The modern road carried us southward, but the land itself seemed to narrow and deepen—as if funneling us into something older, quieter.

We followed the Snake River as it carved its way through a dramatic basalt canyon, cliffs rising on either side like the walls of time itself. The further we drove, the fewer signs of the modern world we saw. No towns, no traffic. Just river, rock, and sky.

About 50 miles downriver, we pulled off into a small gravel parking area—Buffalo Eddy. Even the name felt mythic. We had come here to see the petroglyphs—ancient carvings left by people whose ancestors walked this land long before the Corps ever did. We stepped out of the car and into a silence that felt different. Heavier. More aware of itself.

It was the kind of place that didn't announce its importance—it just waited for you to notice.

A short walk brought us to the petroglyphs etched into black basalt boulders along the edge of the Snake. Unlike pictographs, which are painted, these were cut, chipped, and pecked into the stone itself. They weren't placed on the surface—they were pulled from it.

Some of the images were faint, worn soft by time and weather. Others were bold and clear—spirals, animals, hunting scenes, human forms with arms raised or outstretched. Carmen stopped at one that looked almost like a paddle or a rattle—maybe both. She traced the outline with her eyes, not touching, but feeling just the same.

We stood there for a long time. Not in silence out of reverence, but because there wasn't anything to say. This wasn't the story of 200 years ago. This was the story of thousands of years.

These carvings were made by the Niimiipuu. "The People." Because for thousands of years, in this land, they were *the people*. They needed no other name. This river was theirs. These hills were theirs. These stories, etched in stone, are theirs.

As we walked slowly along the rock face, Carmen reached for my hand. "You can feel them," she whispered.

And she was right. It was art. It was presence. These weren't relics or exhibits or artifacts behind glass. These were messages, left in the open, enduring long after the hands that carved them had returned to the soil.

I looked over at Carmen, the wind gently lifting a strand of her hair, and thought how she had become my guide in so many ways. Her reverence. Her heart. The way she opened herself up to these moments—whether in cathedrals or canyons. Whether at the Grand Tetons or at Buffalo Eddy.

Here, where the Snake carved its way through stone and the Niimiipuu carved their memories into it, we stood inside history.

DRUMS ACROSS THE DIAMOND

As the sun began its slow descent behind the canyon walls, we made our way back up the river toward Lewiston. The land softened as we drove—the cliffs gave way to open bends in the Snake, the sky stretched wider, and so did our anticipation. Not for food, this time—for music.

Our destination? The baseball field at Lewis-Clark State College. Not for a game, though; we were going to hear the drums.

They called it a "battle of the bands," but that hardly captured the weight of it. On one side of the diamond: the Niimiipuu Nation Drummers, seated in a circle on folding chairs, hands raised over taut hides, the pulse of the land pounding out in sync with the songs of their ancestors. On the other: the Old Guard Fife and Drum Corps, dressed in 18th-century Continental uniforms, fifes shrill and bright, snare drums snapping like musket fire.

It wasn't a competition. It was a conversation across time.

Thousands of years of oral tradition and heartbeat rhythm—and a few hundred years of military cadence and colonial march—echoing off the aluminum bleachers and grassy infield of a modern college baseball stadium.

We sat in the stands and let it wash over us—the raw vibration of the drum circle, the crisp order of the fife and drum, the applause of a modern audience. The songs weren't meant to be harmonized, and they didn't need to be. They coexisted—sometimes in tension, sometimes in sync. Like history itself.

Carmen reached over and squeezed my hand. Her eyes were glistening—not from the music, necessarily, but from the weight of the moment. Of everything we were witnessing. Of the contrasts... and the continuity.

That night, the past didn't perform for the present. It stood beside it. And we were lucky enough to be in the stands.

Later that evening, we sat outside the RV, bundled against the lingering chill, the sky overhead cloudless now and sprinkled with stars. The Snake flowed just out of sight beyond the trees, but we could still feel it—moving, steady, patient.

Carmen stirred the ice in her glass and leaned back in her chair, face lit by the quiet flicker of the campfire. Neither of us said much. The day had done the talking.

She glanced at me over the rim of her glass and smiled. That smile.

"This was only day one," I said softly, almost in disbelief.

She clinked her glass gently against mine. "Yup."

thirty-seven
When Stories Move

The skies were still moody that morning, as if the weather couldn't decide whether to clear up or lean into the weight of the stories being told. We headed to Lewis-Clark State College, which had become one of the central gathering points for the Signature Event. This day's events weren't flashy or dramatic—no cannons, no parades. This was a quieter kind of truth-telling.

On campus, we visited a statue depicting the first meeting between Lewis, Clark, and the Niimiipuu. Bronze figures frozen in a moment that carried the weight of centuries. Carmen stood there for a long time, tracing the outlines with her eyes, her brow furrowed in thought. "They make it look so... simple," she finally said. And she was right. One handshake can't capture what really passed between the Corps and the Niimiipuu. Not the suspicion, not the hope. Not the fear. Not the generosity.

Inside one of the buildings, we wandered through the Quilt and Hide Show—cultural expressions stitched, scraped, and painted with purpose. Some of the hides told hunting stories, while others carried symbols I didn't understand but felt nonetheless. The quilts were radiant, a fusion of old traditions and modern forms.

Carmen lingered over a buffalo design stitched in deep reds and golds. "You know," she said, "when women create art like this, they're telling their tribe's stories without speaking a word."

Later that afternoon, we caught three short films. Each one peeled back another layer of the expedition's legacy—not as triumph or discovery, but as rupture and survival. I glanced over at Carmen during one of the interviews, and her eyes were glassy. We were both starting to understand: the Summer of Peace was a pause for Lewis and Clark. But it was a turning point for the Niimiipuu, a pivot between their world and a storm they didn't yet see coming.

The final session of the day was a talk by Allen Pinkham. His presence filled the room before he even said a word. A respected Niimiipuu elder, Pinkham was a direct descendant of Chief Joseph—*the* Chief Joseph. And, according to tribal oral tradition, he also had ancestral ties to William Clark. It struck me like a thunderclap. Two legacies bound in one man.

Here he stood—living proof that history doesn't just echo. Sometimes, it collides.

He spoke not in anger, but with gravity. He spoke of broken treaties and buried stories. Of survival, not as a footnote, but as a legacy. Of the long road from Weippe Prairie to now. And when he talked about the Summer of Peace, it didn't sound like a pause in a journal. It sounded like a fragile miracle. And maybe, just maybe, the beginning of something that's still unfolding.

As we walked back to the car, Carmen was quiet for a long time. Then she said, "I hope that when Allen Pinkham looks in the mirror, he sees more than a bridge between two worlds. I hope he sees the whole river."

We weren't quite ready to call it a day.

THE DANCE THAT LINGERS

We concluded the day at the Lewiston Civic Theatre with a performance titled *Enduring Spirit: Dance of Two Nations*. I still have the program, tucked in with our other keepsakes from the trail. Twenty years later, that folded piece of paper resurfaced, whispering something I must've needed to hold on to, even if the memory itself has faded.

The performance unfolded in three acts.

The first was "Zephyr"—a breath of wind, a suggestion of something larger. It told of a young nation rising, blind to the land it claimed and the spirits it ignored.

The second act, "Tempest," carried a storm. Movements grew sharper, more insistent. The ties between the people and the land were asserted with force and pride, even as forays from the old world crashed ashore in the new.

And then came the third act—"Time." The wind and the storm gave way to the relentless flow of time. Lands were reshaped, reconfigured, reserved.

I don't know why I kept that program all these years. Maybe because something in the performance bypassed my intellect and went straight to the soul. Perhaps because it echoed what Carmen and I were feeling that whole day—that history is never still. It dances.

And sometimes, even when you don't remember all the steps, your body knows it was part of the rhythm.

ECHOES IN THE EMBERS

Back at the RV, we lit a small fire and settled into our camp chairs, bundled in sweatshirts, cocktails in hand. The air was cool, the sky soft with stars. The program from *Enduring Spirit* rested in my lap.

I handed it to Carmen.

She flipped through it slowly, scanning the titles of each act. "Zephyr." "Tempest." "Time." She nodded. "Sounds like our trip."

I laughed. "Or life."

We were quiet for a while. The fire popped and hissed. The Snake River moved just out of sight, steady and unseen.

Then I said, almost to myself, "You know, I've been thinking… about the divide. The Indigenous people were part of the land—woven into it. The statue we saw yesterday—the woman woven into the earth—it wasn't about power. It was about connection. That's the way they see the world."

Carmen sipped her drink, listening.

"But we—white people, Europeans—we came from fairy tales that taught us to fear the forest. The wilderness was something dark. Untamed. And our scriptures told us we had dominion over all of it. It was ours to control, to use, to bend to our needs."

She looked into the fire, then turned to me. "And now we're trying to unlearn it. To hear the stories we weren't told. That's why we're here, right?"

I nodded, eyes on the flames.

Carmen reached over and laced her fingers through mine.

"We're listening now," she said.

The fire crackled again. The river whispered nearby. And we sat there, in the glow of a long day, feeling the gravity of everything we'd witnessed—not just today, but across generations.

And somehow, it felt like we were exactly where we were supposed to be.

thirty-eight
When It Was Time to Go

Friday morning the Summer of Peace Village opened like a circle you're invited to step into: tipis staked in a ring, woodsmoke lifting, drumbeats steady as breath. Children chased stick-and-ball games through the grass; elders watched from folding chairs; hands worked rawhide, bead, and willow. It wasn't spectacle. It felt like a place remembering itself.

This is how I imagine Long Camp, 1806—the Niimiipuu sheltering the Corps near today's Kamiah, Idaho, while the snow held the mountains shut. Two months of pause and exchange: camas root and koos-koos bread traded across fires; foot races and games; a violin pulled down at dusk; Clark tending sickness; knowledge passed hand to hand that would carry the travelers east. We sat for a while and let the village do the teaching. Peace here wasn't signed or staged; it was practiced— children laughing, a drum holding time, neighbors working side by side. When we finally stood to go, I felt the shape of that season settle in: not an event to check off, but a way of being together long enough to be changed.

We drove back to our RV in silence. We'd been on our feet most of the day—walking, listening, taking it all in—and frankly, we were wiped. The couch inside our home-on-wheels had never looked so inviting. We didn't even talk about it; we just collapsed. Carmen stretched out with a sigh, and I sat down beside her, shoes off, eyes closed. Within minutes, we were asleep.

AN UNCHARTED MOMENT, A SPIRITUAL MOMENT

I woke up groggy and disoriented. The kind of nap that leaves a line across your cheek and time slightly out of joint. Outside, rain tapped on the roof—soft, persistent, annoying.

"Dammit," I muttered. "Of course."

We were supposed to attend the Healing Ceremony—outdoors. In a field. On the reservation. One of the only times that land would be open to non-tribal members. I had been looking forward to it since the opening ceremony. And now? Rain. Rain had already threatened to derail so many moments on this trip. I was tired, damp, and irritable—and more than a little tempted to bail.

Carmen, on the other hand, just shrugged and pulled on her jacket.

"We're going," she said, calm as ever. "Spalding's 20 minutes away. Might not be raining there. Let's just go. Who knows?"

I started to object, but then I looked at her—the stubborn set of her shoulders, the optimism in her eyes. She had made up her mind. And to be honest, I trusted her instinct more than I trusted the weather.

So, off we went.

As we climbed the ridge, the light began to change. It was subtle at first—a crack in the clouds, a brightness warming the dashboard. Then Carmen pointed. "Look."

A rainbow had formed, brilliant and low on the horizon.

We followed it as we drove east. And I swear to you, the closer we got to Spalding, the more it felt like we were chasing the tail of something divine. The rainbow wasn't off to the side. It was ahead of us—arched like a gateway to the very place we were headed.

By the time we arrived, the rain had stopped entirely. The clouds pulled back like curtains, revealing a sliver of blue. We parked and made our way to the field—an open stretch of land that, under normal circumstances, we would not be allowed to enter. It was Niimiipuu land, sacred and private. But today, we were being invited in.

There wasn't a formal path—just a fence line and a few loose strands of wire, held up by wooden posts. We climbed carefully through, along with maybe 30 or 40 others. Some were murmuring, others just standing in the tall grass, hands in their pockets, looking up at the sky like it still might have something left to say.

The grass was knee-high and damp. The wind was soft. You could hear the birds. No stage. No microphones. Just a circle forming slowly in the field—people coming together, quietly, reverently, under a rainbow, in the middle of what used to be off-limits ground.

I stood there, next to Carmen, jacket half-zipped, heart wide open.

And I realized: I had almost missed this.

Not the ceremony—this. The feeling of stepping into something ancient, something intentional. Something healing. Not planned, but placed.

We were exactly where we were meant to be.

The circle slowly filled in. We weren't given chairs, but no one seemed to mind. We stood there, in the middle of that sacred field, the rainbow now just a whisper behind us. The ceremony began not with fanfare or music, but with the quiet approach of an elder.

He moved slowly, taking measured steps and maintaining a deliberate presence. He wore a hat adorned with a single feather, with long gray hair resting gently on his shoulders. He reminded me instantly of Chief Dan George in *The Outlaw Josey Wales*. Dignity in every movement. Wisdom in every line of his face.

When he spoke, it wasn't with theatrical volume or practiced cadence. He spoke softly. Honestly. As if the land itself was listening.

"You are standing on hallowed ground," he began. "Not because of what's happening here today, but because of what happened here long before."

He turned slightly and gestured behind him.

"That tree," he said. "That is the whipping tree."

The words dropped into the circle like stones into still water. A murmur moved through the group. Carmen reached for my hand.

"That is where they tied us," he continued, "when we spoke our language. When we prayed in the way of our people, that is where they whipped us—to make us Christian. To make us white."

He wasn't angry, at least not in the way we often think of anger. He was telling the truth, not seeking pity, just letting it hang there, as it deserved to. I looked at the tree. Just a tree. And yet... not.

He spoke for maybe 10 or 15 minutes. About the missionaries. About the pain. About the Spaldings, who arrived in the 1830s to bring the Word of God to the Niimiipuu—though they, of course, called them "Nez Perce." Henry and Eliza Spalding were the first white settlers to build a permanent home among the Niimiipuu. They translated the Bible into Niimiipuu. They baptized. They "civilized." And, as we'd just heard, they punished. They whipped. They enforced silence.

But here's the bitter twist: The Spaldings were also among the first to document the culture they were trying to erase. To love and to wound, all in the same breath. History's cruelty wrapped in irony.

When the elder stepped back, silence followed. No applause. Just the wind rustling the grass and the quiet weight of bearing witness.

Then, another man approached the center. This one in a dark suit and white shirt. No beadwork, no braids, no fringe—just straight, buttoned-up formality. Carmen leaned over and whispered, "Preacher." I nodded. The man didn't speak immediately. He unfolded a single sheet of paper and began to read.

It was a letter.

A letter of apology.

Not a personal one—but a collective one. An official, signed document from the heads of the major Christian denominations in the United States. A letter apologizing to the Niimiipuu for the harm inflicted in the name of God. For the beatings. The assimilation. The attempted erasure of language and culture. The sins of conversion by force.

He read it slowly, carefully, like each word mattered. Because it did.

And when he finished—when he folded the letter and looked up—no one moved.

A gasp. A few audible sobs. Carmen pressed her sleeve to her cheek. My own eyes stung, and I couldn't even tell you why. The truth of it all had landed like thunder in our chest.

There was no benediction. No declaration of "Now we are healed." Just a circle of humans, standing in a field once forbidden, trying to hold the past and the future in the same breath.

Sometimes healing doesn't look like a miracle.

Sometimes it looks like a man in a feathered hat pointing at a tree.

Sometimes it sounds like a preacher saying *I'm sorry*.

And sometimes it feels like standing next to the woman you love, hand in hand, in the middle of a field, beneath a sky that finally made space for light.

After the final words were spoken and the circle gently dissolved, we slipped through the wire fence and made our way back to the car. No one rushed. No one needed to speak. It was as if something sacred had passed through us, and we were still vibrating from the current.

REFLECTIONS ON THE RIVER

Back at our RV, we moved like people in a trance—setting up the chairs, lighting the campfire, mixing our evening cocktails. Carmen was still quiet. So was I. There wasn't much to say that the tears hadn't already said for us.

We sat by the river—the place where the Snake and Clearwater come together. It had become our own quiet sanctuary over the last few nights. The sun had set, but the river was still glowing in places, reflecting the slow shimmer of the lighted boats beginning their parade. Reflections on the River, they called it.

The name felt... right.

As the boats drifted past, their lights dancing in the water like fireflies on a pilgrimage, we both found ourselves staring at the place where the rivers met. It was beautiful—it was powerful. Visibly, audibly powerful. You could feel it.

Two distinct flows. Two different paths. Two journeys, colliding— merging—becoming something more.

We were mesmerized by it. By the exponential force created when two rivers meet. How each one keeps its identity, its memory, its origin... and yet, together, they become something else entirely. Bigger. Stronger. Deeper.

I reached over and took Carmen's hand.

We didn't talk about the parade. Or the elder's words. Or the letter. Not then.

Instead, somewhere in the silence between us, we made a decision.

We would leave in the morning.

No closing ceremony could follow what we had just experienced. No speech or pageantry could touch the ache, the hope, the resonance we felt standing in that field.

It was time. The map listed a hundred side trips. The compass—hers and mine—pointed east.

thirty-nine
Where the Past Lives

We packed up quietly that next morning, the Granite Lake RV Park slowly coming to life around us. The soft hum of generators, the clink of coffee mugs, the shuffle of neighbors preparing to hit the road. But for us, it felt like a farewell.

We rolled onto Highway 12, the Snake River shimmering off to our left, and there they were—the first of the sculptures. Steel figures—larger than life—emerging from the shoulder of the road like ghosts of history. Niimiipuu women and children, hunters and horses, woven into the landscape as if they'd always been there. Carmen sat quietly for a moment, then simply said, "They're watching over this place." I couldn't have said it better.

Just up the road, another metal art installation came into view. We pulled off to the shoulder, stepping out for a better look. This one was unlike anything we'd seen before—circles of silvery hoops surrounding a figure with arms raised to the sky. Animals—fish, birds, elk—cut in silhouette, circling in motion. A prayer in metal. A spirit lifted skyward.

"Look," Carmen whispered, pointing to the heron etched in one of the circles. Our guide. Always with us.

We didn't speak much as we climbed back into the RV. The weight of the week—the Healing Ceremony, the stories, the sorrow and the strength—wasn't something you shake off like dust. It settles into your skin, your breath, your bones.

Just after crossing the Clearwater River, we took a detour up a bluff on the north side. We parked and walked to the edge, looking back at the confluence—the Clearwater flowing into the Snake. Two rivers becoming one. We stood there in silence, watching the currents merge, the water folding into itself like pages of a book. I don't know why, but I took Carmen's hand, not squeezing it, just holding.

A few minutes later, we were back on the road, heading up Highway 95 toward Coeur d'Alene and the long stretch of I-90 that would eventually carry us home. But a part of us stayed behind. Right there on that bluff, at that confluence, in those sculptures, in the echoes of drums and laughter and tears. A piece of us would always remain.

That night's drive was a long one. One of those stretches where we took turns behind the wheel, pushing east on I-90 through the falling dusk and into the dark. We weren't aiming for a destination so much as we were chasing the feeling of the road—the quiet hum of tires on pavement, the familiar shuffle of snacks being unwrapped, Carmen thumbing through the map by the dim glow of the dash lights. Somewhere in Montana, we pulled into a rest stop or a truck plaza. It doesn't matter where, not really. Just two travelers curled up in the RV, the hum of passing semis outside our windows, the weight of the last few days still settling in our bones. We were heading home, but not quite.

The road still had more to show us.

WE DID NOT CLIMB THIS ONE

Sunday dawned bright and clear—Father's Day, and one of those crisp mornings that feel like a clean slate. The kind of day that makes you believe in fresh starts and wide skies. We were somewhere in Wyoming now, turning off the interstate toward our first stop: Devils Tower. That hulking column of volcanic stone rising out of the earth like it was trying to reach the heavens.

As we neared the entrance, a lone prairie dog stood sentinel in the middle of a field, upright on his haunches, puffed chest out, barking our arrival. Carmen laughed, "Well, I guess we're expected." I saluted him, naturally.

According to Lakota legend, Devils Tower was formed when a group of children were chased by a giant bear. To protect them, the Great Spirit raised the ground beneath their feet into the sky. The bear clawed at the sides, leaving deep gouges in the rock, but couldn't reach them. The children were lifted into the heavens, becoming the stars of what we call the Pleiades. We thought about that story as we stood before it, gazing up at the massive striated walls—claw marks frozen in time. Another sacred place. Another reminder that stories—whether told in rock, in wind, or around campfires—are how we come to know the land, and maybe even ourselves.

We didn't climb to the top of this rock. Devils Tower, sacred to many, felt like a place to stand beside, not conquer. After walking the grounds, reading the stories, and letting the hush of the place work its way into our bones, we got back on the road.

WHERE THE EARTH WEARS ITS BONES

This time, we exited I-90 at a familiar spot—Wall, South Dakota. Yes, home of Wall Drug. We'd been through before, and probably would again. But today wasn't about free ice water or five-cent coffee. Today was Father's Day. And my father was born in Lead, South Dakota, not far from here. Somehow, driving the Badlands Loop Road felt like the right way to honor him. To celebrate all the fathers, really—those who came before, and those walking the road now.

The Badlands are something else. You don't just look at them; you feel them. Like the moon dropped down to earth and unfurled its ribs. Eroded spires, ridges, and folds of earth that seem alien, and yet deeply rooted. Dusty pinks and ghostly whites, striated like the pages of a very old book. Carmen called it "beautiful in a strange kind of way." She was right. Surreal. Haunting. Holy.

We paused at one overlook, staring across a canyon of cracked stone and silence. "It looks like Mars," I said. But here on this planet, in this place, we were driving across land sacred to the Lakota and other Indigenous nations of the Plains. This wasn't some forgotten wasteland—it was part of the heartland. The Black Hills, rising to the west, are called Paha Sapa by the Lakota, the center of their world. The Badlands were not far from that center.

We rolled through slowly, windows down, the dry wind wrapping around us. Every turn offered a new view—each one starker, stranger, more awe-inspiring than the last. It was a drive of stillness and magnitude. A moment to be quiet, to remember where we were, and where we'd come from.

By the time we exited the park on the other side, we were humbled by it. Humbled by the Earth's power to shape and reshape itself over eons. Humbled by the stories we'd barely begun to understand. Humbled by how small we are, and how connected.

And so, we proceeded on.

YUP

Our next stop was supposed to be a brief one. A waypoint on the way home. We knew from my grandmother's journals that she grew up on a farm about four miles northwest of Randolph, Nebraska—or maybe it was four and a half miles northeast of McLean. Somewhere in that stretch of Pierce County. I had two photographs of the old farmhouse. One was taken in 1912 by a traveling photographer—my great-grandmother and the children all standing solemn and proud in front of the home. The other was from the 1980s, when Granny returned for a funeral and made a quiet pilgrimage back to the farm. That second photo, grainy and faded, lived tucked away in a folder, more memory than map.

This was back before you could Google Earth your way to anything, before AI could stitch your past together for you. So, before our trip, I did the analog thing: I called the Randolph library.

"The old Hickey place?" the woman on the phone said. "Oh, I'm sorry. That was torn down years ago. But you should still come. Maybe visit the cemetery."

Disappointed but undeterred, we drove south out of Yankton into Nebraska, crossing the wide-open land on Highway 81. Somewhere past the Pierce county line, Carmen pulled out the atlas—yes, an actual paper atlas. She traced her finger across the grid and said, "Well, if it's four miles northwest of Randolph and four and a half miles northeast of McLean, it should be... right about here."

She pointed to the east just as we crested a rise, and there it was.

The farmhouse. Still standing.

Not much to look at—abandoned, run down, swallowed up by weeds—but unmistakably there. We pulled off the road, changed into boots and jeans, and made our way across the brush. No door. Just an open invitation.

We climbed the steps and stepped inside.

I stood there, frozen. I was standing in the room where my grandmother was born. In the house my great-grandfather built. A wave of emotion swept through me so strong I could hardly breathe. Carmen stood beside me, one hand on my back, silent. Just... there. Holding space. Holding me.

We wandered the property. The barn—barely standing—was still in use. Modern farm equipment sat inside, like ghosts of a new generation had moved in with no idea who came before. Someone was using the land. Someone still called it home, in a way.

Back in the RV, I stared down the gravel road. "I think that's the right place," I said, "but the picture's so grainy, it's hard to be sure. We'll ask at the next house."

So we pulled into the next farm. Long gravel drive, house at the end, barns to the side. As we got close, a German Shepherd bounded toward us, full speed, ears back and bark forward. I reached for the door.

"You shouldn't get out," Carmen warned.

"I have to," I said.

I stepped down into the heat of a Nebraska afternoon—must've been 900 degrees—and just then, a big ol' Bubba of a man came waddling out of the house, wiping his hands on his jeans. He didn't say a word.

"I'm sorry to bother you," I said. "Just one question and we'll be on our way." Still nothing.

"Is that the old Hickey place across the road?"

"Yup," he said. A man of many words.

"That's so cool," I replied, smiling. "My great-grandfather built that place."

He extended a hand and nodded. "That's interesting. So did mine."

Turns out, his grandmother and my grandmother were sisters. Somewhere along the way, the families lost touch. Stories that should've been shared got shelved. But now—two great-grandsons, standing in a gravel driveway—those threads were tugging loose from time and tying themselves back together.

"Well," he said, grinning, "you oughta come inside and meet my wife."

I looked back at our RV. Carmen stepped out—my beautiful, blond-haired, blue-eyed wife—and we walked up the porch steps together.

Inside, we were greeted by his beautiful, blond-haired, blue-eyed wife. Also named Carmen.

You can't script that. You can't plan for that. You just open your eyes, open your heart, and let the moment land.

HOMEWARD BOUND

Going back is still a kind of going on.

The drive home was quiet, not because we were tired—though we were—but because we were full.

This trip had been planned as one more leg in our journey to follow the Lewis and Clark Trail. But like so many times before, the trail had a way of turning into something more. It had taken us from the Pacific Ocean to the sacred dance of two nations, from river ceremonies to roadside revelations. From the distant myths of the Niimiipuu to the dusty truth of our own family tree.

And now, as we followed the highway east, it was hard not to feel the pull of home—but also the shift inside ourselves. Something had changed.

We watched the miles slip by in the rearview mirror—Badlands and buttes, canyons and confluences, healing fields and quiet cemeteries. We didn't speak much. The soundtrack was soft, the road was smooth, and Carmen's hand was resting gently in mine. The tiny stone bison rode my pocket as the miles unspooled.

There would be one more trip. More stories to tell. More moments to find. But for now, we simply drove. Hearts full. Spirits steady. Stories deepened.

And home—just over the horizon.

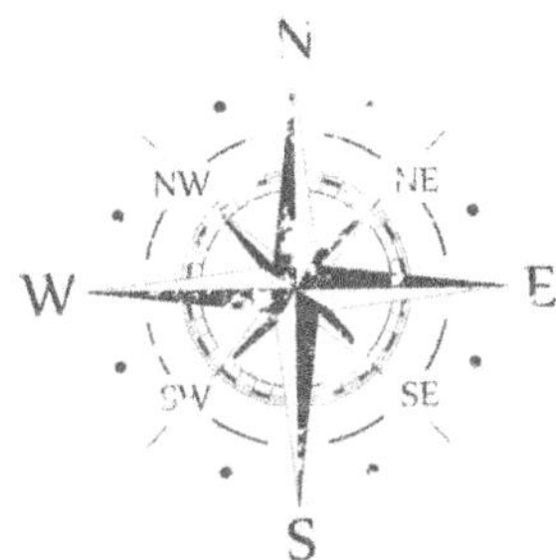
N
NW
NE
W
E
SW
SE
S

What Do You Do When It's Over?

Even endings, it turned out, had echoes.

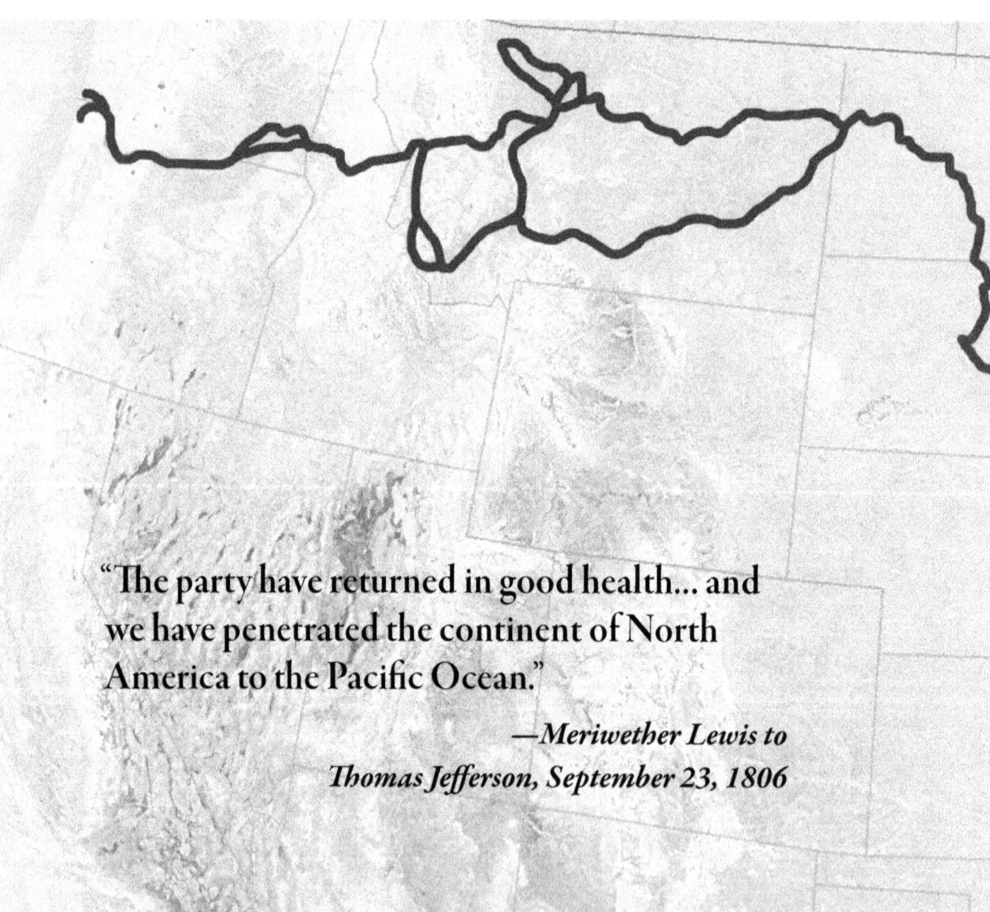

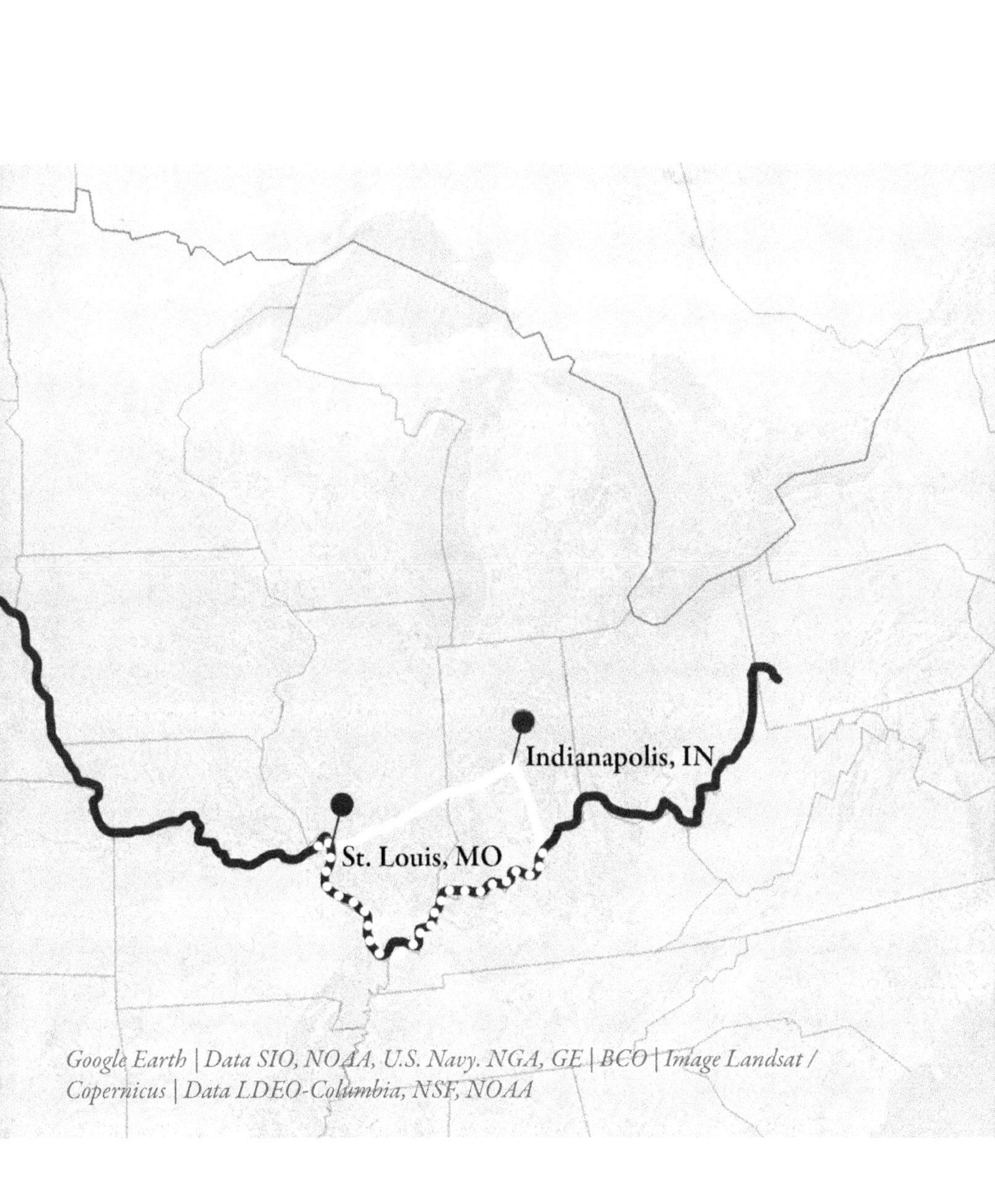

Indianapolis, IN
St. Louis, MO
Google Earth | Data SIO, NOAA, U.S. Navy. NGA, GE | BCO | Image Landsat /
Copernicus | Data LDEO-Columbia, NSF, NOAA

forty
The Road Back

Some journeys are circles. Others are rivers.

This one? It was both.

We drove from Indianapolis to Clarksville at the crack of dawn. It was still early when we left Clarksville, tracing the river south and west, staying near the water whenever the roads allowed. The sun burned through a skin of haze and turned the Ohio into a silver ribbon beside us. Carmen reached across the console and rested her hand on mine—no words, just that gentle press that says everything.

Looking back, I can say what I didn't know to call it then: We weren't just following their route—the road was teaching us our own.

We were tracing the expedition's early route from Clarksville to Camp River Dubois as we made our way to commemorate their return. When our journey had begun a couple of years earlier, we'd skipped the route going southwest along the Ohio River and up the Mississippi in the interest of time. Now we skipped I-70 for the Ohio River Scenic Byway.

Somewhere in that gentle forward motion, a question surfaced.

It had been two years since that night in the tavern—the last open table, sweaty and tired, clinking glasses with two women we'd met on the bus. One of them—smiling over her ice-cold beer—had looked me in the eye and asked: "So, what will you do when all this Lewis and Clark stuff is over?" It had hit like a paddle to the face. Not because it was cruel. Because it was a valid question.

This journey had become more than a curiosity or a shared project. It was the rhythm of our days, pointing us toward meaning, toward each other, toward something we didn't yet have words for.

Even now, with the reenactors days from marching back into St. Louis—flags high, drums low—I didn't have a better answer than I did that afternoon.

It's never really over.

That's what I'd said then. That's still what I believed—maybe more than ever.

Carmen looked out the window, watching the trees slip by in a blur of green and gold. "I think we're close to Metropolis," she said softly, pointing ahead.

Just like that, we were back in the moment. Back on the trail, in the southern end of Illinois. We didn't have language for it yet—the next day we'd hear the Osage speak of the Children of the Middle Waters—but the rivers were already teaching us to listen.

That question from Atchison hadn't just lingered; it had taken up residence.

For six years, this journey had consumed my life, from my one-room apartment in 2000, the walls covered in maps and charts, to launching the real journey with Carmen in 2002 with the mailing of a postcard. The Corps of Discovery wasn't a historical footnote; it was a lifeline. A mirror. A map. I had followed Lewis and Clark's footsteps so faithfully I'd started to feel like I knew them. And through them—through letters, losses, and that dogged press into the unknown—I'd come to know myself, too: that I listen better when the river is talking than when I am, and that partnership—not prowess—is how I want to travel. Carmen's hand stayed on mine; we kept to the slower road.

But now, they were finishing. They were coming home.

So what did that mean for us?

Was this the final page of our chapter, too? Would we close the book and fold back into everyday life? Was the trail fading behind us—or would it keep stretching forward into whatever came next?

I didn't say any of that out loud. I just gripped the wheel a little tighter, watching the river reappear between the trees.

Carmen must've felt the shift in me—she always does. She didn't try to fix it; she leaned back, her hand still warm on mine, and let me drift.

Only—it didn't feel like the end. It felt like a handoff. The chorus quieting so a new verse could begin—not louder, just deeper.

We had miles to go still that day. Forts to visit. Ceremonies to witness.

But somewhere on that quiet stretch of river road, before Fort Massac, the feeling clarified—not closure, but carrying. The river breathed a thin mist off the rocks, and I loosened my grip on the wheel.

And no, we weren't finished. Not even close.

Because it wasn't just about the trail. It never had been. It was about us—about the life we were building, mile by mile, site by site, story by story.

These journeys had become our rhythm. Our sabbatical. Our church pews were driftwood and trail benches; our hymns the wind in the cottonwoods, the hush of museum halls, the laughter over camp coffee. I didn't name it that then; I see it clearly now—we weren't just exploring history. We were making it. Together.

I thought back to the early days, when it started. Carmen hadn't grown up dreaming about Lewis and Clark, but she believed in me. Somewhere between Missouri River overlooks and muddy pull-offs, it became her story, too.

I watched her now, taking it in as we drove—never demanding the spotlight, steady and luminous. She was the one who remembered the extra jackets, asked the right questions, noticed the unmarked graves and the wildflowers others walked past. She helped me see what I might've missed—on the trail, and in myself.

We weren't finishing anything. We were becoming something. This journey hadn't been a detour—it had been the map.

And with every mile, I was more certain: If the Corps had each other... I had her.

The road pulled us forward.

WHERE THE TRACKER JOINED... AND SO DID SHE

The trees began to thin as we neared Metropolis, and the river seemed to settle beside us—steady, familiar, and quiet. This was our first visit to

Fort Massac, though by now it felt like a place we'd long been meant to find—its story already stitched into ours.

This was where George Drouillard joined the Corps.

Half Shawnee, half French Canadian, Drouillard was their tracker—their scout, their interpreter, their quiet strength. He read the landscape in ways no one else could. He didn't need to lead from the front. He simply saw—and that changed everything.

As we stepped through the reconstructed fort, the wooden timbers rising in silence around us, I found myself thinking less about history and more about Carmen.

Over the years, she had become my own kind of Drouillard. Not in buckskins or with a rifle slung over her shoulder, but with an uncanny ability to see the path I didn't know I was walking.

My career had been taking off—promotions, recognition, new ideas finding traction. Outwardly, it looked like I was navigating well. Executing. Leading. But so many of the turns I took, the risks I embraced, the confidence I projected—they came from her. From long conversations at the kitchen table. From her questions. From her belief in me when I couldn't quite believe in myself.

She had a way of uncovering pieces of me I didn't know existed. Like a tracker reading signs in the underbrush, she could spot potential where I only saw uncertainty. And more than once, it was her quiet insight that changed everything.

The Corps found their guide here at Fort Massac.

And somewhere along this journey, I had found mine.

That night, we camped in the state park surrounding the fort—under tall trees and a sky full of stars. We felt one with the expedition... though our accommodations were much more comfortable than the replica beds we had seen in the fort.

forty-one

Where Rivers Join

The next morning, we followed the river south and west, the Ohio on our left, winding steadily toward its final destination. Carmen navigated while I drove, the silence between us full but easy.

As we approached Cairo, the land flattened and opened up. Bridges arched overhead like ribs, crossing from Illinois into Kentucky, and again toward Missouri. The rivers began to stretch wider, as if preparing themselves for reunion.

We parked near Fort Defiance—just a trace of earthwork now, a whisper of its former presence—but it was never about the fort. It was about the place.

The confluence.

Where the Ohio meets the Mississippi in a broad, muddy embrace. Where fresh water and memory collide. Where one journey ends, and another begins.

We stood at the edge for a long while, side by side, watching the rivers meet.

The confluence of the Ohio and the Mississippi isn't dramatic—not like the cliffs of the Missouri Breaks or the thunder of Yellowstone Falls. It's quiet. Unhurried. Two wide rivers easing toward one another, their currents mingling in a slow, inevitable dance.

And yet, the power here is unmistakable.

This isn't just where two rivers meet. It's where they change. The Ohio doesn't simply pour into the Mississippi. It becomes part of it. And the Mississippi, already mighty, is reshaped by the joining.

I looked at Carmen, her hair lifted gently by the breeze off the water. With her hand in mine, our paths stopped running parallel and simply ran together.

It wasn't just companionship. It wasn't just love. It was transformation. I was more me because of her. She gave shape to my current, gave direction to my drift. Together, we didn't just flow—we surged. We carved new canyons. We carried more than we ever could alone.

She was learning to trust that I wasn't going anywhere—the long-haul kind of staying that turns miles into a life. I was learning to own who I am—part geek, part empath—and to step forward without apology. On the road, it looked ordinary—river road over interstate, unmarked graves and wildflowers brought into focus—but back home, it showed up louder: I walked into rooms I used to avoid and spoke like I belonged. Together, we bent the river.

That's what the trail had become for us. A map of our merging. A geography we learned by doing: choosing the river road over I-70, stopping for Fort Massac and the confluence, her eye catching the places history barely bothered to name, wildflowers growing where stories had faded, while I read the dates and names aloud.

We stood with our hands on the rail and let the water have the last word.

LOOKING BACK, LOOKING FORWARD

We drove in silence for a while after leaving the confluence, letting the moment settle.

The land began to rise and fall again, soft hills stretching away from the river like the slow rhythm of breathing. We followed two-lane roads through small towns and vast farm fields, tracing our way north toward Fort Kaskaskia.

Unlike some of the other forts on the trail, Kaskaskia isn't much to look at—at least not in the traditional sense. The original site lies buried beneath layers of time, washed away by floods and forgotten by most. But the bluff still offers one of the most stunning views of the Mississippi River I've ever seen.

We pulled into the small lot and stepped out. The late afternoon sun slanted across the valley below, painting the river in bronze. In the distance, barges moved slowly—heavy with grain, history, or both.

I walked to the edge of the overlook and rested my hands on the rail. Below us, the river curled like a question mark, full of unknowns, full of possibility.

Carmen joined me a moment later. "You can see forever from here," she said.

I nodded. "Almost feels like looking back... and ahead... at the same time."

We didn't need a brochure or a historical marker to tell us what this place meant. The Corps passed this way too.

And maybe that was the feeling we carried, too.

Not finished. Just ready for what came next.

ROMANCE, REWIRED

We didn't have far to go after leaving Kaskaskia. The light was fading, and the day had been full—full of rivers and ruins, questions and quiet truths. We pointed the car toward Alton, winding our way to the KOA we'd booked for the night.

Nothing says romance quite like a KOA near Alton, Illinois.

Hey—I gave her Paris.

What else could a girl want?

The campground was what you'd expect: a gravel pad, a picnic table, a hook-up post painted just slightly the wrong shade of tan. But there was something comforting about it, too—the ordinariness of it. After a day filled with meaning and memories, it felt good to land somewhere simple. Uncomplicated. Ours.

We set up, plugged in, and cracked open a couple of cold drinks. Carmen kicked off her shoes and tucked her feet under her on the little camp chair, the flicker of our lantern catching the edges of her smile.

"I still can't believe we're almost at the end," I said, more to the sky than to her.

She didn't answer right away. Just reached out her foot and nudged mine, gently.

"It's not the end," she said. "It's just another camp."

I heard it as more than a shrug. Going back was still a kind of going forward.

We toasted the day. To Fort Massac. To Drouillard. To rivers and roots and reckoning. And to the road ahead, whatever it might bring.

forty-two
One Last Toast, One More Trail

The day Lewis and Clark returned to St. Louis, they had long been given up for dead. Two and a half years after they departed from Camp River Dubois, they emerged from the wilderness, alive and triumphant. We were here, two centuries later, to honor that homecoming.

We awoke to gray skies, the kind that press low against the earth and whisper of rain. A sharp breeze slid under our jackets, reminding us that fall had turned a corner and winter was already scouting the edges. The ceremony marking the return of the Corps would be held beneath the Arch, in the same spot where we had stood two and a half years earlier for the Three Flags Ceremony.

But first, we detoured upriver.

Fort Belle Fontaine. Just north of St. Louis, tucked quietly on the south side of the Missouri River. Two hundred years ago, the Corps camped nearby before making their final approach to St. Louis. Today, the modern-day Corps—the Discovery Expedition of St. Charles—was camped there, preparing to complete their own long journey.

We wandered into the encampment: canvas, woodsmoke, familiar faces. We weren't reenactors. We weren't officials. But somehow, we belonged. As we left, a fife and drum fell in behind us—it felt less like a pageant, more like a send-off.

After parking downtown, we grabbed seat cushions, blankets, snacks...

and a bottle of Jefferson wine we'd bought years earlier at Michie Tavern, in the shadow of Monticello. We found a quiet perch and settled in above the stage.

Movement on the water caught our eye. Canoes slipped across, paddled by Indigenous reenactors; behind them, the larger boats appeared. The Corps. They landed far upriver, near the base of the bridge, and the crowd surged north. We lifted plastic cups—Meriwether, William, and, with a nod back to Paris, "Mr. Mojo Risin.'"

We didn't cheer. We breathed with the drumbeat and watched the line of paddles lift and fall—slow, exact—until the moment moved past us like a current.

After the dedication on the riverfront, we drifted between stages. The day felt less formal, more alive. On the Native American Stage, we listened to Craig Falcon tell the hardest chapter: on the Marias, an attempted theft, a struggle, two Blackfeet dead—and Lewis placing a peace medal on one of the bodies. After months of peace, that gesture sat like stone.

We walked back toward the Arch in silence—the kind that carries weight without needing words.

At the top of the steps, we paused, looking out over the river and the gathering crowd. The ceremony was about to begin. Carmen slid her hand into mine.

After the presentation of colors, the flags descended the broad steps like a living river. The procession passed close enough to touch. We didn't. We just watched.

Martha Redbone took the stage, her voice rising into the low sky and braiding our old playlist into something older. Later, the band Indigenous sent a current through the crowd. We pulled the blanket tighter and leaned into each other as fireworks stitched light over the Mississippi.

CHILDREN OF THE MIDDLE WATERS

The next morning brought another gray September dawn and a walk onto the Eads Bridge. We weren't there for a view. We were there for a Sunday service—Return to the Middle Waters.

The Osage call themselves Children of the Middle Waters. On the bridge, with the river keeping time beneath us, we stood in that name and listened. No cannons. No parade. Just wind tugging our jackets and words that didn't need raising.

After the service, we drove north to the tower above the Missouri–Mississippi confluence. From the deck, we watched the Missouri's color take the Mississippi—proof that a joining reshapes both. Then we turned toward home.

JUST ONE MORE STOP

The long stretch of I-70 unspooled—flat, familiar. The radio was too loud for most people and just right for me.

But you don't leave a confluence like that and simply go back to normal.

Somewhere near Effingham, Illinois, or maybe Terre Haute, I said, "There's an event in Louisville in November…" It wasn't a Signature Event—the official tour was done—but it marked when Lewis and, at least, Clark stopped there on the way to report to Jefferson.

She raised an eyebrow. "Are you asking?"

"Can we go?"

She closed her book, rested her head against the seat, and grinned. "I figured you'd ask."

The map listed a hundred side trips. The compass—hers and mine—pointed toward what remained.

And just like that, the tour rolled on.

Because the Lewis and Clark Tour?

It never really ends.

The Journey Home

TO: CLARKSVILLE, INDIANA, AND LOUISVILLE, KENTUCKY
NOVEMBER 2006

Without his words, we may never have set out.
Without that spark, there may never have been a journey.

"Since that time maney interesting accurrences has taken place, which I hope to have the pleasure of relateing to you in the Course of about 18 days."

—*William Clark to*
Jonathan Clark, September 24, 1806

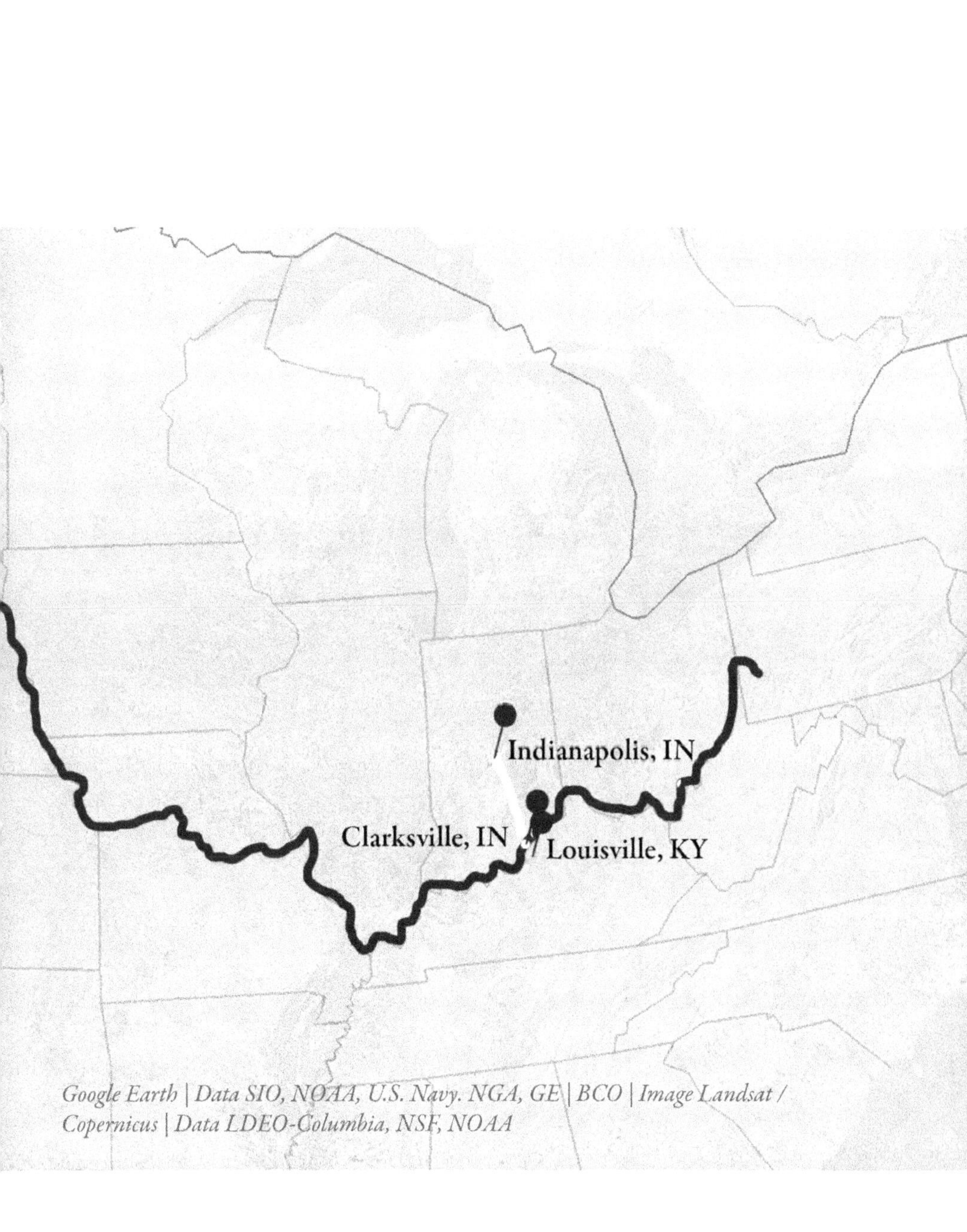

Indianapolis, IN
Clarksville, IN
Louisville, KY
Google Earth | Data SIO, NOAA, U.S. Navy. NGA, GE | BCO | Image Landsat /
Copernicus | Data LDEO-Columbia, NSF, NOAA

forty-three

A Boat, a Blessing, and a Thread of Home

Even though the official series of Signature Events was behind us, we weren't ready to put the journey in park. Six weeks later, we packed the car—no RV this time—for a long weekend in Clarksville, Indiana. Shorter, yes. But in its own way, just as meaningful.

The event was called Lewis and Clark: Homecoming, and that's exactly what it felt like. Not just for the expedition's symbolic return, but for us, too. After all the miles we'd logged, the landscapes we'd crossed, the history we'd immersed ourselves in, it felt like we had come full circle. Back to the beginning. Back to the heart.

We checked into the event's official hotel and didn't have to go far for the first gathering—it was right downstairs, a Friday night dinner in one of the ballrooms. Nothing fancy. But warm. Familiar. A reunion of sorts for people like us who had followed this journey for years. I thumbed the edge of the folded program in my jacket pocket and took in the room.

The first familiar face we saw that night was Phyllis Yeager. We'd never met in person before, but I knew her name well—she had chaired the planning committee for the Signature Event we attended in Clarksville back in 2003.

Long before that weekend, back when this whole thing was still a half-formed dream, I had written to her with an idea that now makes me grin every time I think about it: I was going to canoe the entire Lewis and Clark Trail.

Yes. Canoe.

To her credit, Phyllis didn't laugh—at least not in writing. She responded with genuine interest and even connected me with Senator Baron Hill. There was a moment, however brief, when I thought there might actually be funding for my wild idea.

Of course, the canoe never hit the water. What we did instead was follow the trail in an RV, with air-conditioning, camp chairs, and more snacks than any member of the Corps of Discovery could've imagined. And yet, looking back, I don't think we missed anything essential. Because the spirit of the journey—the curiosity, the wonder, the seeking—was still there. Seeing Phyllis again, years later, felt like closing a loop. Like returning to the place where the dream first tried to take shape.

And then, as if the evening hadn't already packed enough meaning into a hotel banquet room, I spotted another name tag across the crowd.

James Alexander Thom.

There's something surreal about meeting the person whose words lit the match. When I saw his name on the program, that folded edge in my pocket warmed under my thumb.

I had returned from a fateful canoe trip—searching, for what, I didn't even know—when I wandered into the library looking for books about George Rogers Clark and Tecumseh. That's where I first found *Long Knife*. Thom's books didn't just tell history. They let me feel it. The turning point, though, was *From Sea to Shining Sea*—he lived the story he told, traveling the length of the Lewis and Clark Trail, as they did—and as we eventually would. His words carried hardship, brotherhood, hope. I turned the last page and thought, *I want to do something epic, too.*

And now, here he was. Standing just a few feet away, smiling warmly as he greeted readers.

I told him how much his books had meant to me—how his words had cracked something open in my soul, how they had inspired not just me, but Carmen as well. He laughed and shook his head. "You followed the trail in an RV?" he said. "Smart man. I had a lot more blisters."

He introduced us to his wife, Dark Rain Thom, and we talked for a while—about history, about journeys, about how stories find us when we're ready. There was a calm depth to both of them, as if they carried centuries in their bones.

That night, I realized something: Thom hadn't just told the story of the Clark family—he'd helped shape the narrative of ours. Without his words, we might never have set out. Without that spark, there might never have been a journey. And without this journey, who knows what corners of ourselves might've stayed unexplored?

The evening closed with a staged "conversation" among Meriwether Lewis, William Clark, and President Thomas Jefferson—a symbolic debrief of the expedition. It wasn't literal history; it honored the spirit of return. Of reflection. Of legacy. And for us, it was about something else, too: coming home—not just to a place, but to a purpose. To each other. To the story we were still writing.

THREADS OF LEGACY

Saturday dawned cold but not harsh—a mild November morning, jacket weather. We made our way down to Clark's Cabin at the Falls of the Ohio. We had stood here before—October 2003. But this time, it felt different.

There was comfort in the familiarity: the bend in the river, the crunch of leaves underfoot, the path that led to the cabin. But there was also something deeper now. A stillness. A knowing. As if the place remembered us, too.

We paused at the spillway below the locks and dam, where the Ohio surged and foamed, harnessed but still alive. A river tamed, yes—but not silenced. The standing waves lifted and folded, steady as breath. In the wind, the program's corner lifted in my pocket; I pressed it flat and kept watching the current.

The encampment buzzed with life. Tin mugs, wool coats, the ring of a hammer, breath turning white in the air. Just beyond, a canoe carved in the Chinook style rested against the grass—elegant and strong. A small placard noted the coastal roots of the design: one story braided into many.

Near the water's edge stood a modest stone marker. We'd passed it before; this time we paused. These little markers—scattered along the trail like breadcrumbs—had come to mean more than I expected. They were witnesses. Proof. Quiet affirmations that the journey mattered.

New additions framed the park since our last visit—a graceful bridge over the creek below the bluff, flagpoles above the trees. The space had broadened, but the heart of it remained. The path still led to the river. And that's where we spent the most time—by the water.

And then I saw it.

The flatboat wasn't on the river. It sat, high and dry, on a trailer in the grass along the Ohio. But it still had presence—hand-hewn timbers, square angles, a shape more barge than boat. A wooden bridge connected it to the earth, like a gangplank between centuries.

We hadn't expected the sisters—not really. The women aboard wore habits—plainer, older—styled after their 19th-century predecessors. And they carried themselves with that grounded confidence you only find in people who know exactly why they're there.

We walked closer, and Carmen slowed, then smiled in that way she has—like a memory had just taken shape in real time. "They remind me of the sisters at my high school," she said softly.

She meant the Immaculate Conception Academy at Oldenburg, Indiana. Carmen had spent her teenage years there, learning from the Sisters of St. Francis, who arrived in 1851 to teach the children of German immigrants. And here we were, a century and a half later, meeting a group of Ursuline Sisters reenacting their own ancestors' journey—1874, five women floating down the Ohio from Louisville to Owensboro to start a school. Different orders. Different missions. Same fierce spirit.

Carmen stepped up to speak with one of the sisters. They talked for a long while—about the reenactment, about Mount Saint Joseph, about the commitment it took to be part of something so symbolic. I mostly stood off to the side, watching her light up as she made the connection. It was more than shared history—it was lived experience.

Eventually, Carmen waved me over. She turned to the sisters and said, "His people were from Alsace."

One of the women looked at me with a knowing smile. "Ours, too," she said.

Just like that, the past folded in on itself—Alsace, a borderland between

Germany and France that both of our families knew. And now, here we were, in southern Indiana, standing beside a flatboat that had once carried five determined women into the unknown—with Carmen translating between their legacy and mine.

I don't remember all the words spoken that afternoon. I just remember how it felt. Like the trail had cracked open a hidden vein of family, faith, and female strength. Like Carmen had found her people. Like I had, too.

As the sun dipped low over the Ohio, catching the soft folds of the sisters' habits and the slow ripple of the river just beyond, I realized that this was the heart of the whole trip.

There was a moment of quiet. The breeze off the river picked up, tugging at jackets and veils. Carmen touched the weathered wood of the boat. She looked at me, eyes bright.

"These were our pioneers, too," she whispered.

I nodded. For all our tracing of Lewis and Clark—for all the miles we followed the trail—this was something different. Something closer. A different kind of courage. A different kind of discovery. Not mapped. Not measured in miles.

That night, we gathered by the fire in Bicentennial Park. A circle of warmth and flickering shadows. Faces glowing orange and gold. Across the flames, Sacagawea's silhouette stood watch, her gaze lifted toward something distant.

I followed her eyes into the dark and thought, *This isn't just ceremony. This is communion.*

forty-four
And Still, the Rivers Flow

The final morning dawned with a sense of quiet inevitability. It wasn't sadness, exactly—but something close. This chapter of our lives, this long and winding pilgrimage, was drawing to a close. From Monticello to St. Louis, from the headwaters to the mouth, we had followed the arc of history and the arc of us. The official events were nearly over. We had also made an earlier promise—to visit the resting places of Jefferson, Lewis, and Clark on the bicentennials of their deaths. God willing, we still would. But this felt like the end of the trail.

We crossed the Ohio River one more time, heading for Locust Grove, where George Rogers Clark spent his final years. The road shadowed old footsteps.

We arrived to find dozens of reenactors already gathered, immaculate and dignified. Women in elegant gowns and bonnets. Men in frock coats and top hats. In our fleece jackets and jeans, we looked like the ones in costume—like strangers from the future who had accidentally wandered into a moment we weren't supposed to witness.

We waited with the crowd at the edge of the narrow two-lane road. "They're here!" Two boys in formal black attire came running, voices sharp with excitement.

The crowd stirred. A hush fell.

Riders crested the hill—Lewis, Clark, York, and others from the expedition. A black dog—Seaman—walked at a corpsman's side, his fur rippling in the breeze.

We stood still, watching them descend like spirits from the past. For a breath, it was no longer 2006. It was 1806.

Carmen reached for my hand. I didn't say anything. Somehow she already knew what I was thinking:

We made it.

And we're still making it.

They turned up the gravel lane, hooves crunching softly. An honor guard marched in front. A fife and drum corps followed, cadence crisp and clear. The notes pierced time, threading centuries together in a single breath.

On the lawn, the reenactors fanned into a quiet arc. We weren't just watching a performance. We were bearing witness.

Lewis and Clark dismounted. York followed, solemn and tall. Seaman sat at his master's knee. Shoulder to shoulder—just as at the mouth of the Columbia. And now, symbolically, here—home.

An honor guard read a proclamation honoring the expedition's return. Another offered a prayer of remembrance, naming places, rivers, peoples. The silence between those words said just as much.

I glanced at Carmen. Her eyes were wet; her smile was quiet, full. We could both feel it: the culmination of something we'd been chasing since that January day in Charlottesville. Since that first journal. Since that first dream.

George Rogers Clark spoke first, his voice carrying like an echo from another century. York followed—more than performance, it felt like reclamation. William Clark stepped last—the youngest of the 10 Clark siblings, the explorer of rivers, the cartographer of an uncharted nation—now speaking as a man come home.

And then... it was over. No fanfare. No curtain. Just footsteps and low voices as the crowd began to drift away.

We crossed the river one last time and made an impromptu stop at Clark's Cabin, wanting to walk the grounds without the pageantry—just us. The place was still. The river moved quietly, whispering past the banks.

Carmen stood beside a bed of wildflowers, sunlight on her yellow sundress, a wide-brimmed hat shading her face. I took her picture by a Lewis and Clark sign—radiant, grounded, effortlessly beautiful.

As the riders' morning faded in my ears, I slid the program deeper into my pocket.

We stood there for a while longer, listening to nothing but the sound of water and wind. The journey felt complete, but not closed.

We climbed into the car and turned north. The river slipped from view; the meaning didn't.

We didn't arrive so much as agree to keep going.

Echoes of the East

To: Philadelphia, Pennsylvania
June 2007

It started with rivers.
It ends where those rivers meet—and something new begins.

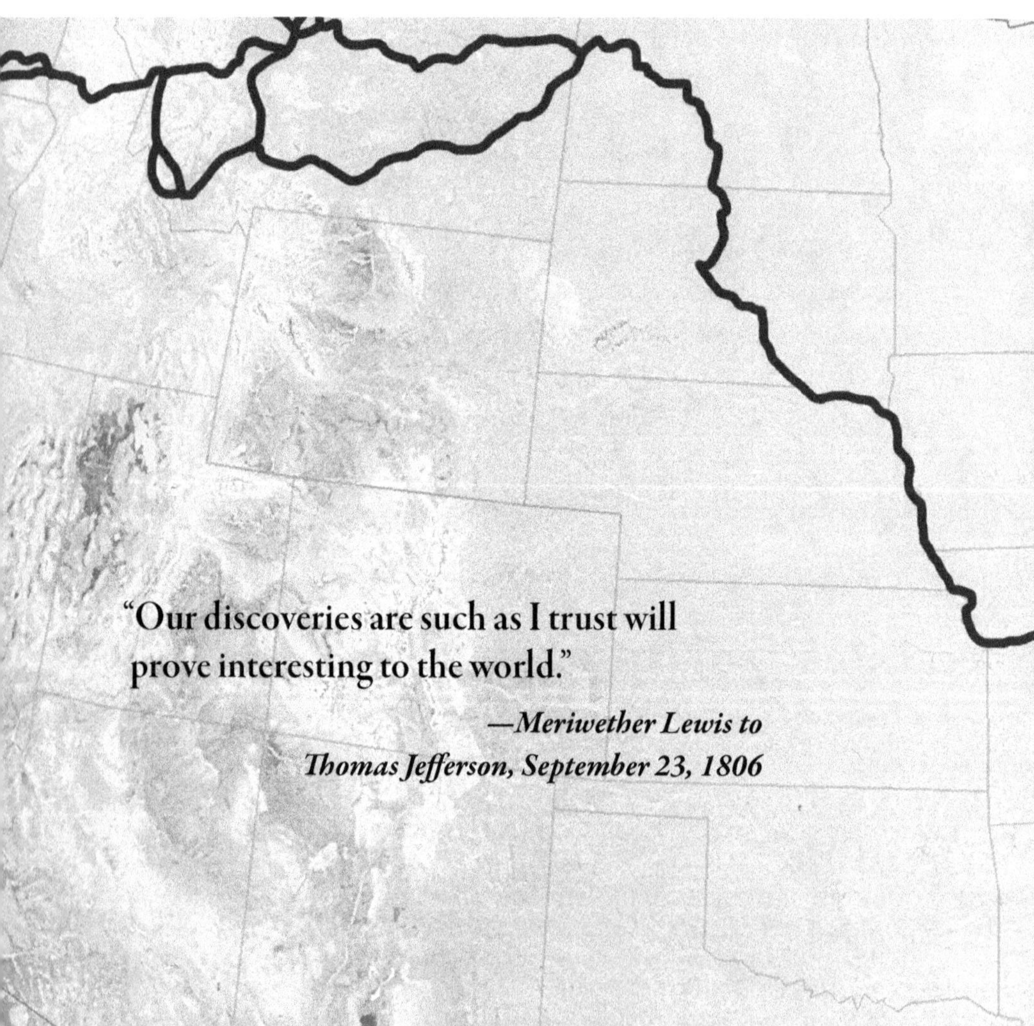

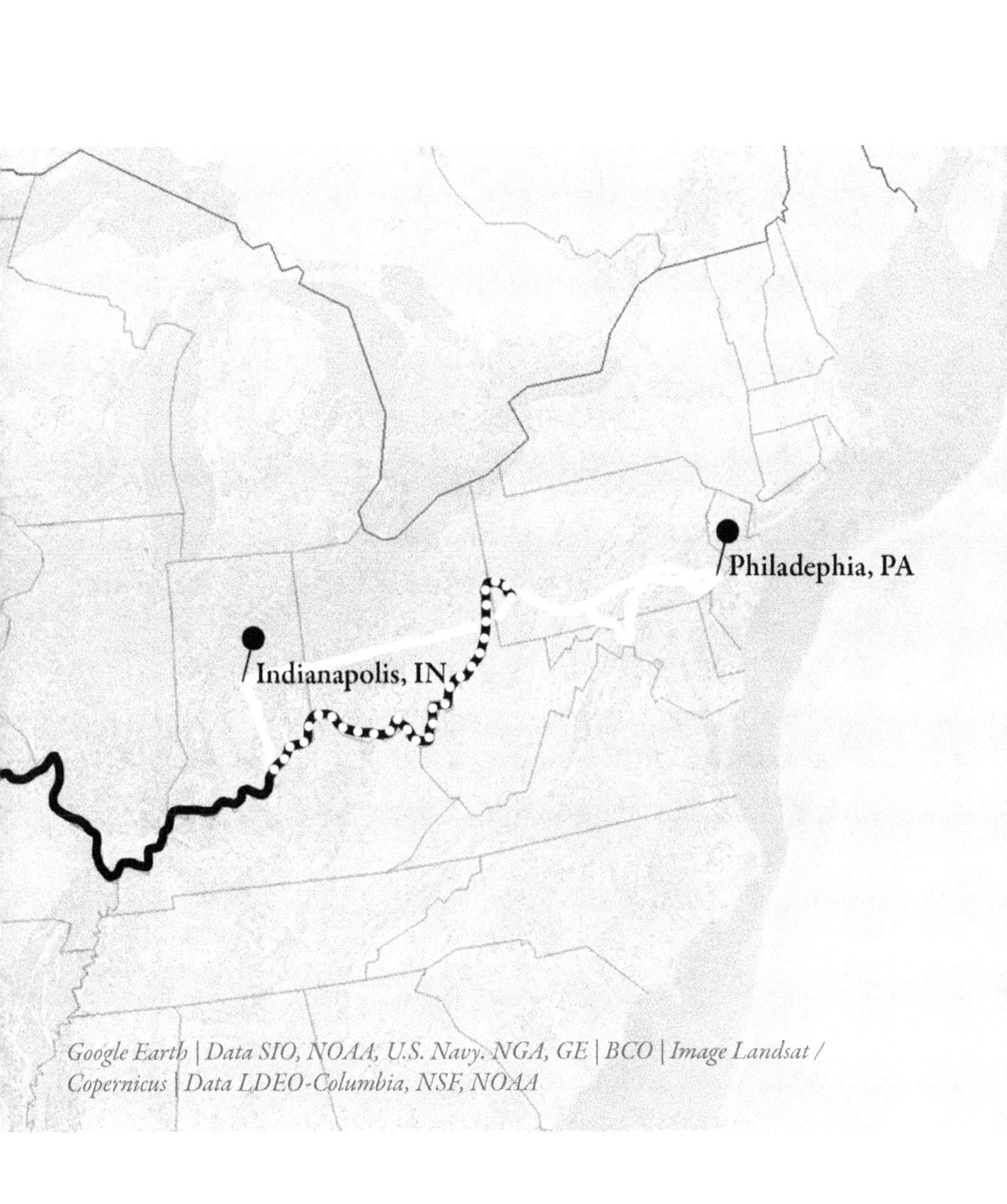

Philadephia, PA
Indianapolis, IN
Google Earth | Data SIO, NOAA, U.S. Navy. NGA, GE | BCO | Image Landsat /
Copernicus | Data LDEO-Columbia, NSF, NOAA

forty-five
The Flag and the Feeling

I couldn't quite process that we had reached the end of the trail. Yes, we had vowed—standing at the foot of Jefferson's grave back in January 2003—to visit the graves of Lewis, Jefferson, and, God willing, Clark on the 200th anniversary of their deaths. But those would be pilgrimages, not part of the epic adventures we'd been living.

After homecoming, life resumed its usual bustle—Thanksgiving, our anniversary, then Christmas—our favorite time of year. On Christmas morning, Carmen and I exchanged gifts before our family arrived. We had a habit of writing playful clue tags. In a nod to Lewis and Clark, her last gift for me read:

> To: Clark
> From: Sacagawea

Inside was a flag—a 15-star, 15-stripe United States flag—and a note: It had flown over Fort Clatsop on February 7, 2006. My birthday. Two centuries to the day. I started to cry.

By New Year's, the flag hung in my office—a daily reminder of our journey, our love, our confluence. Winter rolled into spring—birthdays, dinners with the boys, a visit to Brad in Chicago—and one quiet evening on the back deck, Carmen said, "It feels strange not planning a Lewis and Clark trip. What are we doing for vacation?"

"Well... We haven't really done the Eastern Legacy," I said with a hopeful grin. "Lewis's path from Monticello to Clarksville."

We weren't done with the story; we just needed to follow the river back to where it began and see what it had made of us.

And with that, a new journey was born.

BONE LICK AND BUNNY TOWN

We headed south from Indianapolis on a blistering June morning in 2007, the Ohio coming and going between trees and towns. Charlestown State Park gave us a blufftop overlook and a lazy afternoon. We made a simple camp and let the river steady our breathing.

This leg was about following the water. We stopped at Big Bone Lick, in Kentucky, where bison once came for salt and where fossils later drew the curious—mammoths, mastodons. Jefferson was fascinated; in 1807 he sent Clark to organize a dig. We walked the boardwalks in wet heat, then cooled off in the exhibits and moved on.

Rabbit Hash was a postcard—boarded storefront, smoker going, locals idling. We breathed it in and kept going. Tobacco fields rolled past in waves of green. "My dad grew up on a tobacco farm," Carmen said. "Near Brumfield, Kentucky, I think." We made a note to look it up and add it to the map.

That night, we camped at Lawrence Creek near Maysville. The river breathed; so did we. Every bend seemed to whisper another story.

ROY, BOB, AND THE WILD FRONTIER

Morning brought low clouds and an easy rhythm. We tipped a hat to a boyhood porch with the names Roy Rogers and Trigger Pass, then smiled at a Dutch-style windmill on the Bob Evans Farm—two quick breadcrumbs of childhood and ancestry—and returned to the river.

At Point Pleasant, in West Virginia, Fort Randolph's gates were locked. We circled the stockade, felt the grit of the old frontier, and thought of the killing of Shawnee leader Chief Cornstalk and the ripples that followed— another fort, another story—hallowed, complicated ground.

By late day, we'd reached a quiet campground near Marietta, right on the Ohio–West Virginia border. Stars came out. The river kept its own counsel.

THE YELLOWSTONE IDEA

Dawn never quite arrived—just drizzle and gray. We traced the Ohio toward Pittsburgh, the water a sheet of pewter under a heavy sky. At the confluence, Heinz Field flickered past; we marked the spot for our return.

East on the turnpike, the mountains lifted us through tunnels and cuts. "Range anxiety?" Carmen teased, eyeing the fuel gauge. We laughed, found gas, and split a bag of snacks.

Somewhere between exits, the talk turned to my fiftieth. "Let's plan something epic," she said.

"How about a month on the Yellowstone—Paradise Valley to the Missouri?" I offered.

"What if we learned to fly-fish?" she countered. "Peaceful."

We sketched an outfitted drift of a plan—an RV leapfrog, resupply, nights to dry out and start again. A new dream took shape, still tied to rivers and discovery.

Later, we compared Spanish: her full-immersion summer in Mexico that quietly rewired her courage; my four high school years that taught me mostly how to misplace a gradebook. We crossed into Maryland at dusk and settled into the Hagerstown KOA, the rain finally letting go. We slept to the hum of the highway and the murmur of a plan.

BLOOD IN THE WATER

We traded the meander of the Ohio for Antietam's still fields. Twenty-three thousand casualties in a single day—numbers that stay abstract until you walk the Sunken Road and read the regiments. My great-great-grandfather Sydney Waterman fought for the Union. "He survived," I said. Carmen squeezed my hand. A life rippling forward—to me, to us.

At Harpers Ferry, we paused at the Potomac–Shenandoah confluence, then at the quieter story: Lewis arriving in March 1803, gathering supplies, worrying over an experimental iron boat, and mapping the next steps. Jefferson's Rock looked out over all of it. He once wrote the view was "worth a voyage across the Atlantic." We stood where he stood. "Another fork in the river," I said. "Another beginning," she answered.

We tried to hold that place with respect, knowing we were standing in homelands layered long before our maps had names.

SILENCE AT GETTYSBURG

We let Gettysburg speak for itself—no guide, no audio, just the two of us and the road that threads the fields. At the cemetery, I read Lincoln's 272 words aloud, and they landed the way they always do. We walked among marked and unknown stones. Quiet fit.

By late day, we reached the West Chester KOA. Piña coladas appeared from the RV like a magic trick, and dinner sizzled on the grill. "I think this trip might be one of my favorites," she said. "We've still got Philly," I replied, smiling.

forty-six
The Holy Grail

Philadelphia.

We'd threaded salt licks, battlefields, and river seams all week, but we were here for one room: the American Philosophical Society—Jefferson's society, a keeper of journals and maps. I'd booked a city tour because Philly and Winnebagos do not mix, so the bus scooped us from the KOA at dawn: sunscreened RV people, cameras ready, my pulse already three beats ahead.

We had both flown in and out of this place for years for work—airport, rental car, conference rooms, back out again. But never like this. Carmen slid on her sunglasses and gave me that quiet smile that said *I am loving this*. I squeezed her hand and tried to pay attention as the guide eased us into the 18th century.

Brick lanes. Proper shutters. A house museum with a cradle by the hearth. I stepped into the courtyard for air; Carmen followed, sun catching her hair as I snapped a photo on a low stone wall—grace in a city of revolution. Back to the street. Ben Franklin's church—beautiful, not it. Betsy Ross's house—fitting, after Carmen's Christmas flag to me—still not it. I kept checking my watch between stops like Lewis counting portages. The Philosophical Society wasn't on the tour; we had carved out 90 minutes at lunch, and the minutes were slipping through my fingers.

Then the Liberty Bell—oh, the line. A slow, sweating ribbon of

315

humanity while the clock on our holy grail ticked down. We shuffled forward, read the placards, stood for the photo, and I heard the docent's voice as a metronome of lost time. Carmen squeezed my hand and whispered, "Not yet." She knew.

When we finally spilled back into the sun, I could feel the urgency in my legs. We weren't here to collect stamps. We were here to touch the source.

Lunch wasn't a break; it was a window.

We had one hour.

One hour before we had to meet the group back at Independence Hall.

"Ready?" I asked.

"Set." She smiled.

"Go."

We didn't so much walk as hustle—through cobbled streets and crowds—toward the one place that mattered most to me on this entire trip: the APS!

The holy grail.

And it was finally within reach.

We hustled up the street, threading through clusters of tourists and families with strollers, my inner compass locked on one destination. Carmen matched my pace, even in the heat. We rounded the final corner, the old brick façade just ahead.

There it was.

I practically jogged the last few steps and reached for the handle—only to stop short.

A small, unassuming sign was taped to the glass.

CLOSED.

Not "Closed for Lunch."

Not "Closed on Mondays."

Closed—for three weeks.

While they changed out the exhibit.

Three. Weeks.

I stared at it. "Closed?" I muttered. "Closed?" My voice cracked, somewhere between disbelief and heartbreak. "We drove across the damn country... for this. This was it. This was the holy grail."

I turned to Carmen, who was already one step ahead of me. Literally. She was ringing the doorbell.

I blinked. "There's a doorbell?"

"It's a building, isn't it?" she said with a shrug. "Buildings have doorbells."

Before I could reply, the door opened as a woman stepped out, lunch bag in hand.

Our presence drew her up short.

"May I help you?" she asked coolly.

"We came all the way from Indiana to see the museum," I stammered.

"Well, we aren't open," she said flatly.

"We came to see the journals of Lewis and Clark," Carmen added, her voice calm but clear. "We've spent five years following the trail, from Monticello to Astoria and back."

"The journals?" the woman echoed, eyebrows arching. "We have them, but we don't display them."

"Your website says you do," I said, half-whimpering, half-pleading.

She looked us over, peering above the rim of her glasses with professional skepticism. "Are you academics?"

"No," Carmen said, "we're just history lovers. We've been following the trail for years, part of the bicentennial—"

"Well," she interrupted, "if you're not academics, you couldn't see them even if we were open."

I was stunned. Crushed. My inner child wanted to cry. Carmen stayed steady.

"Isn't there something you can do?" she asked in that way only Carmen can ask—gentle, persuasive, not demanding, but impossible to dismiss.

The woman sighed. "Why don't you go across the street to our library. I'm sure you can look around there."

The library. Not the thing I'd come for. I wanted to see the journals, not a bunch of dusty archives.

"Would you mind walking us over?" Carmen asked. "Maybe you could help tell them our story?"

The woman hesitated, then gave a terse nod. "I suppose so."

She led the way briskly, holding herself upright and proper. I couldn't help but picture the scene in *The Wizard of Oz*—that old biddy pedaling furiously down the road on her bicycle, wind in her skirt and judgment in her eyes.

We entered the library, and she marched us to the front desk.

"These people came here from Indiana," she said. "Could someone show them around?"

"Are they academics?" the woman behind the desk asked, without even looking up. If possible, she sounded even more condescending than the first.

"No, we're not," Carmen replied, steady and sincere. "We've been following the Lewis and Clark Trail for five years. We didn't realize you were closed. We came here to see the journals."

The librarian pursed her lips. "Well... I suppose Nan could show you around." She picked up the phone and dialed an extension.

A few minutes later, a young woman appeared—Nan. Her demeanor was a refreshing contrast: open, kind, curious.

"Hi," she said warmly. "I hear you've come a long way."

We nodded.

"Let me show you around," she offered.

I sighed internally. More books. More *blah blah blah*. On any other day, I probably would have found it fascinating, but I was in a mood. Everything sounded like static.

But then, just as we wandered into yet another room of antique volumes, she said something that brought me back to life.

"So... I hear you're interested in Lewis and Clark?"

"Yes, very," Carmen said. "We've spent the last five years following the trail. It's become a big part of our life."

Nan paused. "Well then... follow me."

She led us through a warren of rooms, eventually stopping in a space that looked more like storage than a library. Metal shelves lined two of the walls—boxes, old AV equipment, framed prints stacked on edge. A third wall held a row of windows overlooking a narrow alley.

But the fourth wall held a vault—a massive, movie-style bank vault door.

Nan motioned to a table with metal legs and a battered Formica top. The chairs were stackable plastic—the kind you'd find in a school cafeteria.

"Have a seat," she said, and disappeared into the vault.

Moments later, she returned carrying several small boxes—maybe six by eight inches and an inch or so thick. She laid them carefully on the table, opened one—

And there it was.

One of the original journals of Lewis and Clark.

We stared in silence, unable to believe what we were seeing. Nan gently turned the pages.

"You can hold them if you'd like," she offered.

"Really?" we both said at once. "But… we don't have gloves."

"Oh." She smiled. "We prefer you don't use gloves. You can't feel the pages with gloves, and you're more likely to bend them."

After seven years of passion. Four years of travel. Thirty-five thousand miles. Countless books. Moments sacred and serendipitous—

We held the original journals of Lewis and Clark in our hands.

I wasn't worried about bending the paper—I was worried my tears would drop onto it.

There was Clark's handwriting. Maps. Sketches. Plant samples. Color. Green trees. Blue rivers. The pigments, we learned, came from native sources. They painted their maps.

"Look at this, Carmen," I whispered, pointing. "The map. The colors."

"Oh? You like maps?" Nan asked.

"Yes," I breathed.

"He has maps on every wall," Carmen added. "Office, basement, you name it."

Nan smiled. "Wait here."

She returned the journals to their boxes and disappeared once more into the vault. When she reemerged, she carried a much larger box— maybe two feet by four feet—and heavy.

She opened it with care, revealing the original copper engraving plate of William Clark's map, published in 1814.

The very plate used in the Nicholas Biddle edition of the journals.

"During the bicentennial, we tried printing from it," Nan explained. "We hoped to raise money for the society. But after about 100 prints, we noticed the plate was being damaged. So we stopped."

She paused. Then asked, almost offhandedly, "Would you like one?"

Would we like one? Are you kidding? We nearly fell over.

She crossed to a shelf and returned with a rolled print.

It was perfect—no fold marks. No tears. No blemishes. Not like the lithograph we had at home. This one was pristine.

Just then, a man entered—Nan's supervisor. I think his name was Roy. He was thrilled at our enthusiasm.

"I've got something else," he said, vanishing into the shelves.

He returned with a print of a document we didn't recognize—the Michaux subscription document.

We smiled blankly.

"It's the only known document signed by four U.S. presidents," he explained. "Washington, Adams, Jefferson, Madison. It's a fundraising document for an expedition meant to be led by André Michaux. Jefferson himself wrote it, back in 1793."

That expedition never happened. Politics with France killed it before it began. But the document remained—its signatures, its dreams—preserved.

And now, we had a copy.

We were floating. Cloud nine wasn't high enough.

We thanked them profusely (we even sent them Christmas cards for years), then hustled back to our group. We had timed tickets for Independence Hall.

With my new map and the Michaux document tucked under my arm, we jogged through the streets of Philadelphia.

I could barely concentrate as the docent described the room where the Declaration of Independence was signed. My brain was still inside that vault. My hands still tingled with the memory of the pages. Our photos came out blurry—my hands must have been shaking. Carmen usually takes our best pictures, but I'd insisted on having the camera—big mistake.

After the tour, we strolled toward the bus, passing a brick garden with fountains. It marked the site of Dr. Benjamin Rush's house. Lewis studied medicine under Rush, using those lessons on the trail. He even carried Rush's "Thunderbolts"—a euphemistic name for the mercury-based laxatives Lewis doled out to treat the Corps and their new acquaintances alike.

As the breeze rustled the leaves overhead, I thought again of that map in my hands, the weight of history, and the path that brought us here—not just along the trail, but through time.

This had been the holy grail of our journey.

An uncharted moment, perfectly mapped.

forty-seven
After the Grail

We reboarded the bus with the poster tube tucked like a violin in the crook of my arm. I felt light and wrung out at the same time—like someone had opened a window in my chest. Carmen, meanwhile, had already spotted the next thread.

"Valley Forge," she said, eyes bright. "Let's go see where they learned to endure."

The National Memorial Arch rose out of the green like a Roman memory. We walked beneath it and read Washington's words carved into stone, the sentences worn smooth by weather and reverence. Carmen stood there longer than I did. I watched her lips move as she reread a line, then touched the edge of the inscription with two fingers as if to make sure it was real.

We crossed a small stone bridge over a creek that had no plaque, but it didn't need one. Its water whispered under our feet, rounding stones that had been here long before winter huts and drill lines, long before the Arch. I set the tube down and finally let my shoulders drop. The air smelled like sun-warmed grass and wet leaves; the breeze carried a faint tang of woodsmoke from somewhere we couldn't see.

Inside Washington's headquarters, the ceilings were low and the floors uneven. We let the rooms tell their stories—a narrow bed; a kitchen hearth with a scarred iron kettle; a window that framed nothing monumental, only a slice of field where someone had once decided to keep going. I pictured lists written by candlelight. Worries nobody saved.

"Pretty sacred," Carmen said quietly, back out in the sun.

She wasn't talking about the Arch.

That evening in camp we clinked plastic tumblers and toasted "George, Thomas, Meriwether, William—and Nan." We added "and Roy" after a beat, and then laughed because it felt right to include the man who wandered in with a presidential signature party under his arm. The fire found its rhythm; sparks lifted and disappeared into a navy sky. I tried to describe what I felt when we first saw the copper engraving plate to Carmen a second time and failed in the same places—how do you explain weight and wonder in a single breath? I didn't have the words.

"It's enough," she said, slipping her hand into mine, "that we got to feel it."

The flames settled. So did we.

STILLNESS SPONSORED BY ROADSIDE ASSISTANCE

We left West Chester early, sun clean on the windshield, the world tidy and possible. Lancaster was our first stop—Andrew Ellicott's modest house, where Meriwether learned the sky. Sextants, charts, a replica desk. Carmen pointed to the instrument panel and grinned. "That's your birthday set," she said. The docent laughed when I admitted we still carry paper maps and a compass on canoe trips. "You and Lewis," he said. I didn't correct him.

Back on the road toward Harrisburg, the turnpike gave way to a two-lane that curled between rock and trees. I stayed a little too polite with oncoming traffic, a little too close to the shoulder. Then—an unkind kiss between rubber and stone. A jolt. A sound you feel in your ribs.

We limped into a parking lot and exhaled. The tire was done. So was my pride.

I tried the jack. The jack tried my patience. The RV did not move. Carmen called roadside assistance because that is why we pay for roadside assistance. "Twelve-thirty," she mouthed. We waited.

There's a special kind of time that only shows up on days like this—elastic, slightly humiliating, measured in glances at a watch you can't change. We drank water. We sat on the curb. We revised our plans in silence and then again out loud. I worked the jack one more time, as if stubbornness could be a tool.

When help finally arrived, it wasn't a gleaming truck with a branded polo. It was a pickup with a toolbox that had seen things and two men who had, too. I caught the faint drift of beer and exchanged a quick look with Carmen that said everything and nothing.

A state trooper pulled in and parked a polite distance away, the kind of presence that makes everyone behave better. The men moved with the competence of people who fix things because someone has to. Lug nuts squealed, the jack sighed, the spare found the hub. The trooper watched the whole ballet with his arms folded, then gave us a small nod as if to say, *On you go.*

Four hours after the rock met the rubber, we rolled. The road felt different under the wheels, less like a promise and more like a gift.

We called it a day early. No grand finale, no heroic push. A hushed campground. A small supper. We sat side by side without a fire and listened to crickets thread the dusk.

"I hate that I hit it," I said finally.

"I love that we're okay," she answered.

The stillness did its work.

WHERE THE RIVERS MEET

Morning heat settled over the road like a hand on your shoulder. We passed Three Mile Island, the cooling towers shouldering the sky—icons you never want a reason to remember. Carmen told me again about the women she'd met who lived through the accident—a meltdown in 1979, how nobody told the truth quickly enough, how terror can be measured in school bus routes and clock hands that slow to a crawl. We rode quietly for a while, then let the road carry the weight for us.

Pittsburgh rose ahead, bridges flung across water like bright ribbons. We parked and walked to the point where the Allegheny and Mononga-hela join and become the Ohio—the old dream braided into a new one. The fountain hissed in the heat; gulls worked their easy spirals. A small Lewis and Clark panel stood against the sweep of the city, unassuming and exactly right.

We didn't talk. Some places ask for stillness, and this was one of them. I took Carmen's hand. The rivers flowed steadily by and, without drama, chose to be one thing.

How do you explain stillness and love in a single breath?

We stood there long enough for the sun to change angles and the breeze to lift a corner of the map in my mind. I tried to honor the layers under our feet—the rivers that were trade routes and lifelines long before our names appeared on any signs; the nations for whom this confluence was not a chapter marker but home. We tried to stand in that recognition with humility.

On the drive west, the countryside unspooled in green and corn, bathed in the afternoon light. We let music fill the places words didn't need to go. A while later, Carmen rested her hand on my forearm and asked, "So... what now?"

"After 35,000 miles, 17 states, and a hundred uncharted moments?" I said. "I used to think I needed something epic—canoe the whole trail."

"You did something epic," she said.

"We did." I glanced over. "And you weren't my Sacagawea, Carmen—you were my Lewis."

She laughed. "You always did need a good navigator."

We drove with the windows down, the air warm and forgiving. The miles stretched between sentences the way a river stretches between bends—quiet, inevitable, carrying what it carries.

"We fell in love with the story," I said finally. "Theirs, our country's... and ours."

Ahead, the word *Home* blinked from the GPS like it had always known. I thought of the flag on my office wall, the copperplate map rolled safe in its tube, the journal pages that felt like a pulse under my fingertips. I thought of rivers we had followed to their beginnings and endings, and of the ones inside us that had learned how to meet.

It started with rivers; it ends where they meet.

It was never only about reaching the Pacific.

It was about falling in love—again and again—with what we found along the way.

And with what found us.

Epilogue

Maps and Meaning

Maps can take you to a place; love teaches you how to arrive.

I didn't know that when we started. I thought we were following a line west and then home again—two people with a shared itinerary and a growing collection of mile markers. Only later—years later—did the shape of it come clear, the way a river only shows you its form from above. It wasn't just a trail we were tracing. It was a life.

The 15-star, 15-stripe flag hangs near my desk—the one Carmen gave me, flown over Fort Clatsop on my birthday. I look up at it when the day goes quiet. It's odd to call a flag tender, but this one is. It's mast and map: something to lift into the wind, something to point a way. If you've read this far, you already know the truth it points to—that the real expedition wasn't only on the ground beneath our wheels; it was in the passenger seat beside me.

When Maps Became Mirrors

There was a day in Philadelphia when a librarian named Nan led us past exhibits and into a small, still back room. She set a copper plate on the table, and the room changed temperature—two centuries of lines pressed into metal. We leaned in, hardly breathing. In that moment, the map became a mirror. I saw what we'd been doing without knowing it: turning routes into meaning, turning miles into a marriage.

Another day, in Pittsburgh, we stood where the Allegheny meets the Monongahela and becomes the Ohio—two currents, one river. Just before the waters join, each river gathers itself in a quiet eddy along the point of land, a brief stillness before the surge. We named it our still point. From then on, whenever we were lost—by season or sorrow—a confluence was the picture we returned to: Two become one and keep moving.

Seeing from the Other Shore

Along the way, we began to see things differently. We went to Louisville expecting to hear Gary Moulton and instead heard Gerard Baker. He didn't scold; he invited. *See from the other side of the river,* he said. Ever since, we've tried to begin by asking: *Who stood on these banks before us? Who still does? What does it ask of us to be good guests?* That question has become a practice as steady as checking a compass.

The Unwritten Journey

If this book is a love story—and it is—then I want to say it plainly. Carmen wasn't my Sacagawea. She was my Lewis. My co-captain. The one who knew when to push and when to pause, who could read the water better than I could, who made the ordinary feel like hallowed ground. She didn't just walk beside me; she changed the way I walk.

We once planned a birthday gift that felt like a dare to time itself: a month on the Yellowstone—from the Park to the Missouri, canoe and cottonwoods, camp smoke in our clothes. We found an outfitter—husband and wife, kids in school, the kind of people who make a river sound like home. Maps spread. Gear shipped. Paid time off denied. *Trim it back,* my boss said. *Two weeks max.* Then a late snowpack swelled the water and swallowed the campsites; the calendar swallowed our window; the boxes came back with our hopes packed inside.

I used to tell this as a near-miss, a shrug, a someday. Now I hear what the river was teaching all along: Not every line on a map becomes a line we live. Some journeys remain conjectural—and still they shape us. We learned to bless the plans that held, and hold hands over the ones that didn't.

The Terrain Ahead

The terrain has changed. We didn't choose it. MSA-C, with its neurodegenerative symptoms, is not a plot twist I would write for anyone. There's the rollator, the careful steps, the voice that now comes with effort. There are appointments and scans and words you never want to hear. Some days, the current feels faster than our oars. And yet—and yet—love remains the water under us.

These days, the grand gestures have given way to small vows:

Love is cooking a simple meal and eating it together.

Love is doing the laundry and learning the complexities of women's clothes.

Love is helping her in and out of the car.

Love is rubbing oil onto her legs and back after a shower.

Love is holding her close at the end of the day.

Love is knowing what's coming and choosing to stay present.

Love is a flag on the wall and a chair by the water.

Grinder's Stand

In October 2009, we followed Lewis's last miles to Grinder's Stand. Memphis first—Graceland smaller than we'd pictured, the Lorraine Motel impossibly large in its silence—and then the Natchez Trace, leaf-colored and slow. The ceremony was called *Courage Undaunted—The Final Journey*. The 101st Airborne played; the Masons read; a rider approached at a walk, leather creaking, the kind of detail that makes two centuries feel like a curtain you can slip behind.

At the grave, there was a wreath, an honor guard, the clean ache of "Taps." Then a single voice rose with "Amazing Grace" and found the trees. We didn't speak on the way back to the car. Her hand in mine, the gravel a hush under our shoes. Looking back, it feels like a funeral for more than one thing—what a country assumes about itself, what a couple assumes time will always allow.

But grief didn't stand alone there. Gratitude stood beside it, steady as an old friend. We had come to honor a man we'd studied and argued with for years, and we left having honored something quieter: the cost of maps, the mercy of companions, the work of proceeding on.

From Trail to Calling

The trail changed more than our weekends; it changed my work—and my voice. I was a chief information officer who dreaded microphones, the guy whose palms sweated before staff meetings. Carmen and my mother-in-law nudged me onto a safer shore: "Tell the Rotary about your trips." We built a tabletop of talismans; I wrote my notes on cards, and a room of strangers taught me that fear can be an oar, not an anchor.

Then another nudge: "Look for the leadership lessons." I reread the journals with a leader's eyes and saw 10 traits I could carry into the office—some as beacons, some as warnings. That little PDF became a keynote, the keynote became a door, and the door opened to an experiential program built with my client FCCS: three days where history tutors the present. I've watched rooms of leaders stand a little taller after a story about York or a decision at a fork.

I thought the river was a hobby. It turned out to be an avocation that became a vocation—a current that carried what I love into what I'm for.

Family, Roots, and Wholeness

How do you summarize 20 years of life? You don't. You name the people, and you let the naming be a kind of gratitude.

Jeremy reconnected with Melissa, a summer-camp love. One afternoon in our living room, they told us a baby was coming; a few months later, they married, moved to Kentucky, and brought Clint and Aly into our family. In September 2012, Braxton Kirby arrived—our first grandchild. Everything they say about being grandparents is true... and more. Our hearts grew.

Brad met Holly at work; love followed. With her came two wonderful kids, Donny and Charity. Carmen cared for them after school, and our home at Whitetail Meadow turned into a wonderland. Our hearts grew. In 2014, Brad and Holly welcomed Jordan Jeffrey. Our hearts grew. Six years later came Jasper Bryant. Our hearts grew again. The marriage ended less than a year later—hard days, serious rapids on the Ton River.

In time, Brad met Katrina. They married in August 2022, right in our backyard. With Katrina came three more gifts: Ariana, Henry, and Avery.

Our hearts grew—fourfold. In September 2023, Hayden Stephen arrived, all grin and motion. Our hearts grew again.

Carmen is a wonderful grandmother. I never knew her Granny, or Grandma Delmo, or Grandma Margaret, but I see them in her—how she listens, how she steadies, how she loves.

The Chair by the Water

If I could leave you with one picture, it would be this: early evening, soft light. The flag on the wall. Two glasses on the porch—sometimes lemonade, sometimes tonic—because tastes change and so do capacities, but the ritual holds. The map on the desk with its penciled arrows. A question we try to keep near the top of the page: *Who stood here before us?* A promise under it: *Listen first.*

The maps were never finished. Ours isn't either. We'll keep a chair by the water. We'll keep asking better questions. We'll begin with gratitude, proceed with humility, and leave room for surprise.

Conjectural.

We proceed on.

Acknowledgments

This book carries the fingerprints of so many people. To each of you—thank you.

Carmen—my Lewis, my compass, my co-captain, my love. Every mile of this journey and every word of this book began and ended with you.

Family—Brad and Jeremy, and the family that keeps widening through children and grandchildren. Thank you for your patience with the long hours at the desk, your humor on long days, and your love that keeps me grounded.

Teachers and keepers of story—Nan and the staff at the American Philosophical Society, who opened a quiet back room and changed the way we saw. Gerard Baker, whose words invited us to look from the other side of the river. Gary E. Moulton, Dayton Duncan, Clay Jenkinson, and countless other historians, authors, and reenactors who gave us entry points into a story larger than ourselves.

My heartfelt thanks to historian James Holmberg, who graciously agreed to read an early draft and offered several thoughtful clarifications and corrections. His insights strengthened the historical foundation of this book in ways I deeply appreciate. Any errors that remain are entirely my own.

The team that made it happen—Books don't simply leap from an author's fingertips; a team of talented professionals shapes them. Pamela Sourelis provided invaluable guidance during the developmental editing process. Lori Paximadis of Pax Studio brought clarity and precision through copyediting. Jody Skinner of Skinner Book Services crafted the interior design and handled proofreading with care. The cover design and interior maps were created by the gifted Jennifer "JVo" Vogel. *Uncharted Moments* was also strengthened by early readers whose feedback helped guide the manuscript: Carmen Ton, Matt Belanger, Lyn Wuethrich, Meaghan Shaffer, Alexandra Rufatto-Perry, Jean Canty Segal, John Regentin, Katrina Ton, Brad Ton, Greg Dorchak, and Carmen Zayas.

Community and partners—Judy and Dave, for the first Rotary invitation that nudged me onto a stage. Ron West, who challenged me to find the leadership lessons. Jean Canty Segal at FCCS, whose note opened a door I never knew existed, words don't begin to express my gratitude. Sean Murray, Matt Walker, Jared Nichols, and the whole FCCS team who built The Lewis and Clark Experience: A New Way Forward alongside me. To my fellow co-creators, thank you for the gift of your insights and experiences.

Mentor and guide—To Dr. Dan Miller, who helped me see the kind of leader I already was.

Care teams—The clinicians and staff at Cleveland Clinic, the University of Chicago Medical Center, and here in Indianapolis at Indiana University Health, who have walked with us through the uncharted territory of MSA-C. Thank you for your clarity, compassion, and care. A special word of gratitude to Jill, Carmen's physical therapist, whose steady hands and kind spirit have supported her—body and heart—through this uncharted season.

Stewards of place—The Lewis and Clark Trail Heritage Foundation, and the many parks, interpretive centers, and local museums that welcomed us and preserved these stories. To the volunteers who clean rivers, the rangers who tend trails, and the community members who keep memory alive—your work matters more than you know.

Finally, to the peoples whose lands and waters we traveled through: Thank you for the patience to teach visitors like us. May we be better guests with every mile.

Lewis and Clark Bicentennial Signature Events (2003–2006)

In 2003, a national commemoration began to honor the bicentennial of the Lewis and Clark Expedition—a three-year journey that helped define the American story. Over the next four years, 15 Signature Events were held along the trail, each marking a pivotal moment in the original expedition. These weren't just history lessons; they were living tributes that brought together tribes, historians, reenactors, and dreamers like us. Carmen and I planned our travels around many of these events. Some we experienced firsthand—standing in the rain, listening to voices that had long been silenced finally take center stage. Others we missed, but we followed their echoes. What follows is a list of those 15 Signature Events: where they took place, what they commemorated, and why they mattered.

1. BICENTENNIAL INAUGURAL: JEFFERSON'S WEST

Location: Charlottesville, Virginia
Date: January 18, 2003

Historical significance: Symbolic launch of the bicentennial, honoring Thomas Jefferson's vision and commissioning of the expedition.

Overview: Opening ceremonies at Monticello introduced the nationwide commemoration. The event emphasized themes of exploration, cultural exchange, and education through interpretive programs, exhibits, and the unveiling of the traveling exhibit Corps of Discovery II.

Our experience: Leg 1: We Headed East to Explore the West

2. FALLS OF THE OHIO: ON THE THRESHOLD OF DISCOVERY

Location: Louisville, Kentucky, and Clarksville, Indiana
Dates: October 14–26, 2003

Historical significance: Commemorated the reunion of Meriwether Lewis and William Clark and the formation of the Corps of Discovery.

Overview: Reenactments, presentations, and community events celebrated the expedition's origins and recognized local contributions, including the roles of York and the Clark family.

Our experience: Leg 4: The Last Jeep to Clarksville

3. THREE FLAGS CEREMONY

Location: St. Louis, Missouri
Dates: March 10–14, 2004

Historical significance: Marked the official transfer of the Louisiana Territory to the United States, enabling the Lewis and Clark Expedition.

Overview: This symbolic ceremony recreated the historic handover of the territory from Spain to France to the United States, with all three flags raised in succession beneath the Gateway Arch. The event included reenactments, cultural performances, and reflections on the international and tribal impacts of the Louisiana Purchase.

Our experience: Leg 5: The World Is Different Now

4. EXPEDITION'S DEPARTURE: CAMP RIVER DUBOIS

Location: Camp River Dubois, Hartford, Illinois
Dates: May 13–16, 2004

Historical significance: Commemorated the departure of the Lewis and Clark Expedition from Camp River Dubois, marking the official start of their journey up the Missouri River.

Overview: Set near the original winter encampment site, this event launched the Corps of Discovery's westward journey. Activities included interpretive programs, military reenactments, and ceremonial farewells. Visitors explored the challenges the expedition faced and the diverse backgrounds of its members.

Our experience: We were unable to attend this event. We did, however, visit all the historically significant sites several times. Leg 5: The World Is Different Now; Leg 6: Two Questions and a Plan; Leg 11: What Do You Do When It's Over

5. PREPARATIONS COMPLETE: THE EXPEDITION FACES WEST

Location: St. Charles, Missouri
Dates: May 20–23, 2004

Historical significance: Marked the final staging and ceremonial departure of the Lewis and Clark Expedition from the last settled community on the Missouri River before entering largely uncharted territory.

Overview: Hosted in Missouri's oldest city, this event featured reenactments, boat displays, and historical exhibits, honoring the Corps' launch into the unknown from the edge of American settlement.

Our experience: We were unable to attend this event. We did, however, visit all the historically significant sites several times. Leg 5: The World Is Different Now; Leg 6: Two Questions and a Plan

6. HEART OF AMERICA: A JOURNEY FOURTH

Location: Kansas City, Missouri; Atchison and Leavenworth, Kansas
Dates: July 3–4, 2004

Historical significance: Celebrated the Independence Day departure of the Corps as they ascended the Missouri River.

Overview: Patriotic festivities were blended with historical interpretation, Indigenous storytelling, and community-wide reflection on the meaning of independence and exploration.

Our experience: Leg 6: Two Questions and a Plan

7. FIRST TRIBAL COUNCIL

Location: Fort Calhoun and Omaha, Nebraska
Dates: July 31–August 3, 2004

Historical significance: Commemorated the first formal council between the Corps of Discovery and Native peoples—specifically the Otoe and Missouria—held near present-day Fort Atkinson in 1804.

Overview: This event honored tribal perspectives and contributions through traditional ceremonies, educational exhibits, and cultural performances. It emphasized Native sovereignty and opened space for Native voices in the Bicentennial narrative.

Our experience: We were unable to attend this event. We did, however, visit many of the historically significant sites. Leg 7: Shakedown Cruise

8. OCETI SAKOWIN EXPERIENCE: REMEMBERING AND EDUCATING

Location: Chamberlain and Oacoma, South Dakota
Dates: August 27–September 26, 2004

Historical significance: Focused on Native perspectives, particularly those of the Lakota (Oceti Sakowin) people.

Overview: Tribes gathered to share their history, culture, and responses to the expedition, fostering dialogue and understanding through storytelling, exhibits, and ceremonies.

Our experience: We were unable to attend this event. We did, however, visit many of the historically significant sites. Leg 7: Shakedown Cruise

9. CIRCLE OF CULTURES: TIME OF RENEWAL AND EXCHANGE

Location: Bismarck and Washburn, North Dakota
Dates: October 22–31, 2004

Historical significance: This event marked a symbolic effort to honor Native cultures and acknowledge the complex legacy of the Lewis and Clark Expedition through a process of truth-telling, remembrance, and cultural celebration.

Overview: Designed as a gathering place for renewal and reconciliation, this Signature Event featured extensive Native participation, including intertribal ceremonies, panel discussions, music, and dance. It sought to elevate Indigenous voices and promote a deeper understanding of the expedition's impact on Native nations.

Our experience: Leg 7: Shakedown Cruise

10. EXPLORE! THE BIG SKY

Location: Fort Benton and Great Falls, Montana
Dates: June 1–July 4, 2005

Historical significance: Commemorated the 1805 ascent of the Missouri River and the Corps' portage around the Great Falls.

Overview: Visitors experienced canoe landings, historical reenactments, and interpretive trails that traced the Corps' route through this rugged landscape.

Our experience: Leg 8: Don't Forget the Coke Money

11. DESTINATION: THE PACIFIC

Location: Long Beach, Washington, to Seaside, Oregon
Dates: November 24–27, 2005

Historical significance: Celebrated the Corps' arrival at the Pacific Ocean in 1805

Overview: Chinook blessings, the Ceremony of the Waters, and hikes along the Fort to Sea Trail offered a powerful conclusion to the westward trek.

Our experience: Leg 9: The Joy Was Us

12. AMONG THE NIIMIIPUU: THE SUMMER OF PEACE

Location: Lewiston, Idaho, and Clarkston, Washington
Dates: June 14–17, 2006

Historical significance: Marked the Corps' return journey and honored their relationship with the Niimiipuu (Nez Perce)

Overview: This event featured traditional storytelling, ceremonies, and educational programs focused on cross-cultural cooperation and hospitality.

Our experience: Leg 10: Summer of Peace, Road of Memory

13. CLARK ON THE YELLOWSTONE

Location: Billings, Pompeys Pillar, and Livingston, Montana
Dates: July 22–25, 2006

Historical significance: Commemorated Clark's return journey and his visit to Pompeys Pillar, where he left the only remaining physical evidence of the expedition.

Overview: Featured reenactments, educational exhibits, and tribal participation focused on Clark's role along the Yellowstone River and the region's Native history.

Our experience: We were unable to attend this event. We did, however, visit many of the historically significant sites. Leg 8: Don't Forget the Coke Money

14. REUNION AT THE HOME OF SAKAKAWEA

Location: New Town, North Dakota
Dates: August 17–20, 2006

Historical significance: Honored Sacagawea's homeland and the contributions of the Shoshone and Hidatsa peoples.

Overview: Community-led programming explored the life and legacy of Sacagawea through dance, education, and intergenerational engagement.

Our experience: We were unable to attend this event. We did, however, visit many of the historically significant sites. Leg 7: Shakedown Cruise

15. CONFLUENCE WITH DESTINY: THE RETURN OF LEWIS AND CLARK

Location: St. Louis, Missouri
Dates: September 23–24, 2006

Historical significance: Commemorated the return of the Corps to St. Louis and their reporting to President Jefferson.

Overview: A grand celebration featured maps, exhibitions, and storytelling, tying the modern commemorations back to the expedition's formal conclusion.

Our experience: Leg 11: What Do You Do When It's Over

Putting Pins on the Map

In addition to the Signature Events, we followed the trail so faithfully that we connected the dots for all but a hundred miles—a narrow stretch in eastern Oregon and Washington that we never quite reached. Along the way, we attended two meaningful events that, while not officially sanctioned by the National Council of the Lewis & Clark Bicentennial, held profound significance for us. We also created two journeys of our own—pilgrimages that deepened our connection to the expedition's enduring legacy.

LEWIS AND CLARK: HOMECOMING
Location: Louisville, Kentucky, and Clarksville, Indiana
Dates: November 5–8, 2006

Historical significance: Recognized the return of Lewis and Clark to their home communities.

Overview: Horseback reenactments, school programs, and solemn tributes were held at the Locust Grove and Mulberry Hill farm sites to mark the expedition's emotional return.

Our experience: Leg 12: The Journey Home

COURAGE UNDAUNTED—THE FINAL JOURNEY
Location: Meriwether Lewis Gravesite, Natchez Trace Parkway, Hohenwald, Tennessee
Date: October 7, 2009

Historical significance: Marked the 200th anniversary of Lewis's death with the first national memorial service at his gravesite.

Overview: Attended by descendants, dignitaries, and the public, the ceremony featured military honors, eulogies, and a formal procession, paying tribute to Lewis's contributions to American history.

Our experience: Leg 2: Of Grief and Gravestones; Epilogue

THE LOUISIANA PURCHASE SIGNING
Location: Paris, France
Date: April 3, 1803

Historical significance: The Louisiana Purchase doubled the size of the United States and enabled the Lewis and Clark Expedition.

Overview: This visit to Napoleon's tomb honored the expedition's European origins, connecting Jefferson's vision with Napoleon's ambition—and the land deal that changed history.

Our experience: Leg 3: City of Light

THE EASTERN LEGACY
Location: Harper's Ferry, West Virginia, to Clarksville, Indiana
Dates: July 4–October 14, 1803

Historical significance: The Eastern Legacy traces Meriwether Lewis's journey from Thomas Jefferson's Monticello to his meeting with William Clark—marking the true beginning of the expedition.

Overview: Retracing this lesser-known leg of the journey brought us to Jefferson's doorstep, through the halls of the American Philosophical Society, and along riverbanks where the Corps took shape. It was a pilgrimage into Lewis's solitude, Jefferson's ambition, and the quiet origins of something monumental.

Our experience: Leg 13: Uncharted Trip—Uncharted Moments

Sources

HISTORICAL SOURCES FOR LEG EPIGRAPHS

The voices of Lewis and Clark have been my steady companions along this journey. The selections gathered here are drawn directly from their journals and letters—words I quoted in the text or placed at the opening of each leg. They serve as touchstones to the expedition itself, to the awe and humility of discovery.

The works listed in the bibliography that follows represent another kind of influence: the historians, authors, and storytellers whose insights shaped my understanding of the Corps of Discovery and the world they encountered.

Leg 1: We Headed East to Explore the West
Lewis, Meriwether, to William Clark, June 19, 1803. In *Letters of the Lewis and Clark Expedition with Related Documents, 1783–1854*, edited by Donald Jackson, 2nd ed. Urbana: University of Illinois Press, 1978.

Leg 2: Of Grief and Gravestones
Clark, William. Letter to Jonathan Clark, October 28, 1806. In *Dear Brother: Letters of William Clark to Jonathan Clark*, edited by James J. Holmberg. New Haven: Yale University Press, 2002.

Leg 3: City of Light
Jefferson, Thomas, to John Dickinson, August 9, 1803. *Founders Online*, National Archives. (Original source: *The Papers of Thomas Jefferson*, vol. 41, 11 July–15 November 1803, ed. Barbara B. Oberg, Princeton University Press.)

Leg 4: The Last Jeep to Clarksville
Clark, William, to Meriwether Lewis, July 18, 1803. In *Letters of the Lewis and Clark Expedition with Related Documents, 1783–1854*, edited by Donald Jackson, 2nd ed. Urbana: University of Illinois Press, 1978.

Leg 5: The World Is Different Now
Amos Stoddard Papers, Missouri Historical Society Archives, St. Louis.

Leg 6: Two Questions and a Plan
Clark, William. July 4, 1804. In *The Journals of the Lewis and Clark Expedition*, edited by Gary E. Moulton. Lincoln: University of Nebraska Press, 1983–2001. Vol. 2.

Leg 7: The Shakedown Cruise
Clark, William. February 11, 1805. In *The Journals of the Lewis and Clark Expedition*, edited by Gary E. Moulton. Lincoln: University of Nebraska Press, 1983–2001. Vol. 3.

Leg 8: Don't Forget the Coke Money
Lewis, Meriwether. May 14, 1805. In *The Journals of the Lewis and Clark Expedition*, edited by Gary E. Moulton. Lincoln: University of Nebraska Press, 1983–2001. Vol. 4.

Leg 9: The Joy Was Us
Clark, William. November 7, 1805. In *The Journals of the Lewis and Clark Expedition*, edited by Gary E. Moulton. Lincoln: University of Nebraska Press, 1983–2001. Vol. 6.

Leg 10: Summer of Peace, Road of Memory
Gass, Patrick. May 11, 1805. In *The Journals of the Lewis and Clark Expedition*, edited by Gary E. Moulton. Lincoln: University of Nebraska Press, 1983–2001. Vol. 4.

Leg 11: What Do You Do When It's Over?
Lewis, Meriwether. Letter to Thomas Jefferson, September 23, 1806. In *The Papers of Thomas Jefferson*. Founders Online, National Archives.

Leg 12: The Journey Home
Clark, William. Letter to Jonathan Clark, September 24, 1806. In *Dear Brother: Letters of William Clark to Jonathan Clark*, edited by James J. Holmberg. New Haven: Yale University Press, 2002.

Leg 13: Echoes of the East
Lewis, Meriwether. Letter to Thomas Jefferson, September 23, 1806. In *The Papers of Thomas Jefferson*. Founders Online, National Archives.

Bibliography

Ambrose, Stephen E. *Crazy Horse and Custer: The Parallel Lives of Two American Warriors.* New York: Anchor Books, 1996.

Ambrose, Stephen E. *Undaunted Courage: Meriwether Lewis, Thomas Jefferson, and the Opening of the American West.* New York: Simon & Schuster, 1996.

Appleman, Roy E. *Lewis & Clark's Transcontinental Exploration.* Seattle: University of Washington Press, 2003.

Beal, Merrill D. *I Will Fight No More Forever: Chief Joseph and the Nez Perce War.* Boston: Houghton Mifflin, 1963.

Bechtold, Karl. *A Current Adventure: In the Wake of Lewis & Clark.* Bozeman, MT: Lewis & Clark Trail Heritage Foundation, 2004.

Biddle, Nicholas, ed. *The Journal of the Expedition Under Command of Captains Lewis and Clark.* 2 vols. New York: Heritage Press, 1962. Edited by Nicholas Biddle. Introduction by John Bakeless.

Chaloult, Michel. *Les Canadiens de l'expédition Lewis et Clark.* Québec: Les Éditions du Septentrion, 2003.

Chuinard, E. G. *Only One Man Died: The Medical Aspects of the Lewis and Clark Expedition.* Fairfield, WA: Ye Galleon Press, 1979.

Danisi, Thomas C., and John C. Jackson. *Meriwether Lewis.* Amherst, MA: Prometheus Books, 2009. Hardcover.

Duncan, Dayton, and Ken Burns. *Lewis & Clark: An Illustrated History.* New York: Alfred A. Knopf, 1997.

Duncan, Dayton. *Miles from Nowhere: Tales from America's Contemporary Frontier.* New York: Viking Adult, May 1, 1993.

Duncan, Dayton. *Out West: An American Journey.* New York: Viking, May 27, 1987.

Duncan, Dayton. *Scenes of Visionary Enchantment: Reflections on Lewis and Clark.* Lincoln: University of Nebraska Press, 2004. Hardcover.

Fanselow, Julie. *Traveling the Lewis and Clark Trail.* 2nd ed. Helena, MT: Falcon Publishing, 2000.

Fifer, Barbara, and Vicky Soderberg. *Along the Trail with Lewis and Clark: Historical Highlights and Color Maps, Where to Stay and What to Do.* Helena, MT: Montana Magazine, 1998.

Fisher, Vardis. *Suicide or Murder: The Strange Death of Governor Meriwether Lewis.* New York: Viking Press, 1961.

Guice, John D. W., ed. *By His Own Hand? The Mysterious Death of Meriwether Lewis.* Norman: University of Oklahoma Press, 2006. Contributions by James J. Holmberg, John D. W. Guice, and Jay H. Buckley.

Gunderson, Mary. *The Food Journal of Lewis & Clark: Recipes for an Expedition.* Sioux Falls, SD: History Cooks, 2003.

Holmberg, James J., ed. *Dear Brother: Letters of William Clark to Jonathan Clark.* New Haven: Yale University Press, April 10, 2002.

Hunsaker, Joyce Badgley. *Sacagawea Speaks: Beyond the Shining Mountains with Lewis and Clark.* Elko, NV: Amargosa Press, 2001.

Huser, Verne. *On the River with Lewis and Clark: The Waterways They Traveled, 1804–1806.* College Station: Texas A&M University Press, 2004. Illustrated edition with dust jacket.

Jackson, Donald, ed. *Letters of the Lewis and Clark Expedition, with Related Documents, 1783–1854.* 2nd ed., 2 vols. Urbana: University of Illinois Press, 1978.

Jones, Landon Y. *William Clark and the Shaping of the West.* New York: Hill and Wang, 2004. First edition hardcover.

Josephy, Alvin M., Jr., ed. *Lewis and Clark Through Indian Eyes: Nine Indian Writers on the Legacy of the Expedition.* New York: Alfred A. Knopf, April 11, 2006.

McGrath, Campbell. *Shannon: A Poem of the Lewis and Clark Expedition.* New York: Ecco Press, 2009.

Miller, Robert J. *Native America, Discovered and Conquered: Thomas Jefferson, Lewis and Clark, and Manifest Destiny.* Westport, CT: Praeger, 2006.

Miller, Robert J., Jacinta Ruru, Larissa Behrendt, and Tracey Lindberg. *Discovering Indigenous Lands: The Doctrine of Discovery in the English Colonies.* Oxford: Oxford University Press, 2010.

Monticello: A Guidebook. Edited by Susan R. Stein, Peter J. Hatch, Lucia C. Stanton, and Merrill D. Peterson. Charlottesville: Thomas Jefferson Foundation, 1997.

Morris, Larry E. *The Fate of the Corps: What Became of the Lewis and Clark Explorers After the Expedition.* New Haven, CT: Yale University Press, 2004. Hardcover.

Moulton, Gary E., ed. *The Journals of the Lewis and Clark Expedition.* 13 vols. Lincoln: University of Nebraska Press, 1983–2001.

Moulton, Gary E., ed. *The Lewis and Clark Journals: An American Epic of Discovery.* Lincoln: University of Nebraska Press, 2003. Abridged edition.

Neuberger, Richard L. *The Lewis & Clark Expedition.* New York: Random House, 1951. Illustrated by Winold Reiss.

Peck, David, and Marti E. Peck. *So Hard to Die: A Physician and a Psychologist Explore the Mystery of Meriwether Lewis's Death.* The Marti and David Peck Family Trust of 1992, 2021.

Phillips, H. Wayne. *Plants of the Lewis & Clark Expedition.* Missoula, MT: Mountain Press Publishing Company, 2003.

Phillips, Marcia Tabram. *The River Calls.* 2nd ed. Raleigh, NC: Lulu Publishing, 2020.

Ritter, Michael Lance. *Jean Baptiste Charbonneau: Man of Two Worlds.* Riverside, CA: CreateSpace Independent Publishing Platform, October 28, 2014.

Ronda, James P. *Lewis and Clark Among the Indians.* Lincoln: Bison Books, 1998. Originally published by University of Nebraska Press, 1984.

Schmidt, Thomas. *National Geographic Guide to the Lewis & Clark Trail.* Washington, DC: National Geographic Society, 2002. Paperback edition.

Strong, Emory, and Ruth Strong. *Seeking Western Waters: The Lewis and Clark Trail from the Rockies to the Pacific.* Edited by Herbert K. Beals. Portland: Oregon Historical Society Press, 1995.

Summitt, April R. *Sacagawea: A Biography.* Westport, CT: Greenwood Press, 2008.

The Daily Astorian. *Fort Clatsop: Rebuilding an Icon.* Portland, OR: Ooligan Press, 2007.

The Salish People and the Lewis and Clark Expedition. *Confederated Salish and Kootenai Tribes.* Lincoln: University of Nebraska Press, 2005.

Wark, Joseph A., and Wayne L. Mussulman. *Discovering Lewis & Clark from the Air.* Highland, UT: Horizon Publishers, 2002.

Wheeler, Olin D. *The Trail of Lewis and Clark, 1804–1904.* 2 vols. Originally published New York: G.P. Putnam's Sons, 1904. Reprint, Scituate, MA: Digital Scanning, Inc., 2002.

Wilcox, Desmond. *Ten Who Dared.* Boston: Little, Brown and Company, 1976. First edition.

Photo Gallery Notes

Leg 1

1. January 2003, Monticello, Virginia. Standing at the beginning, pointing our compass west toward rivers, stories, and the long road ahead. People: Jeff and Carmen; Photo: Unknown

2. January 2003, Monticello, Virginia. Inaugural Signature Event—where a curiosity became a vow to follow the trail together.

Leg 2

3. July 2003, Meriwether Lewis Monument & Gravesite (near Hohenwald, Tennessee). Meriwether Lewis's gravesite near Grinder's Stand on the Natchez Trace. We came as tourists; we left listening differently.

4. July 2003, Meriwether Lewis Monument & Gravesite (near Hohenwald, Tennessee). A preserved stretch of the Natchez Trace leading toward Grinder's Stand—the same path that once carried traders, soldiers, and Lewis himself.

Leg 3

5. September 2003, Père Lachaise Cemetery, Paris. At Jim Morrison's grave, we stood among flowers and quiet strangers, a little awed by how music makes its own kind of pilgrimage.

6. September 2003, Paris, France. Les Invalides—standing over an empire's echo, we felt the difference between conquest and curiosity.

Leg 4

7. October 2003, Jeffersonville, Indiana. Fife and drum rising as the Jefferson statue is unveiled across from Louisville, where beginnings and reckonings share the same shoreline. People: Lewis & Clark Fife and Drum Corps, St. Charles, Missouri

8. October 2003, Clarksville, Indiana. Opening-day ceremony with reenactors on the tented stage—voices rising, flags lifted, and the Corps portrayed in formation as the journey "proceeded on."

Leg 5

9. March 2004, St. Charles, Missouri. Carmen at the Lewis and Clark statue with Seaman, a quiet yes in the cold. People: Carmen; Photo: Jeff Ton

10. March 2004, St. Louis, Missouri. My hand in the Missouri for the first time, a promise I'd keep making. People: Jeff

Leg 6

11. July 2004, Rocheport, Missouri. Overlooking the Big Muddy at a hillside winery, we joked about an RV; the joke stuck. People: Jeff and Carmen; Photo: Unknown

12. July 2004, Atchison, Kansas. Discovery Expedition reenactors landing near Independence Creek on July 4; flags, oars, and a river full of noise. People: Discovery Expedition of St. Charles

Leg 7

13. October 2004, Council Bluffs, Iowa. Wind on the overlook, the Missouri carrying us forward. People: Carmen; Photo: Jeff Ton

14. October 2004, Spirit Mound near Vermillion, South Dakota, where a tale about "little people" became a lesson in listening to land, not legend.

Leg 8

15. July 2005, Lemhi Pass, Beaverhead Mountains—on the Continental Divide at the Montana–Idaho border, near Tendoy, Idaho, and Dillon, Montana. National Historic Landmark, Lemhi Pass—standing on the spine of the West, we felt the river's lessons cross from memory into vow. People: Jeff and Carmen; Photo: Unknown

16. June 2005, Upper Missouri River Breaks National Monument, near Judith Landing, Montana. "Hole in the Wall," White Cliffs of the Missouri—our paddling trip began with a view that asked us to be quiet and pay attention.

Leg 9

17. November 2005, Astoria, Oregon. Fort Clatsop site—an uncharted moment as archaeologists worked where the replica had burned; the past speaking in brush strokes and soil layers.

18. November 2005, Astoria, Oregon. Astoria-Megler Bridge—celebrating Consider the Columbia in November wind, the kind of weather that makes a vow feel real. People: Jeff and Carmen; Photo: Unknown

Leg 10

19. June 2006, Nez Perce National Historical Park Visitor Center, Lapwai, Idaho. Opening ceremony on Nez Perce homelands—elders and leaders carrying flags; we were guests, and our first work was to listen.

20. June 2006, Grand Teton National Park, Wyoming. Sacredness in a small, quiet chapel; the kind of holiness that doesn't need marble to be real.

Leg 11

21. September 2006, Fort Defiance State Park, Cairo, Illinois. Fort Defiance—the Ohio giving itself to the Mississippi. A hard bend in the map, and our favorite metaphor for how two stories can join without disappearing.

22. September 2006, St. Louis, Missouri. Opening ceremony on the steps of the Gateway Arch—color guard, drums, and the reminder that this story belongs to many nations and voices.

Leg 12
23. November 2006, Clarksville, Indiana. Homecoming, November 2006—students and Sisters with a flatboat they called Angela's Ark, tying our journey back to Carmen's school and a lineage of care.

24. November 2006, Clarksville, Indiana. Carmen at the Lewis & Clark marker; the map turning into memory. People: Carmen; Photo: Jeff Ton

Leg 13
25. June 2007, Philadelphia, Pennsylvania. Inside the American Philosophical Society Library, we handled the Lewis and Clark journals and a fresh map pulled from the original engraving plate.

26. June 2007, Pittsburgh, Pennsylvania. View of the Point in Pittsburgh where the Allegheny and Monongahela meet to form the Ohio—the launch point of Lewis's river journey.

Coda
27. The motor home that carried us after the rivers—laughing, listening, proceeding on across asphalt instead of water.

About the Author

Jeffrey S. Ton (Jeff) is an author, speaker, and leadership mentor whose work bridges technology, humanity, and the power of connection. After more than four decades in business and IT leadership, he now writes and speaks about what it means to lead with curiosity, empathy, and purpose.

He is the author of *Amplify Your Value: Leading IT with Strategic Vision* and *Amplify Your Job Search: Strategies for Finding Your Dream Job*. He is also the creator of the long-running blog *Rivers of Thought*, where he explores themes of leadership, love, legacy, and the sacred moments that shape a life.

In *Uncharted Moments*, Jeff turns his storyteller's lens inward, weaving the epic sweep of the Lewis and Clark Trail with an intimate portrait of love, loss, and discovery shared with his wife, Carmen.

A lifelong Hoosier, Jeff makes his home in Indianapolis, where rivers—and stories—continue to call him forward.

www.JeffreySTon.com

Continue the Journey

The story you've just read began as a personal exploration along the Lewis and Clark Trail—but it didn't end there.

Today, I lead The Lewis and Clark Experience: A New Way Forward, a leadership development program created in partnership with FCCS, where modern leaders rediscover the principles that guided the Corps of Discovery—vision, team building, overcoming obstacles, developing resilience, and proceeding on.

If you or your organization would like to bring this experience to your team, the program details follow.

ARE YOU PREPARED TO LEAD YOUR TEAM IN TIMES OF UNCERTAINTY?

Discover a New Way Forward at The Lewis & Clark Leadership Experience.

Explore the key elements of successfully building and leading a team into an uncertain future using the Lewis and Clark Expedition as the historical backdrop.

Learn more about what it means to lead, like Lewis and Clark, in times of unknown and change.

fccsconsulting.com/**lewis-and-clark**